OBSESSION
with INTENT

I hope t
see your contributions
to anti-violence work
in the next book
Lee

In memory of

Bonnie Agnew and Andrea Dworkin

OBSESSION
with INTENT

VIOLENCE AGAINST WOMEN

Lee Lakeman

BLACK
ROSE
BOOKS

Montreal/New York/London

Black Rose Books No. II333

National Library of Canada Cataloguing in Publication Data

Lakeman, Lee, 1946-

Obsession, with intent : violence against women / Lee Lakeman

Includes bibliographical references and index.

ISBN: 1-55164-263-8 (bound)   ISBN: 1-55164-262-X (pbk.)

(alternative ISBNs 9781551642635 [bound]   9781551642628 [pbk.])

1. Women--Violence against--Canada. 2. Sex discrimination in

criminal justice administration. I. Title.

HV6250.4.W65L34 2005   362.88'082'0971   C2004-907110-6

Cover design: Associés libres

BLACK ROSE BOOKS

C.P. 1258	2250 Military Road	99 Wallis Road
Succ. Place du Parc	Tonawanda, NY	London, E9 5LN
Montréal, H2X 4A7	14150	England
Canada	USA	UK

To order books:

In Canada: (phone) 1-800-565-9523 (fax) 1-800-221-9985
email: utpbooks@utpress.utoronto.ca

In United States: (phone) 1-800-283-3572 (fax) 1-651-917-6406

In the UK & Europe: (phone) London 44 (0)20 8986-4854 (fax) 44 (0)20 8533-5821
email: order@centralbooks.com

Our Web Site address: http://www.web.net/blackrosebooks

A publication of the Institute of Policy Alternatives of Montréal (IPAM)

Printed in Canada

The Canada Council | Le Conseil des Arts
for the Arts | du Canada

Table of Contents

Acknowledgements

Credit for the work discussed here belongs to the frontline workers, the women who called them and their anti-rape centres. Special thanks to the CASAC LINKS workers who did the research, analyzed the documents and defended the rights of each woman: Andrea Silverstone, Julie Black, Carolyn Gelhorn, Kerry Gorman, Tamara Gorin, Danièle Tessier, Chantal Robitaille, Lorraine Whalley, Patty Thomspon, Jackie Stevens, Amanda Workman and Jodi Shannahan. The CASAC regional representatives and LINKS workers read every line in draft three times for accuracy and to accrue political agreement.

Like every participant I was deeply dependent on the political work and support of my home collective members, especially of Daisy Kler, who was a key researcher and did much of the work of documenting the references, Tamara Gorin, Louisa Russell, Suzanne Jay, Alice Lee, and from the national LINKS staff, Nicole Robillard. As principal author of the text, except where other women have been recognized for their particular submissions, I am grateful to the entire collective for the economic and political support of CASAC and our Canada wide coalition.

While of course all the responsibility for ideas and notions, wrong headedness and ignorance is mine, I would like to thank some of those women beyond me who tried to educate me about the Charter (its limits and promise) and to keep me company while I tried to educate myself: Shelagh Day, Lisa Addario, Gwen Brodsky, Kim Pate, Liz Sheehy, Sheila McIntyre, Christine Boyle, Nora Currie, Eileen Morrow, Victoria Gray, Sharon McIvor, Judy Rebick, Anne Derrick, Dara Culhane. And thanks to Allan Rock, as Minister of Justice and Attorney General of Canada, for funding the original project.

Finally I would like to acknowledge my personal debt to those women who have encouraged me and other activists to write. We all carry parts of the collective herstory and I no less than others. I am grateful for the belief that I might be able to communicate it to the next women in hopes we could advance their/our struggle.

Preface

This book encapsulates a small part of the thirty years of our Canadian women's rebellion. It centers on the mechanisms of indifference, intolerance and sometimes complicity of government in maintaining men's power over women. The book focuses on the government responses to that part of the power of men over women exercised in criminal brute force: rape, wife assault, incest, and sexual harassment. It counter poses the direct action of women to aid one another and to enlist the support of our community.

This is not another story of the individual men brutalizing told by the valorous women escaping them. But it is of course impossible to tell this story without reference to both. And ordinarily those abuse/domination/escape stories are those that I and other women like me are most likely to tell. In my anti-violence work in transition houses and anti-rape centers since 1973 I have heard and witnessed more than anyone in the world needs to know, of what harm men do to women. My personal knowledge includes branding and hidden bruising, broken jaws and burned flesh, broken psyches, mutilation. It includes callous indifference, excesses of rage, and willful destruction of bodies and minds. It involves damage to old women and babies and practices of cruelty quick and vicious and it involves those cruelties to captives, especially wives and daughters, carefully maintained over years.

Many individual women's stories have moved me deeply. In fact, I have a practice that sustains me when I am least sure of what my life's work has achieved: I recall the names of raped and battered women and children who inspired me, who made me weep with helplessness or with relief at being able to help. I recall those rebels who encouraged me, those who bid me to stand up. I recall them with gratitude and pride in our solidarity. These are women with whom I continue to stand. This book is an expression of that solidarity—between women threatened, raped and beaten and that overlapping group of women working to end such terrorism.

The book is focused closely on only one of our joint set of expectations, frustration and strategies: to make fair law, to make police come when they are called, to make them protect us, to make the detectives do an adequate legal investigation, to make the prose-

cutors effectively put the facts before the courts, and to make judges and jailers and probation and immigration officers hold the abusers humanely in community or if need be,
in state custody, until all women and children are safe from them and until society imag-
ines, and successfully executes, plans to change the conditions of women and to change
men.

I have had the great fortune and tenacity to live and work among the righteous
women of my generation who rebel against the violence that dominates the lives of
women worldwide. Even the research, speech, and judgments emanating from the capi-
tals of the world must now concede the reality of women's oppression that we exposed.
We the women who created the anti-violence wing of the movement in Canada, have mobilized thousands of women to consciousness, self-help, mutual aid, demonstration lobbying, and direct action, both mass and anti-mass in form. We committed our lives and
linked many others to the long-term multi-faceted struggle for social transformation.

Our women's rebellion identified, named, and organized to stop that violence.
Among those I know, are women who rescued those attacked, sometimes by getting between angry men with guns and the women they wanted to shoot. We opened our own
houses and "kicked back" our small salaries to invent feminist shelters: institutions in
which women could hide each other and our children. None of us got rich. Many of us got
no salaries. And of the few who were paid, I know of none who got a pension. Some wore
out with the enormity of our project. Some died trying to escape and trying to help others
to escape. We persist.

We invented, reinvented, and coined words to describe our reality. Femicide among
them. With almost no money we launched messaging campaigns on fences, on bill-
boards, with little stickers in washrooms, on video and public television, on fax ma-
chines, and computers. After Take Back The Night, one of my favorite campaigns from
my own work, is a one-month installation on a construction hustings in my False Creek
neighborhood. We were linking welfare rates, health issues, and violence against women
in this showcase federal housing development. After the nightly destruction of it by
young men, I faithfully repainted and repaired the message wall everyday using my baby
buggy full of staplers, paint brushes, posters and fabric. Another favorite is a scripted bus
trip around our city of Vancouver on an old yellow school bus on which we took media
personalities in 1980, to educate them about hospital shift workers and sweatshop workers and what they needed, to be safe from abuse. We talked about domestic workers
forced to live in, and then attacked on the job in the palatial areas; about women trapped
in prostitution and pornography; about wives and children with no where to go; and
about the deaf student residents at the mercy of their teachers. We called it a women's
"Tour of the War Zone."

Because of that work, expressions like violence against women, battering, sexual
harassment, incest, transition houses, and rape-crisis centres, have gone from being

vague and shameful notions whispered between women to becoming the commonly spoken international political language of human rights. We have spread important information throughout the country so successfully that virtually every college-age woman can cite violence statistics and recognize many dangerous situations. We have made our organizing centres and our political thinking available back and forth across race, class, and regional barriers with enough success that women tell of the sexist violence they have endured from every demographic group within the borders.

Our movement of feminist anti-violence initiatives mushroomed in the Canadian political boom time of the seventies. We had enormous public support. The national federal government was forced to respond to us with some funds and policy and law changes. I, with others, had some success on changes to rape law, including that of criminalizing rape in marriage, the No, Means No, Law and practices about consent and the Rape Shield Law procedures regarding women's private records and the use of women's herstory in rape trials, all of which have been heralded internationally.

Based on our work, Canada claimed to the international community, exemplary government willingness and expertise in combating violence against women. On the basis of that self- generated and self-promoted reputation, Canada has recommended, even pressured with funding arrangements, other national governments for changes in law, in domestic policy, and in their relationship to women's NGO's. While doing so internationally, it co-opted our domestic anti-violence movement substantially. It devastated our network of anti-violence activists. Recently it has reversed much of the government policy that could be a source of pride to any equality-seeking bureaucrat or politician. We have now witnessed criticism from the United Nations of the Canadian treatment of women.

Finding solutions is not easy. Our joint plans as a movement and my personal politics reject "Law and Order" right-wing strategies that violate the human rights and human potential of men, even of accused men (not the least of reasons is the impact on women). But so too do we reject the abandonment of women and children to the lawless sexism of men's current inhumanity. We actively oppose the racism and class bias of the current selective state law enforcement. But in a similar vein, we serve notice to the men of the left that we reject the romanticism of an anti-authoritarian "community justice" or "restorative justice" relying on community as it is, with no affirmative action component (nor even commitment) to advance community organization toward either women's equality or race and class equality.

This book has a special and particular herstory: it began life as only a dull obligation of mine to report back to Allan Rock, a progressive Justice Minister (now Canadian Ambassador to the United Nations) and to the Justice Department of the Canadian government for a small nationally-funded project of which I was coordinator. But all the women involved worked above and beyond the legal obligations of the project to tell the truth of their and other women's enforced situation. They insisted with me that we think about what could be done for the women contacting us for help.

That expanded our work and our report into a contemporary analysis of the relationship between the federal government in the widest sense and the anti-rape movement we lead in Canada. The frontline workers involved in the project valued it. The collective in which I work, Vancouver Rape Relief and Women's Shelter, decided to translate, publish, and distribute more than fifteen hundred copies of the report across the country. A wider group of frontline workers, and then academics, relished it and began to use it in their centers and schools. Demand exceeded that publishing run.

Now it is a report finding relevance in the international community, as it continues to gather steam along the way to a better future for women.

Precisely, this is the story of a group of women over five years who try to enlist the Canadian government (provincial, federal, and international) to aid women like ourselves, to face down, restrain, escape, and correct the violent abuses of power inflicted on women by the men in their lives. But those five years were the culmination of thirty. Women in Canada were, those thirty years, in unique and privileged positions to develop and experiment with strategies to end sexist violence that involved the state.

Like women in England, and some commonwealth countries, we had the social safety net of the welfare state. Besides entitlement to education and health services for all, that welfare state allowed routes to possible state-subsidized incomes for women and their children escaping violent fathers and husbands and bosses. It also allowed specific funds targeted for transition houses from that same social welfare pot. Most women, including American women, had no such source or social tradition.

Add to those material conditions, the "baby boom" population burst and the social democratic job creation schemes like the Company of Young Canadians and the Local Initiatives Project grants reminiscent of the American New Deal. Mix with masses of women on the rise. We had fertile soil. The capitalist economy was booming. There was seed money available for new social projects and much needed social development and some of that was directed toward women, the poor, and aboriginal people. Partly this meant that individual women, me among them, could design the work we wanted to do, like anti-violence programs, and seek government funds to do it. There was more than enough meaningful work to do for most who wanted work, both paid and unpaid. And however unfairly accumulated and unevenly distributed, the country had more than enough resources to sustain everyone and to deliver all needed goods and services.

American women struggled to reform their constitution, as had the black community before them. That civil rights approach didn't yet exist in England or Canada, but the repatriation of the Canadian constitution and the creation twenty years ago of the Canadian Charter of Rights and Freedoms opened that avenue to us too. We had the example of the Black Liberation struggle and new mechanisms of government put in place nominally devoted to establishing the equality of women and mandated to screen all law, policy, and procedures for compliance with women's promised equality. That approach is being reapplied in South Africa, Australia, and other parts of the world. While the Equal Rights Amendment failed in the USA, Canadian women thought we could move ahead securing, then using, a new legal guarantee of equality and our growing analysis of the relationship between men's violence and our position as women in society.

The courts were inherently more closed, appointed, elite, and therefore, theoretically more regressive than the parliament. Still we saw some opportunity in the Supreme Court after the institution of The Charter and, especially once Madame Justice Claire L'Heureux-Dubé was appointed and the critical mass of baby boomer feminist lawyers took their places in academe as well as in the courts.

Even internationally, violence was being recognized as part of the source and maintenance of the oppression of women. UN conferences like Beijing focused on women and the new international agreements fostered there. Initiatives toward a world court held promise, as did the World Social Forums and the so-called anti-globalization uprisings.

Within Canada we had a mostly literate population, a publicly funded media system operating relatively freely, and a public education system that could carry information of women's rights. Both could carry back to government elevated community standards: an increasing expectation of fairness to women, of state action to end the brutal unfairness of violence against women.

In these conditions we needed to answer the question that remains: Why is it so hard, so rare, for Canadian women who tell on their abusers, who ask for help, to get an effective conviction against the men who commit violence against women? And what will we do about it?

With belief in the diversity, splendour and potential of the Canadian Women's Movement,

Lee Lakeman

Introduction: **The Heron Case**

Another woman dead. Another wife. Her husband, of course. Sherry Heron and her mother, Anna Adams, were both shot to death in the hospital. Her husband walked out afterwards and drove himself into the local bush. Everyone knew what came next.

"We were hoping you would speak to the big picture." That is how Laurie Parsons, transition house worker from Mission, put it when she explained to us that she had just referred a CBC national reporter to Canadian Association of Sexual Assault Centres (CASAC) LINKS staff.[1] "We can handle the local details, but we think that CASAC will better express the 'big picture', the systemic issues."

While the murder of wives by husbands is not something we ever get used to, it is not usually an emergency situation for us.[2] We choose, most often, to save our emergency responses for the women still alive.

We knew from experience, however, that women across Canada would be subjected to the details of these events in media reports and might be left more frightened, less sure of where to go. They, like us, would be watching the news media for clues. How would Sherry be portrayed? What excuses would be put forward for the husband? Which authorities would refuse to take responsibility? Which officials would point the way? We recognized a responsibility to ourselves, to those women watching, and to the transition house workers in small and rural centres. We could interrupt our tasks to give this case a few hours.

When I called Sgt. Grant Learned of the Mission RCMP, I explained that as a CASAC representative I was being asked to provide comment to the media and wanted to be as informed as possible before doing so.[3] He was gracious and told me that Sherry Heron had been in hospital for some weeks. Immediately, I asked why? "Well," he said, "she had a serious illness and had also been in a car accident." He knew I was looking for a history of wife beating and told me there was no record of police calls to their house.

He *didn't* tell me that Bryan Heron was a prison guard for thirty years who supervised others and so the likelihood of his wife calling the police for help was slim, whether she needed them or not.[4] Sherry's husband had been assisting her in dealing with her medical condition for months, he said, and there seemed to be some recent "interference" from her family of origin as to who should be her primary care person.

Sherry's mother was sitting at her bedside when the husband arrived with a gun and shot them both.

The police were trying to establish, Sgt. Learned said, just when Mr. Heron received the restraining order that had been issued against him and whether that was what "set him off." He said Sherry had expressed worry about Heron's temper and what he would do when he was served the order.

How, I asked, did a woman confined to a hospital bed get a restraining order and, why would she need one? Well, he explained, her sister had come to the Mission detachment of the RCMP to inquire as to what help was available for Sherry as she was "considering leaving her husband." An officer from the domestic violence unit had been "sent directly to Sherry's bedside to take a statement." The Sergeant reassured me that Sherry had specifically been asked whether or not there had already been any domestic violence and she had said no.

But at a press conference, the Sergeant is quoted as admitting that Heron was "harassing his wife." The police understood that to mean harassing as "annoying." "Had there been any suspicion of violence, we would have either gone with a peace bond or, better yet, we would have arrested the individual as we normally would in threats of violence."[5]

The police claimed the statement-taking officer had no grounds for a criminal charge. Their hands were tied. Not wanting to seem insensitive, or to leave her and her family dissatisfied, he had thoughtfully involved the RCMP Victim Assistance worker.

> RCMP victim services assisted her in going through the motions of obtaining
> a restraining order...nothing in the restraining order warned of the possibility
> of violence.

I didn't ask whether the police had advised Sherry of the existence or usefulness of the local transition house, but the fact that he didn't mention it seemed to tell the tale. That was the end of police involvement until after the murders.

Two versions of this woman's experience were being constructed. In our version, it was obvious that Sherry was leaving her husband and was scared. Women scared of leaving their husbands usually have good reason. We wondered what those reasons were and why the officer didn't find out. We knew their house was remote and that Heron had been trying to split Sherry from her family. It seemed to us that after she was hospitalized, Heron was no longer able to keep her family away. From her sickbed, Sherry talked to her sister and mother and agreed that her sister would go and check out the situation with the police; see if they would act against a fellow law enforcer, and if they would perceive the crimes that had already been committed. Perhaps her sister was confident there was legal help available to Sherry by right.

Sgt. Learned failed to tell me Sherry had told police from her hospital bed that her husband had threatened her life, restrained her, isolated her from her family, and threatened them with harm, especially if she attempted to leave him. She told them of these criminal activities in order to get protection. She told them he owned several registered guns and was a prison guard accustomed to using force. Sherry also said he had been depressed lately. The police failed to see the criminal activity and the danger to life and liberty for Sherry and claimed their hands were tied. Sherry, her sister, and mother did not give up. Sherry got advice from someone, likely the volunteer Victim Assistance worker, to contact and hire a lawyer.[6] If criminal law enforcement wouldn't help, maybe they could do it on their own with a civil restraining order. She did that.

Through her lawyer, Mr. Parmjit S. Virk, Sherry told the court in an affidavit that, among other things, she was "fearful that (he) could come after (me) with his weapons… within the last year, (he) has on numerous occasions said to me, 'if you leave me, I will hurt you and your family'…he will not be pleased once he receives the pleadings in this case." This is from her affidavit filed in B.C. Supreme Court, May 16, 2003. According to this document, Sherry had been separated from her husband for two days.[7]

The restraining order was granted. Heron was directed to stay away from Sherry's place of residence. If he did not, he would be defying the courts and that would be considered a crime. The remaining problem for Sherry and her family was what to do when Heron exploded, as she had expected, and told everyone that he would.

When I called the hospital, Mr. Don Bower of the Fraser Health Authority told me the hospital staff had been very brave and fully active.[8] The restraining order had been attached to the clipboard containing her medical chart at the end of her bed. Security staff had been notified. A nurse had spotted Mr. Heron. She had seen him there pretty much every day. She read the chart and knew there was a restraining order issued that day so she called the security guard. The unarmed guard entered the room, I was told, and asked Heron to leave. When he wouldn't, I was also told, the guard backed up a few steps so that he could see the nursing station and yelled for them to call the police.

After Heron shot his wife and mother-in-law to death, he walked out of the hospital. The security guard, I was assured by the hospital public relations man, had quickly and successfully locked the wards "to protect the staff and patients of the hospital." I said, "You mean the other patients of the hospital." Both police and hospital officials assured the public that everyone had done a fine job and we could all be proud.[9]

We were encouraged to think it was all terribly tragic and unavoidable. There was just a hint that "if only Sherry had been willing to reveal any real violence," or "if only Heron had sought medical help," or "if only her family had not interfered," or "if only

Sherry had not needed long-term home nursing from her overburdened husband," things might have been different. If only.

CASAC went on national television the next morning to say that any transition house worker in the country would have spotted Sherry Heron as an ex-wife in danger.[10] Any anti-violence worker could have described the many criminal charges that could and should have been laid against Heron when Sherry and her sister first reported to police. Such charges might have saved three lives.

Sgt. Le Maitre from RCMP headquarters participated in the interview with me; he rolled his eyes at the TV camera saying, "hindsight is easy," and he did not know "where I was getting my information." He repeated that the problem is that the public just doesn't understand the difference between a civil restraining order and a criminal law peace bond. He was shocked when I said women don't care about the difference and shouldn't have to study law in a crisis moment to get equal protection of the law.

Heron had displayed the proprietary and aggressively controlling attitudes that would make him prone to wife abuse. He also had weapons and was depressed. He had made threats to harm Sherry and her family, and he had what it took to carry out those threats. Heron was a man in political circumstances and personal conditions that increased the likelihood of his acting out his sense of entitlement and righteousness.[11]

We at CASAC identified, even from our distance, that Sherry was asking her family, community, and government for help. She understood terribly well that an individual man armed with a marriage license and guns overpowered her. She got the family and community response one might hope for. But she also sought and needed state protection of her liberty and security in order to function as an autonomous person. The State, in all our names, failed.

The police are not the only public officials who failed what we think of as equality obligations. Hospital officials should have made the decision to move Sherry, either within the hospital or to another hospital, so that she would not have been so vulnerable to her ex-husband's immediate temper. They could have done it just to protect her privacy. We do it all the time in transition houses and other women's services. Everyone involved could have been spared. It would have been much better than having to provide hospital staff with trauma counselling afterwards.

It took us another couple of days to consider that it was a useless infringement of her privacy to place her legal restraining order on her medical chart as though it could be expected that some nurse could and would enforce it. This was an act, we suspect, designed to cover the hospital legally but not to affect Sherry's privacy or security of person. At the very least, it constituted an indignity.

Sherry did everything anyone could expect and was advised to do by her family, community, and the State to establish her autonomy. She had her own income from her own job. She got herself into public space and out of the sanctity of his home. She ended her marriage. She involved her family, checked her legal rights, talked to the authorities, and notified the public institutions charged with her care and protection of the danger she knew so well.

Since the failure to protect was so blatant, we began to suspect that someone might be set up as a scapegoat. We contacted the unions so as not to get caught in the predictable next move to blame the least powerful individuals: the front line cop, the security guard, or the nurse who spotted Heron and called hospital security. That's when we discovered that the security man was new, in a privatized position through Windsor Security, and possibly the only person on security duty in the hospital.

It is highly unlikely that a private company would be more informed, vigilant, and ready to act on Sherry's human rights as promised in the Canadian Charter of Rights and Freedoms, than the police and public hospital staff.

The next likely fall guy would be the low-paid lawyer working on her civil order. Like the other individual criminal justice professionals involved, he did not do the best possible job.[12] All these people share some amount of personal and professional responsibility.[13] But we were more interested in moving further up the power chain.

While we thought our way through this, we watched as a manhunt unfolded for Heron who had gone to the bush. At this point, the police had no trouble using Sherry's information about how dangerous Heron was.[14] To secure the warrant to search his house and cars, they produced that information before a judge, including the list of his guns that included the .357 magnum he used to kill Sherry and her mother.[15] It must have been the other four rifles that made him seem a huntsman to them. Now there could be helicopters, dozens of cops, SWAT teams, and uniforms displayed at regular press briefings. Nothing was too much to put into Heron's capture, now that Sherry was dead. When a police dog dragged him out of a tree stump, he shot himself.

Again, we failed to convince the authorities.

The police refuse to acknowledge that it would have been wiser to spend law enforcement dollars to prevent these three deaths rather than on the wild manhunt in which we were all caught up. Why not assign a local police officer to her security, once her sister apprised them of the situation? Yes, we do know how many Sherry's that could mean. Why not consider the whole hospital her home from which he was barred by the restraining order? They could have had a police officer or a security guard stop him at the door of the hospital. Yes, we do know what he might do; isn't that the reason women go to the police? Why not move her from one room to another, or one facility to another? Yes, it would cost money. Why not remove his guns? Was there a civil liberty at stake here greater than Sherry's right to life, liberty, and security of her person? Why not at least enforce the possible criminal charges and the likely bail order that would follow?

It took us ages to understand the world-view that allowed the police to repeat, as though it explained everything, that Sherry had only told the court (in her affidavit) about the violence done to her. In their minds, she had not told them (the police). That the advice to tell the court came from a Victim Assistance worker employed by and answerable directly to the police is an unavoidable reality.

That Victim Assistance worker has never been heard from again. The police were blameless, in their own minds, and no one else is allowed to judge them.[16] "The brilliance of patriarchy," says Robin Morgan, "is disintegration."[17]

The new Liberal B.C. Provincial Attorney General, Geoff Plant, had softened the pressure on police to arrest by changing the Wife Assault policy in the first week of May 2003.[18] Only a few days after the murder, he opined that any increase in violence against women that we were attributing to his announced policy reversal was our fault. His move had been the first blow to the best policy on violence against women in the country, the Attorney General of B.C. Violence Against Women in Relationships Policy.[19] We were "irresponsible" he said. It was not his change in political policy, but the spin we were putting on his policy change that was dangerous.[20]

In any case, we had all witnessed the RCMP refusal to enforce the VAWR Policy.[21] The RCMP wrote their own policy after the Vernon Massacres and Sgt. Le Maitre told me in the waiting room of the CBC that he teaches this policy and procedure to police.[22]

For days, we entirely failed to consider the role of the judge hearing the affidavit of the violence already committed against Sherry. (Sometimes it is difficult to conceive of the equality we have never experienced.) The obvious inadequacy of the solution before him: an application for a civil restraining order (and the sloppiness of this one in particular) apparently gave no rise to questions as to what was going on and no advice to anyone regarding the equality issues at hand. Regardless of what the officers of the court were putting before this judge, surely it was obvious that Sherry was seeking her inherent constitutional and inalienable woman's rights.

The combination of three public institutions (police, hospital, courts) providing inadequate service is grim. But the failure of these institutions and the persons working therein to deal with equality issues can be deadly. Private legal advice and privatized hospital security removed any fail-safe.[23]

Since he died in custody, a coroner's inquest has been called into Heron's death. This is a matter of law. An inquest is required for anyone who dies in the care of the state. To date, no inquiry has been called into the deaths of either Sherry or her mother. Apparently, despite the facts that they were in a public hospital, before the courts, and asking for police protection, and were being advised by a police-based victim assistance worker, they were not in the care of the state.

Notes

1. Personal phone call logged, May 21, 2003, from Laurie Parsons calling from the Mission Women's Resource Society that operates the transition house.

2. Women We Honour Action Committee. (1992). *Women Killing: Intimate Femicide in Ontario 1974-1990*, Toronto: Author.

3. Personal communication by phone from the CASAC office, May 21, 2003.

4. Canada.com network print story, (May 22, 2003), available online <www.canada.com/components/print>.

5. Hunt for Killer, (May 22, 2003), *Penticton Herald*, p. A2.

6. This is speculation, but the Victim Assistance worker has not been heard from since.

7. Richards, G. (2003, May 28). Woman Slain in Hospital Feared Husband's Wrath. *The Globe and Mail*, pp. A1, A7.

8. Phone call personal communication, May 22, 2003.

9. Ramsey, M. (May 22, 2003). Guard Who Saw Killing, *The Vancouver Sun*, p. A4.

10. CBC National TV, Lakeman for CASAC, with Alison Smith, (May 22, 2003). Interview tape available through CASAC.

11. Lakeman, L. (1993). *99 Federal Steps Toward an End to Violence Against Women*. Toronto: National Action Committee on the Status of Women.

12. He could have asked for terms about how the order should be handled for instance.

13. Culbert, L. (2003, Nov. 13). RCMP's Learned gets new posting: The force's top spokesman was accused of an off colour remark, *The Vancouver Sun*, p. A15.

14. Pemberton, K. (2003, May 24). Mission Murder Suspect Shoots Self, *Times Columnist*, p. A6.

15. Search Warrant issued by the Province of B.C., May, 21, 2003, on the information of Corporal Edward Anthony Preto.

16. This is in spite of insistence from women's groups for years that we must have some effective means of civilian review, and complaint of police policy, not just personal behaviour.

17. Morgan, R. (1990, c1989). *The Demon Lover: On the Sexuality of Terrorism*. New York: Norton.

18. His policy, now called Spousal Assault Policy, was announced at a press conference, May 1, 2003.

19. This policy began with recognition of the holistic nature of any solution and clearly identified wife assault within the continuum of violence against women. It did not compel, but did advise arresting and prosecution. It was a political policy imposed and was never fully supported by crown or police.

20. Personal communication to Suzanne Jay, and the women of the B.C. CEDAW Group, in Vancouver meeting, June 6, 2003.

21. Woods, J. (1998). Recommendations for Amendments to "E" Division, RCMP Operational Policies Pertaining to Relationship Violence and the Processing of Firearms Licences. Royal Canadian Mounted Police.

22. Personal communication in the lobby of CBC Vancouver, May 22, 2003.

23. Fail-safe is a mechanism by which when predictable failures happen there is a plan B. Sherry should have been saved by the call to police, but failing that, the hospital and lawyer action should have worked to support her interests.

The Background of Relations Between the **Canadian Government** and the **Canadian Women's Movement**

Our CASAC Approach

C ASAC women live with distress and a certain sense of ever-present emergency. Often lives are at stake. Always, the *quality* of women's lives is at stake.[1]

Yet there have been times over the thirty years of our herstory when opportunity has gladdened us and made equality-seeking work easier, even thrilling.[2] There have also been times of peril that have shaken our sense of confidence that we can ever improve the status of women and reduce the sexist violence that holds us all down. Sometimes we would settle for, but cannot seem to achieve, an advance in the treatment of women already beaten and raped. But usually, we have our eyes on freedom and the prevention of another generation of women being abused and threatened. Other times, we can feel the political ground shifting and fear for us all.

We have always attended raped and battered women within a wider framework that has included the shaping of national discourse on violence against women when we could, and taking our rightful place in the public political discussion of what constitutes equality and freedom. We, as do caring, intelligent people everywhere, consider which social change strategies to use to end violence against women and to achieve dignity and liberty for all women…in particular, those we are charged with assisting.

Much of our CASAC activity is direct action: resisting imminent violence, creating escapes for women, breaking the isolation of women by developing affinity groups and mutual aid arrangements, and organizing ourselves into small, democratic groups. We maintain a consciousness-raising component among ourselves and constantly organize new women for our rescue, crime prevention, status-changing discussion, and work. We assist each other in acquiring access to the services of our communities and of the state. Similarly, we participate in mutual aid coalitions to join forces for us all. As early as the Justice for Women Campaign (1992), we worked with other national groups as an equal partner to fight to protect the equality-seeking component of the funding for our member centres.[3] We lobby for the effective and fair distribution of the resources of the state (including but not limited to the delivery of services). We participate in lobbying, law reform, and federal government consultations, when that is financially and politically possible, and when it seems to us to be productive.[4] Productive, for us, means there would be movement toward reforms consistent with our long-term goals.

While we do not expect women's liberation to be a product of governments, we do not exempt our communities, or our governments from responsibility for assisting women, as we resist repression. We expect our government to respond appropriately to women's legitimate aspirations for peace, freedom, autonomy, and economic well being. It is in this spirit that our work to examine violence against women was carried out.

This work reflects a moment in the transformation of Canada, the worldwide women's movement, and the bridging of centuries of women's struggle. We are participating in what is often referred to as the end of the second-wave women's movement, and we are reconstituting ourselves in the international movement of the new century.

We have lived through dramatic change imposed on us, not only by the violence done by individual men, but also by a decade of government responses to women's insistence on equality. We have endured five years of neo-liberalism. The significance of the details presented here must be read within this context. Otherwise, careful readers might miss the point.

This book intends to inform those who are committed to the advancement of women. Of course, it is designed especially to promote and support those working anywhere to assist women, in Canada, and the rest of the world, to emerge from this period of violent repression of women's aspirations.

A Few Keys to Our Herstory

The Canadian Parliamentary hearings that resulted in the *The War Against Women* report was a, then normal, consultative government process that paid the expenses of representatives of organized collectives and groups to go to Ottawa to present their opinions.[5] In this case, it was primarily women's equality-seeking groups consulting on the subject of women's needs in relation to violence against women.[6] That inquiry had grown from a cross-party deal between elected women on a parliamentary standing committee. In part, they were responding to the uprising of women in the community against sexist violence expressed in the media after the Montreal Massacre.[7] They were also responding to the attempt to harness the energy of that uprising in a call from some women for a new Royal Commission on the Status of Women.[8]

The significance of the first Royal Commission has been documented in other places.[9] For the purpose of this book, readers need to know that the federal sub-ministry responsible for the Status of Women, women's program funding, the Canadian Advisory Council on the Status of Women and the provincial Advisory Councils on the Status of Women as well as the women's equality sections in all government departments resulted from that more than twenty-year period of Canada-wide organizing work. Largely, women at a Strategy for Change conference conceived these initiatives.[10] Eventually, they served as the first sources of funding and government policy papers on sexist violence (but not for several years).[11]

The commitment to women's equality on the part of the Trudeau Liberal federal government had been hard won and was still boxed in by notions of formal equality, which framed many women's issues in terms of women's equal citizenship.[12]

The National Action Committee on the Status of Women (NAC) was the initiative of the voluntary sector of women activists in Canada. It was the first such national coalition. This coalition, along with others, pressed the government to implement the recommendations in the *Report of the Royal Commission on the Status of Women* as well as those that were not documented in the report or even clearly articulated yet by the movement at large.[13] Women's centres, which were nearly all members of NAC, provided the local organizing base needed to build support for grassroots women's demands and to illuminate new ones as they lobbied for change.[14]

Other women, including CASAC members, were responsible for simultaneously building the anti-violence initiatives and women's emergency centres. Class largely differentiated the two groups of activists: the anti-violence workers often being the poorer, less formally educated and less privileged. Neither was fully integrated in terms of race although aboriginal women and women of colour participated in and contributed significantly to both. Never the less, the work on violence was underway. The Winnipeg study fostered by CASAC members at Klinic[15] had recorded incidences and theorized about rape in a report to CASAC as early as 1980.[16]

In that same time period, aboriginal women and women of colour had launched other organizations and other feminist struggles that would lead us. To mention only three: In 1970-75, black immigrant leader Rosemary Brown was elected to the B.C. Legislature, India Mahila Association started work with the B.C. immigrant women population from northern India and Pakistan, and Jeanette Corbiere Lavell launched her fight against Section 12 (1b) of the Indian Act.[17]

Dawn Black, federal MP for the New Democrat Party (NDP), stated in the course of those parliamentary hearings of the 1990s, that the Royal Commission of two decades earlier had not addressed the issues of violence against women and that was an important reason why there should be a new one. Those 1990s parliamentarians were perhaps aware that even the limited government commitment to women's advancement, as it was laid out in the first *Royal Commission on the Status of Women*, was already waning.

CASAC took those parliamentary hearings as an opportunity to meet with feminists from across the country who were working on violence issues. We sat through many days of powerful presentations and then met with the presenters. We took home copies of everything to share with other frontline women. We could hear the marvellous consensus building among women across the country and across class and race divisions about what needed to be done about violence and its underpinnings and about how change should be accomplished. LEAF (the Legal Education and Action Fund), NAWL (National Association of Women and the Law) and NAC, among many others, delivered sophisticated analyses that interlocked with others to present a holistic picture that was powerful and achievable. While the *The War Against Women* report expressed a much watered-down version of that consensus, it nonetheless created a benchmark of community understanding. There is no reason to retreat from that benchmark. In the course of the hearings, CASAC learned how to use national meetings called for other purposes and heard that emerging consensus. We heard it and used it to mobilize support for abused women for the next decade.

Each presenter was asked, in turn, whether his or her group endorsed the call for a new *Royal Commission on the Status of Women*. CASAC agreed but expressed our concern that we had not really considered the matter and that it wasn't what we had come to say.[18] We wanted to carry forward the accumulated knowledge of the organizations, including rape crisis centres, from across the country. We thought allowing the government to go back to mass meetings and calls to individuals would be a tactical error that would cost women in terms of delayed action.

The press for something like the Royal Commission was, of course, a deal already constructed in Ottawa between parties. Obtaining the agreement of national women's groups was only window dressing. But even the women who were elected members of Parliament were disappointed when what we got from the incoming Conservative government was not the mainstream organizing opportunity of money and prestige associated with a Royal Commission style of government inquiry, but The Blue Ribbon Panel on Violence Against Women.

Individuals on the Panel were isolated from their groups, declared personal experts, and paid more than they were likely to have received by continuing in their community work. Some had come from frontline groups. The government refused to appoint women chosen by the movement (as we had organized ourselves), to authorize our groups as the authorities or experts or to use the spokeswomen we chose. Instead, they insisted on tokenizing the movement as a whole, including racialized and groups of disabled women.[19] Feminists failed too. There were a couple of groups that kept control over the member they knew but the process, as a whole, was terribly destructive for the anti-violence movement. The ten million dollar Panel, in its interim report, called for the federal government to provide funding to rape crisis centres and shelters for abused women. But the carrot also came with a stick. Just before the final report release date, Mary Collins, the Conservative Minister Responsible for the Status of Women, warned us "physically and sexually abused women could be further victimized if Canadians reject the Charlottetown agreement on October 28." The Minister said she simply wanted women to consider how a "no" vote (regarding the Accord) could affect them. "If there is a 'no' majority, you can't just pretend it never happened," she said. "It's just like in the family. I mean, if you have a huge argument you just can't pretend it never happened." CASAC and NAC had just withdrawn support for the Panel and were actively involved in the "no" campaign.[20]

The Panel published as its research and final report, a plethora of work that had already been done by the anti-violence movement.[21] The Panel published facts, analysis, and maps of the problem. But facts and analysis cannot be understood outside of their context. The main impact of the Panel was to counteract the accrued influence of the unity worked out in the movement. This was particularly true of the unity built in the feminist caucus at the Kim Campbell conference, and the *The War Against Women* parliamentary hearings.[22] Quickly, the Panel was called upon by the media, professional associations, and government officials alike to substitute government-authorized "experts" and "expertise" for troublesome, independent women's anti-violence advocates.

For the federal government, it established a successful model for consultations meant to restructure Canadian voluntary self-organized groups. It also played a part in ridding the federal government of the meddlesome movement of feminist activists. It carried within it, much of what has been wrong with consultations carried out by the Canadian government ever since. The Panel, in its work and final report, got just enough money to secure more media attention than the movement groups could secure and just enough government endorsement to replace or cloud what little natural authority had been accorded the pan-Canadian anti-violence women's groups in Ottawa. By then making sure that the chosen formation did not have the infrastructure and funds to do its job properly, the government shot down the authority of the Panel itself. The power of the anti-violence movement groups to speak on the issues and create pressure for government change was greatly diminished. The Panel itself was never given the prestige or power within the bureaucracy that might have assured cooperation for even the best ideas. The change of government, at the time of the release of the final report, further guaranteed its limits.

CASAC has never been granted national operating funds. At this time, all core funding to women's groups has been suspended. NAC has effectively been closed. It had endured aggressive attack since the beginning of women's resistance to the restructuring of Canada in the Charlottetown Accord by participating vigorously in the *No* campaign. Mulroney's Conservative government attacked in the form of rumour campaigns, funding of others who undermined its work and refusal to cooperate with NAC's annual Ottawa lobby. The re-election of Liberals did not relieve that attack; the restructuring continued without the proposed national accord. NAC, once the largest national women's coalition, recently struggled for more than two years without any government money.[23] The Federation des Femmes des Quebec one can speculate is facing similar and growing pressures. Currently there is no such national coalition as NAC (of pan Canadian women's groups) functioning in Canada. Provincial associations of service and advocacy groups cannot fill such a void.

Women centres have also been on the cutting block. Women centres have been in trouble since the federal government's decision to off-load their funding to the provinces. The crushing of staff and organizers at the Alberta Status of Women also temporarily silenced many. An act that clearly threatened other women. And whether or not they (federal officials) meant to set such an example to other governments they did. Those women were accused of working for the advance of the women of Alberta while receiving only UIC payments. Then the federal government hounded them as though they had committed fraud. Who didn't know that the provincial governments, especially those of Premier Ralph Klein and Mike Harris, had no commitment to women's equality or the enactment of the Charter? Even those provincial governments who were amenable to supporting women centres were faced with less money in the transfer pot.

The cutting of federal funding for women centres as equality-seeking organizations and the subsequent redefining of them as social service providers in terms of provincial funding criteria was key. That transfer/cut enforced their dependency on the provinces and consequently restructured their programs and operations from one of support for the advancement of women as a group to one of service delivery to individuals.[24]

The final blow in Alberta was the threat of the federal government to criminalize the remaining women's advocates in the centres. This technique of threatening low paid staff and volunteer advocacy boards with personal pressure on themselves and their organizations (as well as their families should criminal threats be pursued) has been repeated with NAC board members.[25]

Other processes took over. Some of the community outrage on behalf of women and feminism that was visible after the Montreal Massacre had also fed the Justice system's enthusiasm for Kim Campbell's conference, Women, the Law and the Administration of Justice. Kim Campbell was the first female Federal Justice Minister and she wanted to mark the occasion. At least this was a conference where the claim that "all stakeholders are welcome" was serious and not cynical. Judges from all levels were cajoled, seduced, and encouraged to attend, including those who proposed to educate other judges. Prosecutors and those directing prosecutors, police and those who educate police, were all nudged into sitting with women's equality advocates from the fields of law, anti-poverty organizing, law reform strategists, women's anti-rape centres and so on. A number of key women leaders from the aboriginal movement were convinced to attend. So were immigrant women leaders. Regardless of the glamorous settings used to lure the privileged as well as its mixed intentions and lack of direct outcomes, there is no doubt that this was a useful government activity related to violence which propelled some reforms in judicial education, rape law, the federal-provincial discussion of prostitution, and child care guidelines, among other things. It has never happened since.

The CASAC representatives from Quebec and B.C. and the Yukon approached Kim Campbell at that conference regarding the need for a new Rape Shield Law. The Supreme Court had just struck down the decision in the case of *Seaboyer and Gayme*. She told us she had received more mail on that subject than any other and she would be tabling new law. She wanted the public support, or at least to neutralize the public criticism, of women's groups. She invited four or five national groups to meet and advise her. When we neared the tabling of a draft, CASAC insisted that many more women and their advocates needed to be consulted as part of any meaningful process to create useful legal strategy meant to address women's oppression.[26]

This was during the era of the 1993 Violence Against Women Survey that confirmed our two decades of rape crisis centre and transition house statistics tracking by finding that:

- Fifty-one percent of Canadian women had experienced at least one incident of physical or sexual assault since the age of sixteen, and of those almost sixty percent were the victim of more than one such incident;

- The VAWS found that twenty-five percent of Canadian women had experienced violence at the hands of current or past spousal partners (married or common-law) since the age of sixteen;

- Sixteen percent of Canadian women had experienced violence at the hands of dating partners, twenty-three percent at the hands of other known men, and twenty-three percent at the hands of strangers;

- Forty-five percent of women had experienced violence by men known to them—twice the proportion by strangers;

- Over half of all women who reported violence reported more than one incident;

- The violence occurred more than once, and one-quarter to one-third involved more than ten episodes.[27]

CASAC used the opportunity afforded its own group to include those we thought must be consulted on rape law, a new and much wider configuration of feminists. The CASAC representative asked directly for the funds to meet and the power to choose who would meet and about what, as well as the control of government official attendance or not in return for some serious attention to her law initiative. We won from Campbell the costs to invite, gather, and facilitate a pan-Canadian meeting of those working on violence and those most affected by the violence.

We wanted all women who worked on the subject to participate, even if it was not their primary or only work. Aboriginal women, women prisoners and their advocates, women from Quebec, and domestic workers were invited to comment on their own needs, as were prostitutes and their advocates, battered women and their advocates, immigrant women, black women, students, welfare recipients, disabled women and so on.[28]

There were two lists created: one for groups of women with particular constituencies in terms of, for example, race, language or a specific burden and so on and another list for groups of women clustered around a specific demand or objective such as childcare or prisoners rights or refugee settlement needs. This early attempt to reconfigure the wider movement of feminists behind anti-violence initiatives was later attempted by NAC in the Barrie gathering to discuss violence issues and by the Canadian Association of Elizabeth Fry Societies (CAEFS) in their "Human Rights of Prisoners" consultation processes. It was facilitated by CASAC leadership with assistance from all those attending the "justice consultations."[29]

CASAC women found it enriching to work out joint positions within these coalitions and to meet the government on such terms. These gatherings exposed the complicated web that held sexist violence in its Canadian place in much the same way that consciousness-raising works in a small group. Each woman spoke from her group's concerns, expertise, and experience and listened to the others for similarity and overlap.

This also provided a very efficient way to work out recommended reforms of policy and procedural adaptations and initiatives that could advance the use of Justice resources toward women's equality and the reduction and amelioration of violence against all women.[30] We won, among other things, an agreement from Allan Rock, Minister of Justice, to undertake an "en bloc" review of those women in jail who had not had the benefit of being considered as survivors of wife assault who had needed to defend themselves. For more than two years, other national groups had assisted CAEFS in a post card campaign proclaiming, "Jails are not the shelters that battered women are seeking." During both the 1995 and 1996 consultations, women lobbied Rock and by the second year while we met in the Delta Hotel in Ottawa, Rock had assured us a review. This too became a fight with the bureaucracy, which substituted considerably less than the review modelled on the Legatt Inquiry, which we had been seeking. The Ratushny review, never the less, advanced some of the cause for women who were jailed. During the same years, we protested the lack of legal aid, especially for civil and family law, the overly quick introduction, and uselessness of the stalking law as well as the drunk defence and pushed for improvements to child support guidelines for divorcing parents, among many other significant reforms.

Those consultations established a forum for debate, discussion, and unity building.[31] We were developing a new form of consultation. Grabbing the willingness of Kim Campbell and the Ministers that followed through Allan Rock paid off. Every year, it allowed the movement to meet as never before on these matters, even though there was no pre-existing government consultative or supportive policy that allowed us to do so.[32]

Through that work, we established some terms that could make government consultations productive for non-government, equality-seeking groups.[33] Answering government's questions and supplying an audience, whether for bureaucrats or politicians, could not be our only agenda. Neither could lobbying ever be our sole purpose when meeting was so rare and expensive.

In the years immediately preceding this project, there was a certain satisfaction and sense of progress for CASAC in hosting the annual consultations between women's groups and the Justice Department. For several years, we had been able to invite feminist representatives from across the country to meet for three days and then to present a joint set of positions and messages to the Minster of Justice and his officials.[34]

Little did we know we were living through the beginning years of new across-government policies to refuse citizen engagement with policy decisions. NAC had already been attacked and cut and the national lobby which NAC's member groups had organized annually on Parliament Hill regarding the status of women in Canada was soon to be eliminated. The last NAC lobby was held in 2001. Funding seems to be generally limited now to projects sponsored by professional associations and non-government groups accepting contracts to research what the government would like to publicize.

It had never been the position of CASAC that violence against women should be considered by government only or even primarily as a matter of criminal justice or even that this was the most productive lens through which to view the problem. We were accustomed to the vacillation in government policy in the 1970 to 1990 period of insisting on the construction of sexist violence as either a matter of women's health or a matter of law and order.[35] We had argued since the 1970s that although violence brings health and justice into the picture, we should, as a community, assess and approach this as a matter of women's freedom. We can view it best from a position, ministry, or group committed to women's liberation. Only for a very short period of Canadian government policy did we achieve an equality approach and then it was a very limited, formal equality approach to women as equal citizens.[36] Still, the opening we had in the Justice Department, especially under Liberal Minister Allan Rock, was too valuable to dismiss. Occasionally, we could use it to get timely access to the ears of staff[37] or other relevant ministers of the federal government or federal-provincial working groups.[38] Those meetings created a precious record of the conditions of women in Canada and the changes proposed by women's groups.

Ongoing processes, similar to NAC's annual lobby, are being implemented. New anti-globalization processes like CEDAW accountability groups through the Feminist Alliance for International Action (FAFIA) and the construction of the demands and processes of the Canadian and International World March of Women are already in operation and more are coming.

The Justice consultations ended with the new policies on citizen engagement issued by the Treasury Department under Minister Anne McLellan's leadership. The Justice Department work suffers for lack of information and lack of pressure from frontline anti-violence organizations. The women's movement suffers being asked to present our opinions regarding women's equality and freedom from violence only within the context of a Victims of Violence model, if at all. And all women waiting for relief from violence (in law, especially) suffer from federal neglect and disregard.

The Canadian Government was Decriminalizing Violence Against Women and Criminalizing Women's Self Defence

It was on the way to a special CASAC meeting with Minister Allan Rock that we first articulated to ourselves, and then to him, that we were living in a pivotal moment in which violence against women was being decriminalized and women's defences against sexist and racist violence and impoverishment were being more and more criminalized.[39]

The occasion was the 1995 tabling and discussion of the amendments to the Sentencing Bill. The bill would bring us "conditional sentences."[40] Among other things, it discouraged imprisonment for crimes considered less serious: that is those that would ordinarily get less than a two-year sentence. Since, for many reasons, most violence against women receives sentencing of less than two years, we knew this would have disastrous results for women trying to hold men accountable and trying to find personal safety.[41] The bill was being fast tracked to avoid critical debate. In our minds, the bill was part of a new deal struck behind closed doors between the provinces and the federal government for the handling of criminal violence.

That year 85,000 women and children had used shelters to escape a violent man. Easily another 100,000 had used anti-violence crisis lines. Violence against women was more evident than it had ever been before. We were already worrying about the substitution of short-term municipal shelters for staffed transition houses committed to women's equality needs.[42] Not only would they fail to deliver (since it wasn't their raison d'etre) what women needed individually but also they could undermine the ability to track how much violence was going on since they did not record it as violence against women. CASAC had already been swamped with the needs of women facing mandatory counselling and unbalanced mediation with abusive fathers, brothers, sons, and husbands. The drunk defence as an excuse for violence was being considered and wasn't yet defeated.[43]

In the mid 1990s, we tried to confront the mess of science, junk science, and the law as DNA testing affected violence cases. Since DNA was becoming a useful tool in exonerating men who had been wrongly convicted by police manipulated informants, it was a difficult case to make. But since then, the defence bar has begun to join us in the argument that DNA is often a distraction. While the science has improved, it is still evolving and far from conclusive in most cases; the focus on it often detracts from the cases that do not involve DNA but where women are willing to provide evidence of their abuse and are in need of criminal investigations and prosecutorial diligence to make their case. To many police and prosecutors, those cases seem initially to be much less of a sure thing. Yet cases focused on a disagreement about consent are the norm, not the exception. Usually a woman knows who her attacker is and his identity is not in question.

Increasingly, federal justice officials promoted what was described to progressive people as a "declaration" strategy we "should" embrace called "Restorative Justice"; many of these we saw as unfair practices, including diversion before and after court.[44] The critique from left progressives was slow to come.[45] Many women's groups were offered contracts to examine and consider the practices. When it did come, the sham of restorative justice was somewhat revealed.[46] I am aware of no equality-seeking women's group's paper or position supporting the changes promoted as Restorative Justice in this bill. But the speed of the passing of the bill and the funding of its promotion suggests that the Justice Department was fully aware of the likely opposition.

We were already dealing with lawyers holding "whack the complainant" workshops given by and for the defence bar; these workshops advised lawyers how to demolish the credibility of any women complaining of sexual assault.[47] This was part of an accelerated campaign to frighten off women wanting to complain about violence to the courts. Jane Doe was trying to hold the Toronto police accountable and we were unable to prevent her being pilloried in the press and in the courts through the use of her health records.[48] There is no doubt that the continued use of records is to bully women with the fear that all their personal history will be searched for any material that might be used to call up sexist illusions and bias in the court or press. Those illusions are then raised to challenge her credibility. The use of these records has been particularly virulent in cases of incest but they have frightened and warned off many other women dealing with other types of sexual assault.

We were dealing with several women/wives/girl-friends who, after being violated by their male partners for years, were being threatened with or were already serving time in jail for their defence of themselves or their children. We were planning and thinking of their defence.[49] Our defences were being constructed as pre-meditation by the Justice system.

We protested the conditional sentencing to Justice officials at a meeting called by David Daubney of the Sentencing Reform Team.[50] We appealed to them that they could and should make it clear to all that violence against women was a serious crime and that conditional sentences such as house arrest and serving sentences in the community should not apply. We were told that was impossible.[51] But eighteen months later, when a conditional sentence was applied to Lillian Getkate's conviction, then prosecutor Andre Berzins challenged it and threatened to appeal it. He claimed it was very important that she not get a conditional sentence because this was a case of "domestic violence" and the sentence would send the wrong message.[52] Apparently, for the public good, according to this restorative justice model, exceptions could be made to the decarceration strategy to jail women who had defended themselves from horrific sexist violence but not to jail men who committed violence against women.[53]

Women were calling us from Ontario because their welfare checks were being reduced or restricted and they were being forced into "workfare."[54] The pressure to stay in abusive situations was mounting. We were dealing with an increase in child prostitution, street level prostitution, and the police meddling in local "neighbourhood" politics by fostering "shame the john" campaigns, with no regard for the effect on the women. Federal plans were unresponsive to our demands for protection of women being trafficked and for women being criminalized.[55] They made no commitment to interfere with prostitution itself.[56] Women found soliciting were being herded about the cities, if not jailed, while the men who abused them, if charged at all, were diverted without records or publicity to John schools.[57]

Domestic workers and farm workers were being held hostage in situations of sexist violence by immigration and labour legislation.[58] Legal aid was being limited more and more and had never been properly available for civil cases.[59] Women were being charged or threatened with being charged with welfare fraud and soliciting as well as being threatened with "mutual arrest strategies," and public nuisance charges.

The week the expression "decriminalizing violence against women and criminalizing women's self defence" came to mind, we were dealing with the police threat to jail our colleagues at the Windsor Sexual Assault Centre for shredding the confidential records of a woman who did not want her rape crisis files revealed to her attacker in court.[60]

It took a while for us to realize that the moment was created by the interaction of several initiatives on the part of global capital, federal government actions by both officials elected and bureaucratic, by the defence bar and the judges, before whom they argued, by the police and their political organizations. For a while we didn't see all that. We just knew that more and more women were calling us, with more and more need for advocacy to get what had been assumed for a generation to be available in Canada: subsistence income, basic health care, access to non-government advocacy to use the law.

CASAC met with Minister Rock in the Members' Lobby of the House of Parliament for half an hour to describe the problem and the hoped for solution. Minister Rock was aware that CASAC had no funds for a national office, no paid national staff, no lobbying funds, no public relations budget and no travel budget, so he agreed to make time to meet whenever CASAC could represent itself in Ottawa.

We pointed to the danger in the Sentencing Bill and our concern that it was being rushed through the House. We asked for immediate intervention to protect violated women and their advocates from the imposition of criminal charges, particularly regarding welfare fraud, victim records, and prostitution. We warned against the changes being proposed in criminal law defences and policy that would excuse men's violent, sexist behaviour as the outcome of passion or intoxication on top of their sense of sexual entitlement to women. We warned of the law and order wolf under the sheep's clothing of "restorative justice."[61]

We asked him to define restorative justice, to prevent the use of pre-conviction diversion in cases of violence against women until a public consideration of the predictable impact on women was undertaken and to avoid post-conviction diversion until further assessment of the success of the programs. We told him that each of these things was destructive for women, in and of themselves, but in combination, they would be formidable.

We didn't express the panic we felt that the equality-seeking efforts of women could be set back by years and that these Justice Department moves, in combination with what was being promoted in other parts of the government, had the potential to break the feminist anti-violence movement in Canada and to hide, once again, the very violence we were fighting.[62]

Notes

1. All CASAC women answer crisis calls and deal with women in life threatening and life changing moments.

2. CASAC history since the 1974 founding is available in CASAC office and online <www.casac.ca>.

3. Lakeman, L., letter from The Native Women's Association of Canada (NWAC), The National Organization of Immigrant and Visible Minority Women (NOIVM), The DisAbled Women's Network of Canada (DAWN), NAC, and CASAC, to Michele Landsberg, September 14, 1992.

4. Two good sources on the relation between the anti-violence movements and the state: Dobash and Dobash, (1992), *Violence against Women and Social Change*, London and New York: Rutledge, which assess that work in both England the USA, with some reference and many applications to the Canadian scene. Also see Lakeman, L., (1990), *99 Federal Steps*, which is both a programme, and a record of CASAC agreements of its time.

5. Department of Health and Welfare, (1991), *The War Against Women*: First Report of the Standing Committee on Health and Welfare, Social Affairs, Seniors, and the Status of Women to the House of Commons, Ottawa: author.

6. Lakeman, L., February 12, 1991, CASAC presentation.

7. *Maclean's Magazine* (1989, Dec. 18) online: <www.rapereliefshelter.bc.ca/dec6/Maclean's.html> and <www.rapereliefshelter.bc.ca/dec6/leearticle.html>.

8. This project was initiated by Metro Toronto Action Committee (METRAC). This whole period is extremely well documented and analysed by Andrea Levan: Levan, A. (1996). *Violence Against Women*. In Brodie, J. (Ed). Women and Canadian Public Policy. Toronto and Fort Worth: Harcourt Brace and CO., pp.320-355.

9. *Womenspace*, website of herstory online: <www.herstory.womenspace.ca/timeline.html>.

10. *Ibid.*

11. For instance, MacLeod, L. (1987). *Battered But Not Beaten…: Preventing Wife Battering in Canada*, Ottawa: Canadian Advisory Committee on the Status of Women (CACSW).

12. In this day and age we would be unsatisfied with less than substantive equality for all residents and a gendered approach to immigration, settlement, and support for the women of the Global South.

13. This not to be confused with the current use of the term, "Voluntary Sector Initiative," a government programme that delivers the only available government dollars to those who agree to produce some project work consistent with a pre-existing government policy initiative.

14. Not that centres were sub-NAC groups, in fact, the model for the NAC AGM lobby came from Vancouver Status of Women's successful B.C. lobby. For more information see Womenspace online: <www.herstory.womenspace.ca/timeline.html>.

15. CASAC member group in Winnipeg, Manitoba.

16. Brickman, J., Briere, J., Lungen, A., Shepherd, M., and Lofchick, M., (1980, May), *Winnipeg Rape Incidence Project: Final* Results, Paper Presented at the Canadian Association of Sexual Assault Centres, Winnipeg, Manitoba.

17. Silman, J. (1987). *Enough is Enough: Aboriginal Women Speak Out*. Toronto: Women's Press.

18. There is again a call for a new Royal Commission on the Status of Women initiated by the Status of Women Councils in Atlantic Canada. While we recognize the need for money and attention, CASAC has not endorsed this call. We prefer to support the call for funding autonomous women's groups.

19. Letter from Judy Hughes for the Panel on Violence Against Women to Joan Meister of DisAbled Women's Network Canada, October 7, 1992.

20. Vienneau, D. (1992, October 12) No vote called a threat to women. *Toronto Star*, p. A2.

21. Minister of Supply and Services. (1993) *Changing the Landscape: Ending Violence-Achieving Equality*. Final Report of the Canadian Panel on Violence Against Women. Ottawa: author, cat. sw451/1993E.

22. At the Women, Law and the Administration of Justice conference held in Vancouver, June 1991, Shelagh Day went in front of the conference and called for the women delegates of the "equality-seeking groups" to meet. In the caucus called by NAC, women discussed, for instance, why a national government programme to register the fathers who were not paying their support bills would be a bad idea for poor women. The group who had adopted the idea in the caucus dropped the suggestion from their proposals after they were convinced of the newly understood implications for the poorer women.

23. Personal communication (September 30, 2003) Abou-Dib, M., NAC executive member at the meeting of the Canadian formation of the World Women's March in Ottawa.

24. Two articles that were particularly helpful in the 1980s when we were beginning to analyse cooptation: Flakas, C., and Hounslow, B. (1980). "Government Intervention and Right Wing Attacks on Feminist Services," in *Scarlett Woman Magazine*, and Sullivan, G. (1982). "Funny Things Happened On Our Way to Revolution," in *Aegis Magazine*, spring (4), 12-22.

25. In both cases, the groups were starved for funding, and then the individuals were criminalized for their adaptations. In Alberta, the women were accused of working as advocates for the women of Alberta for free, while collecting UIC payments for part of the year. In the NAC case, the board members were accused of not paying the employers' share of the contribution to the Receiver General. They paid the workers and the small business people they owed first. They are being threatened personally with a $70,000 bill to the federal government.

26. McIntyre, S. (1994). *Redefining Reformism: The Consultations that Shaped Bill C-49*. In Roberts, J. and Mohr, R. (Eds.), *Confronting Sexual Assault. A Decade of Legal and Social Change*. Toronto: University of Toronto Press, pp. 293-327. Many have written about this process, including Judy Rebick, and Justice Minister Kim Campbell. Campbell, K. (1996). *Time and Chance: The Political Memoirs of Canada's First Woman Prime Minister*. Toronto: Doubleday Canada. We look forward to writing the CASAC version someday.

27. Johnson, H. (1993). *Violence Against Women Survey*. Ottawa: Statistics Canada.

28. CASAC has the lists of original invitees and of those who participated over the five-year period.

29. These became annual events through five different Justice Ministers from Campbell in 1992 to McLellan in 1998.

30. Smaller groups were always being proposed by Justice personnel, perhaps to satisfy political bosses, and perhaps to avoid hearing the context that could not be avoided in the larger consultations.

31. Although LEAF had become involved through the work of defending Donald Marshal, Anne Derrick, for instance, was keen to question anything that promoted a right-wing agenda that minimized the civil liberties of the men accused. But she also taught us that it was the state, in all cases that had wrongly convicted in Canada, not vengeful women. Fely Villasin was key in introducing the connection of domestic workers, rape, and the live-in caregiver programme, and the new questions of landed rights as a solution. Karen Mladenovic, for the prostitutes, warned of undermining of their Charter rights in anything that eroded their agency in the name of protection, and also of anything that sacrificed them as women in order to use them as witnesses, or abandoned them as inevitable sex slaves, instead of criminally challenging this violence against them. Shirley Masuda introduced the complexity of agency and consent for disabled women.

32. Status of Women consultation processes and Women's Program funding, which had allowed consultation through the NAC lobby, was threatened as early as 1993, in spite of public support, and was crushed by 1995. See online: <www.herstory.womenspace.ca/timeline3.html>.

33. We learned, for instance, that consulting with government was worth our time if we got to meet on our own terms (alone) first so that the government agenda did not overwhelm our own.

34. In 1993-1998, CASAC hosted annual consultations in which the government paid the expenses of some sixty to seventy women's groups chosen by CASAC for their expertise and interest in violence against women as a matter of equality. We met for two days alone to work on our own agenda, and then met for a third day with government representatives, sometimes as many as five ministers and many bureaucrats. We presented our issues and opinions of reform as a group. CASAC taped both the closed and open sessions and retains those tapes. Tapes of the open sessions were also taken by the Department of Justice Officials.

35. Both have specific dangers and can be used by government to over rule women's agency and self determination (as a group and as individuals). Law and jails can, obviously, be turned on women as well as men. One of the first persons determined as a dangerous offender was a very young and very "undangerous" woman, Lisa Neve. See CASAC conference material for Lisa Neve. And sometimes the fascism comes in with drug therapy and regulation, for instance of prostitutes and drug users mothers, aboriginal women immigrants, and so on.

36. Lakeman, L. (2000). Why Law and Order Cannot End Violence Against Women and Why the Development of Women's (Social, Economic, Political and Civil) Rights Might. *Canadian Women Studies,* 20 (3), pp. 24-33.

37. Consultations with staff on: provocation, self defence, mandatory minimum sentences, drunk defence, no means no, rape shield.

38. There was a spin off consultation series with Equality-Seeking Women's Groups held by Solicitor General Andy Scott, Vancouver April 21-23, 1998, under the leadership of CAEFS. CASAC attended.

39. We discussed these impressions and confirmed it immediately afterward with women's advocates gathered by METRAC to discuss the "records fight." It was a fearful insight then and there has been a growing body of evidence since.

40. The Sentencing Reform Bill, September 3, 1996.

41. Crnkovitch, M. (1995, October 11). *The Role of The Victim in Criminal Justice System-Circle Sentencing in Inuit Communities.* Paper presented at the Canadian Institute for the Administration of Justice, Banff Alberta.

42. Gadd, J. (1995, December 2). More Women, Children Using Shelters. *The Globe and Mail,* p. A9.

43. Still, L. (1992, April 24). Drunkeness Proposed as a Defence. *The Vancouver Sun,* p. 3.

44. Lakeman, L. (2000); Canadian Association of Elizabeth Fry Societies and Canadian Association of Sexual Assault Centre conference proceedings, Ottawa, October 1-3, 2001. Plenary/Roundtable on CD. Victoria: Time and Again Productions, 2001. Also available online: <www.casac.ca>.

45. Oglov, V. (1997). *Restorative Justice Reforms to the Criminal Justice System*. Draft Discussion Paper. Prepared for the B.C./Yukon Society of Transition Houses.

46. Department of Justice. (2000, May 7). *The Changing Face of Conditional Sentencing: Symposium Proceedings*. Ottawa: Author.

47. The public sponsor of this tactic was lawyer Michael Edelson. See Schmitz, C. (1998, May 27). Whack the Complainant at Preliminary Inquiry. *Lawyers Weekly*.

48. Doe, J. (2003). *The Story of Jane Doe: A Book About Rape*. Toronto: Random House Canada.

49. Sheehy, E.A. (1995). *What Would a Women's Law of Self Defence Look Like?* Status of Women: Canada.

50. Department of Justice. (2000, May 7).

51. A meeting called in Ottawa Justice offices in 1995 by David Daubney, former Conservative MP who authored the bill. Among those present: Kim Pate, CAEFS; Prof. Elizabeth Sheehy; Andre Berzins, Chief Crown in Ottawa and a figure in the Restorative Justice community; Lee Lakeman, CASAC.

52. A meeting called by feminist advocates with Andre Berzins and his staff in the Ottawa crown office (March 1997). This was eighteen months after the Justice meeting with Daubney. Those in attendance included a transition house worker from Lanark County Transition house, and Leighanne Burns, from the now closed second stage house, plus Kim Pate, CAEFS, Professor Elizabeth Sheehy, and Lee Lakeman, CASAC.

53. This was a case of an abusive husband who worked as a psychologist for the RCMP who had wired the house with a bomb device. The state could not see the self defence logic in the killing (of which she was accused) of her husband in his sleep. What were her options?

54. Workfare is a term first used by the Ontario government that refers to the loss of the right to welfare and the replacement of welfare with a government subsidized work plan in which non profit and profit making ventures could use unemployed people.

55. CASAC responded to the white paper on prostitution to the consultation possibilities with staff, such as Lucie Angers, and also protested loudly, even rudely, when women who were trafficked into the country were held in jail, even as we met in Ottawa. In personal communication with Don Perigoff, Rick Mosely, Yvonne Roi, throughout 1997-98, and with Rick Mosley in Canadian Embassy in Cairo, Egypt on the occasion of the UN meetings to discuss crime.

56. Increased licensing of massage parlours and their ads, for instance, merit no discussion in the white paper on prostitution by the Justice department.

57. Criminology Professor John Loman of Simon Fraser University is the best Canadian source on the use of John's Schools as an escape route from prosecution.

58. Lakeman, L. (2000).

59. These issues were raised in the consultation presentations to the Minister of Justice Allan Rock and his officials. Legal aid work was often led by Lisa Addario. See: National Council of Welfare. (1995). Legal Aid and the Poor. Available online: <http://www.ncwcnbes.net/htmdocument/reportlegalaid/reportlegalaid.htm>.

60. Personal communication (1997) with Fiorini, L., executive director of Windsor Sexual Assault Centre.

61. Lakeman, L. (2000).

62. Without anti-violence centres there would be no count. See Lakeman, L. (1993), and Dobash, E. and Dobash, R. (1992).

Pickton, the Police, the Pig Farm and the Missing Women

Suzanne Jay

ON FEBRUARY 8, 2002, the collective that operates Vancouver Rape Relief and Women's Shelter, invited other local women's groups to respond in a press conference to the latest move by the Joint Police Task Force.[1] The Task Force was investigating the notorious "missing women case" and had begun searching a pig farm. Three weeks later on February 22, Robert William Pickton (one of the farm owners) was arrested and charged with the first two of now fifteen cases of planned murder.

Six years earlier, with others, I had organized a Valentine's Day March through the downtown eastside to protest and mourn the missing women. My role has expanded over the years to include informing the local and international media about this violence against women.[2] I've spent many hours in the courtroom at Pickton's preliminary trial and I've started to write about what it has to do with us.[3]

I have been discussing the case with Deborah Jardine since last November. The first indication that her daughter was missing came from social workers with whom Angela had kept regular contact. On December 16, one of them called Deborah to say that something had happened. They were worried. Later they told this distraught mother that they had gone to the morgues at Burnaby and Surrey and that Angela's body was not among the "Jane Does." Although it was comforting that social workers would actually go looking for a destitute woman, it's telling that they expected Angela's disappearance equaled her death. Angela is not one of fifteen women that Pickton is now charged with killing, but Deborah considers her daughter to be among the murdered.[4]

In January 1999, Deborah spoke with the victim assistance workers and the community policing office in the downtown eastside. The social workers had directed her there when she called the Vancouver Police Department about her daughter's disappearance. Deborah's daughter was gone from the downtown eastside by November of 1998. Angela disappeared after attending a public meeting that became the documentary *Out of Harm's Way*. Organized by the Portland Hotel and the Carnegie Centre, the event to promote "harm reduction strategies" was attended by 700 people (partly because they were given an honourarium of $5). The officer told Deborah that Angela was one of eleven women to go missing that year. He told her about the possibility of a serial killer operating in the downtown eastside and then directed her to a detective in the Vancouver Police Department's missing persons section. That detective explained that they had not contacted Deborah about Angela's noted disappearance because Angela was an adult.

They had, however, called the Sparwood RCMP (Angela's old home town) to see if Angela was known to that detachment (presumably as a criminal). The detective did not take a statement or interview Deborah for information about her daughter. Deborah had this discussion in January, a full two months after Angela's disappearance. She pressed the detective to make a missing person's poster. He declined her offer of a recent photo of

Angela, telling her that they had one on file. Looking at the photos that police used for the missing women's poster, it's easy to see that they are mostly "mug shots." Many of the missing women had been arrested at some time or another for petty crimes.[5]

Victim's Services reply to Deborah's request for help was that they could not help her as she was not the victim. Since then, the victim services workers involved in the case have been criticized by family members unhappy with the lack of resources, information and help.

Through long distance calls to the Portland Hotel (in 1998), where Angela had lived, Deborah discovered that the police had visited the building but they had not looked through Angela's belongings, nor interviewed the caretakers of the building, which had a rigorous sounding security system, including security cameras and a sign in/out system. She found out that Angela had picked up a welfare check three days before her disappearance but the police had not talked to that worker either. She talked with Angela's dentist and found that the police had still not requested her dental records five months after her disappearance. Officers assigned to the case explained that because Angela had been sighted several times since November, investigators had not pursued that investigation actively.

Deborah made her own phone calls and found that a woman named Sereena Abbotsway physically resembled Angela. Sereena had called our crisis line in September 1996 seeking shelter. She was being released from hospital after 10 days in a coma. A man named "Dave" had raped, beaten, then thrown her from a car off the Georgia Street viaduct. Since we were full, the volunteer answering the call found Sereena another place to stay knowing that the police were already involved and investigating. Regretfully, we don't know any details about the police investigation into the man who almost killed Sereena that time. Sereena Abbotsway was last seen August 2001. She is one of the fifteen women Pickton is charged with murdering. At the time of her disappearance, Sereena was wanted on a warrant for failure to appear on a charge for stealing chocolate bars.

Deborah decided to use the Police Complaints process. She explains:

> I filed a Formal Complaint against the Vancouver Police Department for Neglect of Duty in July 1999. It took considerable time, effort, researching codes, conduct and police regulations. Prior to filing I wanted to be positive I followed all protocol. It was essential my complaint would be taken seriously and not discarded because of a technicality.[6]

The letter explaining the dismissal of her complaint informed her that an investigator had talked with the officers she had named, and each officer denied saying the things that Deborah had documented. Each officer described Deborah as unreasonable and emotionally distraught in addition to being a liar. The Commissioner noted that Deborah was the only family member of a missing woman to complain about the police. Deborah's appeal of the decision painstakingly documented the behaviors of investigating officers and the sections of the Police Act that Deborah believed they had contravened. Despite her offer of tape recordings of disputed conversations, her application was rejected.

As we prepared for the February press conference, we learned that Pickton had been charged in early 1997 for confining (and handcuffing) and repeatedly stabbing Wendy Lynn Eisteter. At that time Judge Kenneth Page released Pickton on a $2,000 bond and bail conditions including no contact with Wendy Lynn and that he not leave his farm.

Those 1997 charges against Pickton were stayed. The crown judged that there was no likelihood of a conviction. And apparently he decided there was no redeeming social interest in the prosecution. The crown said and we all knew that it meant Wendy Lynn, who was described in all the media reports as a drug-addicted prostitute, was not considered a credible witness to the events that left her injured and half clothed on a country roadside at 1:45 a.m.[7]

Various sources noted a dramatic increase in the number of women who went missing from the beginning of 1998 to 2002.[8] One newspaper reported that "more than 30 of the women have disappeared since police first looked at Pickton as a suspect in 1997."[9]

In 1998 a second officer was assigned to the missing-person's section of the VPD to help deal with the sharp increase in missing women. In the same year the Vancouver police department issued a press release saying that police did not believe a serial killer was behind the disappearances. Since then, a wrongful dismissal trial has revealed that senior officers disregarded the theory of a serial killer out of professional jealousy and that the missing women investigation was in disarray, was understaffed and subject to infighting among officers.[10]

In April 2002, the Police Complaints Commissioner, Don Morrison was forced to resign from his position after serious allegations about his biased handling of complaints and an over zealous coordination with police. His bias surfaced only because staff blew the whistle during a routine legislative committee reviewing the complaints process. After his resignation, the Commission announced that there would be a review of those complaints reviewed by Morrison. Deborah filed a request to re-open the investigation into her complaint. Deputy Commissioner Barbara Murphy denied the request noting that on completion of the police investigation, Murphy's office may recommend a public inquiry.

Various other political figures including the Vancouver Chief of Police Jamie Graham, Members of Parliament, Libby Davies and Tony Bhullar have also proposed a public inquiry. We insist too that there must be public inquiry including legal support for equality seeking groups like us to participate fully and meaningfully. But in any case, the end of the police investigation is not in sight. Public scrutiny needs to begin now and the police must be more forthcoming immediately.

On April 23, 2002, Karin Joesbury filed a civil suit naming the Government of Canada, British Columbia, the City of Vancouver, the Vancouver Police Department and the City of Port Coquitlam. The filed claim states that they

...willfully failed to properly investigate all information received knowing that such willful failure to investigate would allow the killing to continue, or alternatively the Vancouver City Police and the Royal Canadian Mounted Police were negligent and such negligence allowed the killing to continue and such negligence amounted to gross negligence.[11]

Pickton is charged with Andrea Joesbury's murder.

On June 2, 2002, a worker in our center saw a poster in her neighborhood asking for information about a missing woman. We contacted the sister who had put up the posters. She had reported her sister's disappearance to the Vancouver Police but had been told that the police get many missing reports a day and that there was little to nothing they could do. The missing woman was struggling with drug addiction and was prostituted. Her boyfriend had kicked her out of their home after a fight and she had not been seen since. Our women's group call to pressure police for action resulted in a same day pick up and distribution of a photograph of the missing woman. The next day she was found.

Notes

1. Groups: Downtown Eastside Women's Centre, Justice for Girls, Aboriginal Women's Action Network.

2. This story has been covered by world wide media. My assignment has meant interviews with CBC, CNN, the BBC, the *New York Times*.

3. Jay, S. (2003, March 03) Reject Red light Speech to Raging Women Conference, Vancouver.

4. <http://www.vanishedvoices.com>.

5. Hume, M. (2002, May 7). 54 lives, 54 mysteries in B.C.: The mind works overtime as police search pig farm. *National Post*, p. A1. A reporter for the *National Post* confirmed this hunch when he checked several women's police and court records. A visit to the vanished voices website is from a guard at the B.C. Women's Correctional Centre, a provincial prison. The guard notes that s/he knew many of the women on the list of missing because they had each spent time in prison.

6. <http://www.vanishedvoices.com/complainttoPolice.html>.

7. Hume, M. (2002, May 7).

8. In June 2002, a reporter gave me a list of missing women that he had compiled (Ron Benzce, personal communication, June 13, 2002). He recorded a huge leap in the numbers of women gone missing from 1997. According to his documenting, seven women disappeared during 1995/96 and ten women disappeared in 1997 alone and ten again in 1998.

9. Middleton, G. and Berry, S. (2002, June 25), Police first suspected Pickton early as 1997: Vancouver police and RCMP argued over resources and territory, *The Province* A4.

10. Brought by former Detective-Inspector Kim Rossmo.

11. Berntsen, D. (personal communication 2002, June 26).

Bernardo and Pickton:
Making the Cases of Monsters

In other places, we have tried to begin to come to terms with the making of monsters. Obviously, these men are born children, as innocent as others, and so we must, as a society, account for their distorted adult selves. As individual men, they must take responsibility for their own choices and the consequences of their actions. However, no child could warp into such a man without the intentional collusion of some, the mindless cooperation of many, and the indifference of even more. And we are not talking about their mothers. We must ask ourselves, who introduced them to pornography, to weapons, to abuse, to being abusive, to sexualizing abuse, to abusing for sexual gratification? Who ignored, or even rewarded their actions, as they became more terrible and more terrifying. As for their attitudes toward women, "they had to be carefully taught."[1]

Since the publication of Jane Caputi's book, *The Age of Sex Crime*, CASAC women have known about the relations between the media, police, and serial killers built on modern "Jack The Ripper" propaganda. This is a theory of the social construction of such serial crimes of woman-hating in the modern industrial city. The commercial media coverage affects, and is essential to, both police investigations and killer behaviour. The nature of modern policing is essential to the success of, and is changed by, the killer and the media. Similarly, the sensationalizing of the killer is important, if not essential, to both media profits and police budgets; a hideous theory with entirely too much supporting evidence. In both the Paul Bernardo and Robert William Pickton cases, we see the modern community and this three-way interdependence at work. We need a Caputi-like analysis of these two cases. We can see some of the Bernardo triangle already and the Pickton construction is just beginning to be unveiled.[2]

We would need to examine: the taunting of police in the media, the media campaign for evidence by police, the struggles over using the video footage of abuse as evidence in open court, the media ban struggle, the defence bar withholding of videos, the police budget demands, the promotion of DNA testing for all women working in downtown prostitution, the media spectacle of the farm search, the police provision of media tents at the crime scene, as well as the provision of tents with controlling Victim Assistance staff in which family can mourn at the dig site, and the "leaks" to the media from the police.

The technological changes available in North America since the publication of Caputi's book offer new insights. It is not just a hideous side bar that both men used video pornography extensively. That they made video and photographic images of the abuse of women is known. That those images of rape, degradation, and destruction were likely headed for the commercial market is easy to guess. Bernardo had money and no regular income, and Pickton was known to entertain biker gangs with drugs, pornography, and prostitution. Members of Hells Angels partied at "Piggy's Palace."[3] And gangs, including the bikers, own not only most of the drug trade, but most of the pornography and prostitution industry in Canada. Certainly they are implicated in anything going on in the east end of Vancouver.

A powerful chapter of the Hell's Angels also have a stake in the area. One high ranking member of the East End chapter had an interest in the No. 5 Orange strip club, and Starnet, an internet gambling and pornography company that was busted in the late 1990s. Starnet was located near the heart of the downtown east side on Carrall Street. The company streamed live sex shows online from No. 5 Orange, and was also known to distribute pornography depicting sadomasochistic scenes.[4]

But we are concerned with the legal issues of their stories and the questions of how the system avoids conviction in cases of violence against women. We are specifically concerned with what happens at each of the five stages: 911, police reports, investigations, crown counsel decision-making, and finally, in the courtroom.

In both men's lives, before the final hideous charges are laid and the horrifying sexist collusion of other men is revealed, there is the everyday mindless cooperation of the system with the abuse of women and before that, the everyday indifference to women and our complaints of violence.

In the mindless category of cooperation with their sexist violence, is the legion of mistakes of criminal policing chronicled in both cases. One of the worst examples is the wilful interference with the Charter rights of the accused and the rights of prisoners. No breaching of the rights of others will serve us well. In fact, in high profile cases, it often provides the legal escape route later for the men (see: Regan defence). Most often, mindless actions took the form of police territorial wars, failure to co-operate between detachments, failure to follow policy and procedures, and failure to use common sense. In this category too, is the failure to adjust to technological change: to test DNA handed to them, to record evidence technologically, and to communicate with others electronically.[5]

The most worrisome category of complicity in the making of monster cases is the continued indifference to women's equality and violence against women. In both the Bernardo and Pickton cases, this came in three forms. The police (and some other authorities) refused to take seriously other earlier complaints against these men. They ig-nored criminal abuses of women that were happening in front of them as though no one had complained.[6] Even after the murders, women's issues are still ignored. The police construct these events as being about families rather than women. The horror of the Bernardo murders and the vulnerability of women have been, with the help of the media, made into the individual tragic story of two families. That leads directly back to the gov-ernment promotion of the Victims of Crime Office in Ontario.

Once having caught the man, the police, and the media, search aggressively for a fe-male victim to construct as an accomplice as though that was the only way to convict.

In both cases, ex-girlfriends had already repeatedly reported the men for violence. Usually the system avoided arrest, never mind conviction. In both cases, women who had escaped these men had handed the authorities extra-damning evidence: some of seeing bodies, of being stalked on foot and in cars, of enduring sexualized strangulation, of being attacked or confined. These women handed over their word, their stories, for evi-dence, as well as addresses, descriptions, license plate numbers, and so on.[7]

Responsible, ordinary women reported both men to authorities for sexist violence long before their final crimes. These were women seeking help against more normalized forms of abuse and violence. They were largely ignored. Their evidence was wasted. Their motives were impugned. Their sense of danger challenged.

There were also men, in both cases, who reported to authorities that they feared for women and could attest to the danger to women.[8] That was ignored too, as though it was an everyday occurrence![9]

It seems to us that once the men have become monstrous and monster crimes have been committed, once the community is in shambles and women are dead, the cry for prosecution is mounting, and then all resources are finally mustered. The police and me-dia, at that point, need to find a way to make sense of their failures, and to explain how things could go so far. They seem to find comfort in using the media to construct the case as a singular crime of the century carried out by a genius of evil with equally evil female accomplices. They need her as both a source of evidence and to serve as a dramatic ele-ment. Apparently, they can believe this woman, perhaps only because she is already pegged as an evil woman. We saw it with Bernardo and we are seeing it now in the use of Dinah Taylor in the Pickton case.

We do not condone the behaviour of women complicit in the abuse of other women, whether it is pornography, prostitution, or murder, but since reporting violent men is so unlikely to be convincing to authorities, and actually leaving them is impossible without legal help, we wonder just what these women could have done? How to avoid complicity and still be alive?

It is not just desperate women and the police who over-looked abuse, allowed themselves to be complicit. Local musicians and partiers, including politicians, all used

Piggy's Palace, in spite of what they saw of illegal drug damage, prostitution, and violence.[10] No. 5 Orange is across the street from the Vancouver Courthouse. Prostitution is rampant in the biggest cities in Canada. It is evidently not newsworthy or worthy of legal action that women report dangerous men to police, on a daily basis, to no effect.

Notes

1. Pop song from Tin Pan Alley musical, South Pacific, about teaching racist attitudes to children.

2. Caputi, J. (1987). *The Age of Sex Crime*. Ohio: Bowling Green State University Popular Press.

3. Piggy's Palace was a clubhouse style nightclub in a converted barn owned by David Pickton (brother of) in Port Coquitlam.

4. CTV website link: <http://popups.ca/content/publish/popups/bc_missing_women/content_pages/articles/article7b>.

5. Justice Archie Campbell's report of the policing, in the Bernardo case to the Ontario government, is featured in: Jenish, D. (1996, July 22). Bernardo: How the police bungled the murder case. *MacLeans Magazine*, pp. 40-41.

6. Bailey, I. (2002, February 16). Killer Stalked Prostitutes, Police Told. *National Post*, p. A8. Makin, K. (1995, September 1). Police Had Bernardo link in 1990. *The Globe and Mail*, p. A1.

7. Bailey, I. (2002, February 16), Makin, K. (1995, September 1).

8. Bailey, I. (2002, April 12). I Tipped Police to Pickton in 1998: Former Employee. *National Post*, p. A10.

9. Makin, K. (1995, September 1).

10. Middleton, G. (2002, February 10). I played 'Piggy's Palace.' *The Province*, p. A6.

What is **CASAC LINKS?**

What We Were Trying to Do

CASAC LINKS (from April 1, 1998 through March 31, 2003) was a five-year project of the Canadian Association of Sexual Assault Centres to: unite several Canadian feminist anti-violence groups, using shared crisis work, shared research and documenting it, and shared political activity. It was also an attempt to bring forward and amplify the voice of anti-violence workers, and the women who call them, in the national discussion of women's equality and rights. It is another step in the ongoing effort of the women of CASAC to end violence against women and move the world toward a peaceful, egalitarian freedom.

We act always as part of the international women's movement and so are always moving within and building new coalitions of allies. We planned, as part of this project, to engage women in the wider pan-Canadian women's movement in discussions of violence against women and how to stop it. We planned to be active discussants on movement building including the resistance to sexist violence within NAC. We planned to consider whatever we might build anew, whether it is with the International March of Women, both at the Canadian coordination level, and on the International Sexist Violence Committee, with FAFIA, not only in the think tank process, but also as part of the committee preparing an alternate report to the UN on CEDAW compliance. We planned to lead discussions in the FFQ and in the post-Beijing gatherings. We planned alliance activities with labour and human rights organizations.

CASAC LINKS uses the Charter of Rights and Freedoms as a point of discussion, a legal lens, an overarching law, an entry into international affairs, and as a promise to Canadian women. The project, as a whole, examines and partially answers the research question of how the Canadian state avoids identifying, arresting, prosecuting, convicting, and properly sentencing those men who commit violence against women. We were aware that everyone else knew how few cases of sexist violence are acknowledged and authorized as valid by the system. We thought that documenting that injustice would be pointless. The Statistics Canada staff was already undertaking severity and incidence studies so we could move on to other documentation.

Making Deals and Getting Money

In this decade, securing any federal funds for effective anti-violence work has become a victory in itself. It had been a source of great irritation to women in anti-violence work that many millions of dollars had been channelled through the Family Violence Initiative Fund. Justice was to have an initial cut of 7.1 million.[1] The government has used too little of that money to make a difference. In 1991 the federal government claimed to be spending 136 million dollars on an initiative that was just getting underway. Through the name alone, the public was encouraged to believe that millions were being spent on the problem. One might assume that in frontline organizations we had received much of the money and that, any minute now, we would hear from some that "the government is throwing money at the problem."

But as far as we could tell, most of that fund's money had simply circulated from one government department to another and was being used to little effect on violence against women issues. A staff person in Justice, or Health, or the Solicitor General's Department, had a title changed to reflect something related to violence and that department acquired a new part of the fund. Justice officials claimed to need the money to review the Criminal Code and the Divorce Act to see what could be done to make victims safer. They were to better inform frontline workers on how the law could be used to secure women. They were to train judges and so on.[2] Or an extended arm of government enriched itself; for instance, a meeting of hospital administrators or teachers or police chiefs to discuss violence against women became the reason for a special grant from the fund.[3]

For thirty years, violence against women has been visible, and considerations thereof should have been made part of the normal course of governing. It requires only a redistribution of priorities and resources already available within government departments. Police chiefs meet on a regular basis and, after all, women are 52 percent of the population: this is one of the critical issues of law and law enforcement facing women. Why hadn't it been a priority all along? Why does time allocated to this topic in existing meetings justify increased police budgets? Why is violence against women not a key topic in all police meetings? Why does attending to the normal require extraordinary funding? We suspected cynical posturing about new programs and approaches. Very little of that public money, so widely promoted as a special fund to address family violence, was actually used to support the services and advocacy that constituted the only proven and new (in these past thirty years) community force for change—the services and advocacy created by the independent women's movement.

As representative to CASAC, from B.C. and the Yukon, I brought my ideas and plan to the Regional Representative Committee of CASAC (representatives chosen by member centres in B.C. and Yukon, the Prairies, Ontario, Quebec, and the Atlantic regions). They endorsed the outline, agreeing that CASAC should seek funds from the Family Violence Initiative Fund through the Federal Department of Justice. Allan Rock, Minister of Justice, encouraged us. He said he respected frontline service providers and that he saw that we (CASAC) could "hold government officials feet to the fire."[4] He was referring to the consultations we had organized. After several meetings, he suggested he would approve the money, but that we needed to prepare a project that met the departmental requirements. We recognized Rock as a politician who seemed determined to have a positive impact on community development. He knew it would be our objective to funnel as much of that money as possible into the preservation and development of existing local equality-driven services.

Of course, what we really needed was a step toward core funding for the centres, and for our national coalition. But all levels of government continued to refuse. So we designed a project that would reinforce our infrastructure and enhance national dialogue among ourselves. The increasing government withdrawal of financial and political support from equality-seeking groups meant we would have to restructure our communications and interaction. Maybe this project could increase our capacity to do so.

The withdrawal of government-funding commitments and consultative processes risked not only the future of our national anti-rape infrastructure, but also the very existence of the network of women's centres, shelters, and anti-rape organizations in Canada. No matter what we designed to sustain national dialogue, we knew we wanted to preserve the basic availability of centres in which feminists can take calls from desperate women, organize with them, educate our communities, and ourselves, and mobilize some effective community responses.[5]

The original proposal was tailored to the available money in the Family Violence Initiative Fund. It required us to shape the project around research. We didn't particularly want more research or want to do more research. We needed action. Still, only the technical requirement had to be met. Allan Rock already agreed about the principal of action first, and research only as a means to record it.

What remained of the fund would not have been enough, even if we had it all. Certainly what was left of the multi-million-dollar fund at that point was much larger than the final agreement between CASAC and the Federal Department of Justice. Our project, in its first draft, would have required five million dollars over five years, and would have seconded workers from twenty member centres full-time to the project. There was to be one centre from the capital city of each province, plus a second, smaller city. In this way, the smaller centres could compliment the voices of the larger centres, like Vancouver, Toronto, and Montreal.

There is no doubt that anti-violence work would have benefited from this larger amount, both as a way of responding to more women in each province, and as a way of strengthening the work of CASAC as the largest non-governmental feminist anti-violence organization in the country. The final agreement with the Department of Justice allowed for two million dollars over five years and our project was tailored accordingly. We have often wondered what those other three million dollars were used for. Has anyone heard? Was it something useful? Did it leave a legacy of improved community relationships and increased possibility for social change? We have seen no sign of where that money to end violence against women went. Did it save lives? Ours did.

Finding a Reform Strategy Consistent with Our Transformative Intent

We planned the project to focus on the application of the spirit of the Canadian Charter of Rights and Freedoms to women's issues.

The work began with CASAC's consideration of *The Equality Deficit: The Impact of Restructuring Canada's Social Programs*.[6] We read all the research published at that time by the Status of Women Canada regarding Canada Health and Social Transfers (CHST) and its impact on women.[7] We found this provided helpful explanations, documentation, and theorizing about what we were experiencing in our work and the rest of our lives.[8] We chose *The Equality Deficit* as one of our starting points for shared work because the authors had consulted us (CASAC), and had tried to include our frontline experience in their analysis. It seemed to us that *The Equality Deficit* addressed the particular herstory and achievements within Canada that were being damaged by structural adjustment policies.[9] We had observed the authors' efforts to include in their construction of a feminist understanding, both the impoverishment, and racializing of women being intensified by those policies.

Over the next five years, we, as CASAC representatives, LINKS workers, and citizens participated in many fora,[10] read many accounts of the end of the welfare state in Canada, and of the globalization process in which Canada has played a role, and which has engulfed the women living in Canada.

We operated with some hope of improving the treatment of women and children through the application of the Charter and Criminal Code of Canada. We knew we could suggest guidelines that would address the systemic issues of inequality. These might improve the policy development of police and crowns in relation to spouse assault, criminal harassment, peace bonds, and sentencing. They could be of assistance to the victims of male violence, including single women (without the social requirement of a male overseer, father, husband, sponsor, etc.), those beaten and raped within the family, those at risk on their jobs due to harassing bosses, and those driven into prostitution. The project was interested in ensuring that Charter equality issues related to violence against women were attended to and advanced in consultation with the Federal Department of Justice, the centres, and the community.

The project was also conceived to benefit rape crisis centres, many of which have existed for years in service to their communities with too little or no federal government funding, despite the start up funds of the 1970s, which identified these centres as being vital to the advancement of the equality of women. Independent, feminist, rape crisis centres, transition houses, and women's centres are still the best resources for women to decrease their isolation and vulnerability in the face of male violence. That usefulness and the demand for centres is evident in the number of women who call centres every year, who want to be involved with the independent women's movement, and who want and need information about the law and their rights under the Charter.

LINKS made it possible for eleven centres across the country (initially 12, one from each province, and two from Ontario and Quebec) to work united in learning about the Charter and its potential role in ending violence against women. It also allowed discussions of all the influences, particularly those involving the federal government, concerning the issue of rape in Canada. For the first time in many years, women could describe what was going on in each city, and begin to compare notes on the changing situation for women. Although CASAC had maintained a system of regional representatives and managed to raise funds for them to meet occasionally, it had been several years since we had been able to afford to meet nationally as representatives of centres and as frontline workers. This horizontal communication had always been the backbone of CASAC and was sorely missed. In this project, we moved back toward that structure, not only by modeling it in the project, but also by meeting with Regional Representatives and attending the national convention that accompanied our conference "Women's Resistance from Victimization to Criminalization."[11]

CASAC LINKS paid one worker from each of those eleven centres for half of her time; this was dedicated to LINKS work with other centres. Using the language and promise of the Charter of Rights and Freedoms, she discussed her crisis interventions and her community. She recorded some of that work in the research component; other parts on the Internet, and in local public education materials. Of course, she discussed her findings and new approaches with other workers in her centre as well as with other centres. We speculated, with some assurance, that she would use her understanding to respond with more confidence to violence against women in her community, and make LINKS between her experiences and what was being done in other parts of Canada and the world. We hoped she would be welcomed into Canadian political debates about the Charter and its future, the relationship between criminal courts and the Charter, as well as, social change and the Charter.

The project made it more likely for workers in rape crisis centres and transition houses to develop and strengthen their work with the women who use their centres. We hoped that, as usual, workers would make use of the expertise and knowledge of each caller and research interview participant to benefit and inform other women across the country. That was often the motivation expressed by the interview participants. Help and information about the law, as it affects women victims of male violence in both criminal and civil cases, is a compelling factor for women escaping abuse and women establishing personal safety, independence, and any other actualization of her promised equal legal status within Canada.

The target groups for the project were and have remained the women who call the centres, and stay in transition houses, the paid staff and volunteers who work at the centres, and the feminist allies in the women's movement both within Canada and on the international scene. We, of course, hoped to effect at least some positive change for all women. We expected to make some small advances for women in Canada.

Engaging the Digital Revolution

Computerization of the centres, the establishment of a national web site, and the promotion of ideas and opinions within the Canadian context, were central to the LINKS project. CASAC had participated in and followed the early work of Womenspace.[12] We had developed and managed an early Internet network among those who were invited to the women's groups' consultations that informed the Justice Department.[13] That network facilitated the digital communication of only one woman from each national group. From that experience and our discussions with those groups, we knew that even if women had the hardware, they also had specific needs in the area of training for full use of the Internet possibilities and for comprehension of the digital revolution that was underway.[14]

Under-funding and under-staffing paralyzed most women's groups and certainly the anti-violence groups. They had no economic opportunity to adjust to this moment: no computers, trainers, sites, or networks dedicated to advocacy work.[15] To the extent that centres had any computers at all, it was likely to be found sitting on the desk of a bookkeeper (being used like an overgrown adding machine). Consequently, we had very little hope of using digitalization to advance the cause of women or of the non-government sectors or civil society at large. We were and are in danger of falling out of the loop (actually of being pushed *out* of the loop) of law reform initiatives, public education opportunities, movement building, and community building. We designed LINKS as a modest pilot initiative to explore what the digital revolution might hold for us.

During the five years of the project, LINKS centres were each able to buy a computer.[16] In the beginning, neither the Regional Representatives nor the LINKS worker groups could communicate by email or Internet. Basic training was our first hurdle. Each of those computers was dedicated for the use of the LINKS worker while she was doing the crisis counselling and research that would become national work. Otherwise, they remained available 24-hours-a-day and accessible to all other workers in the centre, including volunteers, and, in some cases, callers, and users of the centre.

We suddenly saw public legal education possibilities within the anti-violence workers' networks, and for us with other communities regarding male violence against women and women's equality. One of our most effective tools was the development of our web site and web-capacity building; we discovered ways to educate the educators and to promote progressive dialogues. Maybe we could keep the web sites and information depots interactive, and, therefore, current and widely accessible. Of course, our main target audience was our membership, but the sites could be widely used by women (and some men) in Canada and well beyond. We would face an enormous problem of how to continue this work without money for salaries after the project, but the initial achievement would stand, nonetheless.

The overall CASAC LINKS project was developed and approved at the level of regional representatives meetings. It was vital to keep political control in the hands of our elected executive and not allow project funding to reorganize us. The representatives and the research team, in consultation with established feminist researchers, could develop the research study component of the project, which was participatory in nature. The research team, also known as the LINKS workers and the national staff, would participate in all levels of the creation of the research model and the tools used for interviews and analysis.

The High Media Profile for Some of Our Cases Affects Us All

During the course of this project, many Canadians have been affected by numerous high-profile cases of violence against women. Such impact is unavoidable. The national staff hoped to add to the project some understanding of these cases since they constitute such a large part of the context in which we were examining responses to violence in Canada. Initially, we imagined a more distanced analysis, but when we realized that we were, as frontline workers, involved in many of the cases, we worked with centres and workers to communicate a sense of the story from our perspective, to augment the commercialized and sensationalized story most women endured, and all public officials were watching:

- The Jane Doe rape in Toronto and struggle with Metro police;
- The May/Iles wife murder and subsequent inquests, and then the murder of Gillian Hadley;
- The Fujian boat women trafficked from China;
- The rape cases of Hilton in Quebec;
- Jill Gorman's fight against Tyhurst, the psychiatrist rapist in B.C.;
- Rozon (Just for Laughs) sentencing in Québec;
- Bonnie Mooney's brutalizing in B.C. and the civil suit about the policing responsibilities at three levels of government;
- Paul Bernardo's case of avoidable murders (although out of the time period of the project, this was still a major ideological and political influence);
- Robert Pickton and "the missing women" of Vancouver;
- Nellie Nippard's ongoing fight for protection from her husband in Newfoundland;
- McKeowen and Leclair murders while 911 listened in Winnipeg;
- Regan cases in Nova Scotia.

The Power/Politics Within the Project as We Begin

The lines of political authority for the project were settled in our contract with Justice. We refused to change our decision-making process (Regional Rep's as an interim decision-making body between conventions, consistent with policy and conventions, with one centre/one vote to establish policy whenever possible); this was our attempt to minimize the dangers of limited project funding, especially in the absence of core funding. The Canadian Association of Sexual Assault Centres has never received core funding from any government, provincial or federal. There have been a few funded projects, but it has usually had to rely totally on the voluntary participation of its members. Our project budget and work plan, therefore, included meetings of the national decision-making group: the Regional Representative Committee. We hired LINKS and a national staff from within our current membership and obtained office space from which the project would be conducted.

The national staff was hired in Vancouver to allow effective over-seeing by the responsible regional representative, requiring as little time as possible. CASAC insisted that the project meet the political standards of our organization, so it was essential to have a bilingual coordinator.[17] It was also essential that the national staff be experienced as much as possible in frontline anti-violence work. The coordinator, half-time office manager, and web-site staff, all had to be able to understand and lead a discussion with frontline workers in the midst of a cross-Canada dialogue stemming from the everyday, normal experiences, opportunities, and frustrations of anti-violence work. Since CASAC didn't have a permanent national office and since it was crucial to spend what funds we had on supporting the centres, we housed the project in the basement of the Vancouver centre. Space and equipment for the project was rented from Vancouver Rape Relief and Women's Shelter, where the infrastructure of phones, copier, fax, and computers meant less money had to be allocated to the overhead expenses of running a national office. In fact, there were only two desks facing each other, equipped with computers, etc. and sharing a phone. The Vancouver Rape Relief Collective supplied reception services, security, and all staff personal needs.

The Regional Representative Committee maintained the final political authority over both the project and the publication of any outcomes. Each year, the committee met five or six times to discuss our progress and to advance the work of the regions in relation to the LINKS project. We also used those meetings to steer our organization, as best we could, and to advance the coalition's work well beyond the terms of the project.

Pan-Canadian Issues

The Regional Representative Committee agreed to propose and choose together which centres would participate on the basis of several criteria. They were to be already functioning and established anti-violence centres, which had long-term staff who were familiar with the current legal information and practice needed for everyday advocacy regarding violence against women, and who could also be released from other duties to dedicate the time needed for the duration of the project. The centres needed to have an existing internal organization that would promote group discussion of new possibilities and recurring questions. The role of groups and grouping was essential to our design and execution of the project and research.[18]

We agreed that we would choose one from each region and two more from the most populated provinces/regions. The choice of a range of centres was especially important because we wanted some level of involvement from the whole organization, not only in administrative support, but also in terms of political involvement in the discourse we were creating. We needed the reputation of the centres in their communities, their relationships with professionals in their communities, and their crisis support work. We wanted the work of this project to have long-term implications that would be visible in the long-term work of the participating communities and centres.

A Regional Representative approached each centre to enlist their participation and agreement to second a staff person half time to the project and to enter into an agreement with the National Office in which the National Project Office would take responsibility for sending quarterly payments and receiving reports as well as financial and political accounting. The national staff would not have a direct "boss" relationship to the workers. The coordinator and director of the project took responsibility for suggesting directions for the LINKS portion of the worker's time; the centre and their established system of accountability would remain in place for all other aspects of her work. Any relationship with interviewees, including disbursements for their expenses and honorarium, would be conducted through the centre.

We had agreed that staff seconded from the centres to work on the LINKS project were to be long-term workers (paid staff or volunteers) who had experience with the legal system in their roles as anti-violence advocates in their centres, and who could lead the rest of the centre in the work coming out of the project. In the end, only half the workers fit these particular criteria; in part, because the funding pressure on centres was already having an impact. Once the centres were chosen, the project was underway.

Centres Selected

Vancouver Rape Relief and Women's Shelter was chosen from the beginning and remained with the project throughout.

Calgary Communities Against Violence left after the first year of the project because they did not want to participate in the research portion of the project...the centre feared punishment from local authorities and had spent a lot of time and resources building a relationship with the authorities in Calgary.

AWO'TAAN Native Women's Shelter was asked to be part of the project and remained with it until the end of the five years.

Tamara's House (transition house in Saskatoon) stayed with the project until the LINKS worker resigned in the second quarter of the fifth year of the project; the decision was made at that time, because of lateness of the project, to not replace the centre.

KLINIC Sexual Assault Counseling Program, Winnipeg was chosen from the beginning and remained with the project throughout.

Toronto Rape Crisis Centre/Multicultural Women Against Rape left after one-and-a-half years because they had made an internal decision to focus the energy of the centre on local and provincial alliances.

Timmins Area Women in Crisis replaced Toronto in the second year of the project.

Ottawa Sexual Assault Support Centre left the project in the second year for fear the project would further victimize women; they feared that women's anonymity could not adequately be protected, and that too many details that would reveal the women would have to be included. We were not successful in interesting another centre from Ontario. They were totally engaged in protecting themselves from the Harris government agenda. After the second year of the project, we accepted that Ontario would have one centre instead of two.

Montreal Mouvement Contre le Viol et l'Inceste participated in the project from the beginning and remained throughout the five years of the project.

CAPAS de Chateauguay participated in the project from the beginning and remained throughout the five years of the project.

Fredericton Sexual Assault Crisis Centre participated in the project from the beginning and remained throughout the five years of the project.

Avalon Rape Crisis Centre, Halifax participated in the project from the beginning and remained throughout the five years of the project.

Newfoundland and Labrador Sexual Assault Crisis and Prevention Centre (formerly called *St-John Rape Crisis Centre*) participated in the project from beginning and remained for the five years of the project.

PEI Rape Crisis Centre participated in the first year of the project and decided to withdraw in the second year of the project; the centre had gone through many years of lack of funding and did not have an adequate staffing level to dedicate one woman's position half-time to the project.

Antigonish Women's Resource Centre came on board the project in the second year and remained with the project until the end of the five years.

Having centres in as many provinces and regions as we had gave us the opportunity for pan-Canadian discussions. It helped to highlight what social, legal, and political policies affected women across the country.[19] We had no idea, at the beginning, that we would also be chronicling the disintegration of national standards and removal of what state protections for women had been won in law and policy in the previous fifty years. It was a failure of design not to anticipate this and not doing so has slowed us down considerably. Centres closed, words about rights lost meaning, women who called us, volunteered with us, and worked for us, were more and more impoverished and desperate. Centre workers were in a constantly escalating crisis of having to attend to individuals in need of help due to diminishing services, increasingly hostile governments, increasingly contentious media, and communities in uproar.

We hoped and planned that the financial benefit of LINKS to the centres would be significant. The centre in Newfoundland did not have the money to rent a permanent space.[20] It had been operating for years, but was floundering. The women who had sustained the collective with volunteer hours were under ever more severe economic pressure, preventing volunteer organizing. The women who called them needed more and more daytime advocacy.[21] The changes in the condition of women in Newfoundland meant that their anti-rape collective collapsed under the weight of no paid help.[22]

The Strength of Frontline Feminist Experience

We knew that by involving experienced long-term members of the centres, whether their experience had been as paid staff or as volunteers, we would have access to a tested and flexible analysis and praxis about violence against women and women's equality which we might be able to reinforce and authorize with the national discussion, and which would then reinforce that voice within each group of local organizers. We knew that equality-seeking activists were in need of some think-tank-like possibilities and that strategies and tactics, campaigns, and recommendations would logically flow from any contact between such women. The voices of the individual women we would interview would be critically important, but the voice of women who had met with thousands of such women would be no less so. The callers would give us an individual snap shot and the workers would confirm its context and present a collage.

Practiced, long-term rape crisis, and anti-violence workers bring a level of expertise and analysis to research interviews, allowing for more detailed information, and accurate judgments about the situation for women using the justice system. More practiced crisis workers would teach the language and practice of anti-violence work to the newer members. Newer members would have the opportunity of the project, through the research and national conversations, to develop themselves as advocates and organizers within their own regions.

They would bring to their work a level of data and comprehensive analysis they could not develop in isolation. Not only would workers be much better at navigating the legal systems, and much better advocates for the centre and its clients, but they would locate their work in relation to the international women's movement, the international struggle for human rights, and the struggle against international globalization. Our main hope was that practiced women would be able to spot and analyze what was happening to women in Canada, juxtaposing the promise of the Charter against the current crisis in women's equality, especially in the area of violence against women. Since we built the plan on the participation and leadership of whole centres, we were dependent on both their success locally and their membership responsibility within CASAC.

Opportunities for grouping women in response to their experience in the system, as well as opportunities to organize women in the women's movement were expected, as was action outside of the terms of the project.[23] We were looking for opportunities and actions to take what was learned about the Canadian Charter of Rights and Freedoms and use that knowledge in the advocacy for individual and collective groups of women.

Getting Started Always Means Reconnecting with Older Political Agendas

Even as representatives discussed the project with centres in their regions and with closely allied groups in their area, the work began. The profile of CASAC was heightened. Questions about when and when not to work together as anti-violence groups were raised.[24] Pressure against us working together came from many sides. The Ontario Harris government, for instance, had tried to force together services for abused women, and raped women, to confine the already small budgets of both under the guise of One Stop Shopping. While we debated whether or not to consider "violence against women" as a category more useful in the political context than "wife assault," or "incest," or "rape," since it reveals who did what to whom, and, therefore, what and who must change, we did not argue for combining services for efficiency of cost or service delivery. We might sometimes need specific services and combined political formations. Many governments, including the Harris Tories, had imposed community "coordination models" on local centres that impaired the ability of non-government groups to advocate for the women who needed them by tying funding to impossible partnerships.[25] Discussions began as to which professionals could be trusted for cooperation and which agencies would be helpful. Some old struggles were re-ignited.

The project had to bridge the gap between the unilingual English-speaking centres in Canada and the centres in Quebec, which were either bilingual or French. Bilingual and French centres were growing in Ontario and B.C. The language and culture gap was challenging enough. We began to manage some meetings between the dominant Anglophone group, with two Quebec centres, and one bilingual centre in Ontario. Opportunities for learning about the unique coalitions and groups in Quebec were essential to the rest of the centres. And our picture of the Canadian context was simply impossible without the women of Quebec. Ordinarily, as a matter of policy, Regional Representatives work in centres. We decided to allow the participation of a Quebec provincial coalition staff person as a Co-representative who did not meet our criteria of "centre based" as a concession to the collective needs of Quebec.[26] This proved both problematic and useful at various points in the five years. We had the opportunity and the challenge of bilingual meetings of Regional Representatives and of LINKS staff from centres, sometimes with professional researchers and consultants hired for the project. Materials both written and digitalized had to be translated with very little money. We started with a convention that the meetings would remain in the Ottawa, Toronto, and Montreal triangle, in order to save funds for travel, translation, and meeting space. The hosting region or centre would supply the administrative needs of the meeting: chair, minute-taker, personal supports, translation, meeting space, etc. We hoped that we might strengthen the commitment of the centres to a bilingual practice and interest local members of local centres in the workings of CASAC.[27] The plan was a moderate success. Translation was always a problem, and is very difficult, if not impossible, to solve without extra dollars.

The women from Quebec often had to manage an exhausting situation full of political double meanings. The Anglophones had to handle a situation in which they carried the anger from many other moments of English domination that had offended intentionally. The current unintentional harm, therefore, was always additionally destructive and suspect.

But most of our energy, from both sides of the language divide, went to meeting the challenge of two criminal justice systems, two Charters, and our ignorance of each other's reality. Certainly, very few workers in English Canada were aware of the progressive history of criminal justice issues in Quebec or the history of the development of the systems of community building and public popular education organizations. None of us were fully aware of the breadth of women's groups and their coalitions being funded in Quebec.[28]

The Quebecoise and, increasingly, the Ontarians were not fully aware that many of the issues they were confronting at the provincial level were being led and often controlled at the federal level in policy and law. Nor were they aware of the differing access to federal funds for women's groups as experienced especially in the west and the Atlantic regions.[29]

Penniless Regional Organizations

We knew we could reduce the isolation of the centres across regional boundaries, but we could not address the lack of contact within CASAC regions.[30] We could try to assist regional meetings, and we could and did plan digital networking to be of some assistance, especially in those regions, like B.C., and the Atlantic, which could not afford to meet face-to-face as they needed to. It could not replace access to national conferences and pan Canadian meetings to which they might be invited or that interested them, but it could help.

Penniless National and Local Women's Movement

In the original conception of the project, we planned to broaden the base of the alliances, both within and outside of CASAC by funding the participation of shelters and women centre's equal in number to rape crisis centres. We also planned to add to that mix, a number of visible minority immigrant women's groups as well as aboriginal women's groups that would not ordinarily meet our membership criteria as providers of emergency and usually twenty-four hour services.[31] We hoped to speed the formation of a broader and ever more intelligent movement of women who work against violence against women from a feminist perspective. We thought it might be time to intensify the feminist political link and loosen the link to service models or even to community development models.[32] We had some hope that out of the informal dialogue that always accompanies shared work we would define a new basis of unity for the future.[33] Very tight budget restrictions limited that option. Nonetheless, over the five years, we did find ways to advance that agenda too.

We had a sample of women centres and transitions houses within the project where we could begin that dialogue. Several years earlier, in the work to form a situational coalition to help construct the new rape shield law, we had included an even wider selection of service/political formations committed to ending rape, but without more money, our experiment in LINKS was limited.

Race and class differences between us and between groups of callers had to be faced in our discussions. Planning honoured our intentions for a world without class and race oppression, but we knew we would not over-come the historical differences within Canada. We were wary that economic forces were creating a gap between the women who use our services and those who collectively operate them. Our main advance, we thought, even after the budget restrictions, could be in the alliance work among national organizations. We did work on and achieve some increased race integration of staff and services, and other progressive changes at the local level,[34] but we under-estimated, by far, the changes happening to other groups with whom we hoped to build alliances: Pauktuutit Inuit Women's Association, Metis National Council of Women, Native Women's Association, Congress of Black Women. All have suffered economic blows and political restructuring that have reshaped their functions under new government regimes.

Some of Our Organizational Weaknesses

Centres leaving the project during the course of the five years led to some instability. It was always a huge problem since we had invested so much. New centres had to catch up with a project already familiar to the others. Work was delayed. Some of the original concepts of the project were lost as a result. Losing Toronto as a centre meant that the project could not benefit from the unique experience of a women calling a rape crisis centre in the most culturally and economically diverse city in the country. The leadership on race integration questions that might be expected from Toronto was absent and had to be offered from weaker centres. To be fair, LINKS had less to offer to the Toronto centre. It was better funded than most, had more access to the national media than we could achieve, and would have found itself working to educate some of the others. It was CASAC that suffered for lack of Toronto. Although it is still the opinion of the participating members that Toronto would have gained too in positioning itself in the national discourse. Vancouver, and Montreal Centres, that carried similar, if less, community power, decided to participate for reasons of their own. Losing PEI Rape Crisis Centre left that province out entirely from the benefits of financial stability and regional coalition building. And, more importantly, it isolated the PEI centre from our human rights discourse.

Still, we missed opportunities for public education through the media in response to high profile cases as a result of this lack of representation of the biggest centre in Ontario. But we also lost voice because the consolidation of ownership of the media was working against us. The cuts to the CBC and the changes in print media ownership all cost us influence with the public. We were still extensively covered. Most media coverage focused on the Vancouver and national staff. It was hoped that more of this would come from the regions when high profile cases were publicized in their cities. Opportunities became available in Montreal from time to time, but the language barrier was often an issue.

There was an obvious problem of execution in our plan in that many of the workers assigned were much newer than we had hoped. It was usually the result of local economic pressure on the centres, but sometimes a pan-Canadian skepticism crept in regarding what could be achieved in a project based on law. Centres expressed fear for women, and some participating centres expressed a distrust of any partnership with research professionals, or government agents. The worldwide experience of government intervention in the women's movement had taken its toll.[35]

The work we planned and imagined required skillful practice as an anti-rape activist. We presumed those skills based on experience as a counsellor, media spokeswoman, lobbyist, and alliance builder. Virtually every long-term worker has those skills. But new women were more or less skillful. They lacked even the confidence that would make them jump to action in particular ways. Consequently, we missed opportunities for public legal education with our groups and through the media. We also missed opportunities for using regional coalitions and coordination within cities to advance equality for women and anti-violence work. Research interviews, in some cases, lacked political judgment in terms of follow-up questions and probes. Perhaps most important, there were missed opportunities for grouping women within the centres around the issues coming out of the research and the project. We missed some opportunities to organize callers and users of the centres. There was a certain level of denial or self deception or deceiving each other about this, instead of facing it squarely, which prevented us from solving the confidence and skill-sharing problem. For instance, more involvement from the

Regional Representative might have supplemented the needs of the newer staff without sacrificing opportunities.

Every change in LINKS staff meant more difficult group building for the national team. Since we had very little money to meet, it was important that we remember each other from one meeting to the next, and be satisfied with email connections in-between. With a stable work force, this would have been barely sufficient, but any change in personnel disrupted whatever culture we had established, and renewed any unresolved fears and discomforts. The team building was, nonetheless, very successful, and hopefully, lasting.

Power Politics Not of Our Making: The Giant in Our Midst

We did not imagine how fast and how totally the social fabric of Canada would change. Consequently, we did not plan to research that impact on women, and on our organizing for women's equality. But the knowledge gained in communicating with each other, nonetheless, does record some of the consequences of the withdrawal of Canada's safety net, as it applies directly to women raped and battered, and as it applies to the infrastructure of services and advocacy organizations which had been built during the period of the existence of that net.[36]

What, after all, can a transition house mean for most women when there are so many less jobs for women? When there are few jobs at all, and we lose the right to welfare, pensions, and UIC? Transition to what? Who can protect women's legal Charter rights in an undocumented mediation or alternate dispute resolution (ADR)? Do mediators get equality training? How do we challenge a mediator's failure to apply Charter law, without legal aid, or provincial test case litigation funds? What can violence against women still mean when city governments promote the legalization of prostitution in massage parlours red light districts and escort services for tourist dollars? What can gender mainstreaming mean when a federal budget can be imposed which does not consider the impact on women? What are we to do with the increasing fear in racialized communities of the imposition of police state tactics? What does it mean to criminalize violence against women, then charge, as nuisances, the women who complain of the violence? What is the impact of a targeted criminalizing practice? What does it mean to target international trafficking as organized crime, and then to jail the victims?

Government changes have affected each woman's and each centre's use of the state in the protection of her rights and freedoms. Our project could have been much better designed to consider and triangulate these changes, these blows. In the lead up and over the course of the project, centres would have to deal with the impacts of:

- Father's rights groups;[37]
- Victim's rights groups;[38]
- Right-wing law and order agendas that cared little about women's equality;

- The downsizing and secreting of government decisions;[39]
- The rhetoric of mainstreaming equality;[40]
- No money to women's groups;[41]
- Relentless cuts to public sector programs[42] and jobs;[43]
- Back-tracking on the fifty years of small steps of income redistribution that had been achieved;[44]
- Fundamental reorganization of education and health care;
- All centres were threatened and cowed by the increasingly punitive responses to women's advocates;[45]
- Women in need being targeted, particularly for welfare fraud, prostitution, refugee claims, for being trafficked women, and for unsuccessfully complaining of violence;[46]
- Such pressure from the government and the public hindered some centres' participation and led to some distrust between officials and the centres.

Some of Our Criteria for Success

In the end, our co-workers and callers will judge. Did we do the job? Did we reinforce the centres to do their job? Do we understand better the discussion of rights? Can we better understand what callers are asking of us? Can we better articulate women's demands for equality—for freedom from sexist violence? Do we know each other better as centres, workers, and advocates? Do we understand the achievements and failures or weaknesses of the movement that won the Charter of Rights and Freedoms? Can we understand and use that achievement without losing our place in grassroots organizing? Can we survive the restructuring of information in the digital revolution? Can we make the digital revolution work for us? Can we unite to better the protective net that shelters and anti-rape centres offer? Can we unite to advocate for systemic change to prevent violence against women? Can we unite in an even greater force to demand the protection of our sisters and daughters, our mothers, and neighbours, our friends, and lovers, from the violent tyranny of sexism? That is, after all, what we really set out to do.

Notes

1. In spite of many requests and some publicized versions, we have never seen a real accounting of the Fund monies, or how it was used except in an internal document, which Allan Rock offered me to analyze in his constituency office (1997). See Minister of Supply and Services Canada. (1991). *Family Violence in Canada: A Call To Action*, cat. H72-21/66-1991.
2. I can never understand the need for more public dollars to educate the most privileged and most formally educated members of society. Why not simply require it as a job-performance factor?
3. I saw briefing notes prepared for the Minister in which that grant was revealed. Those notes were shared with me by Allan Rock in his constituency office as we prepared for a meeting with George Thompson, Deputy Minister, to press him to deliver on the Minister's promise of funds in 1997.
4. Allan Rock, Minister of Justice, personal communication (June 1995).

5. In April 2003, B.C. funding ended for Victoria Sexual Assault Centre, Kamloops Sexual Assault Centre, and Terrace Sexual Assault Centre, leaving only two free-standing feminist rape crisis centres in B.C. The others were replaced with Specialized Victim Assistance Programs whose funding is based on the population base since they are charged with servicing criminal justice victims, not preventing the victimization of women. Their funding too has been curtailed.

6. Brodsky, G., and Day, S. (1998) *Women and the Equality Deficit: Impact of Restructuring Canada's Social Programs.* Ottawa: Status of Women Canada.

7. By 1998 nearly all federal funding directed to women's equality was being used to support professional or para-professional research.

8. But we continue to protest the policy change that directed what little women's programme money remained, to research only. This practice has divided activism from analysis, and has intensified the race and class divide in the movement. It has also blocked the integration of the intelligence of working class women from the current debates.

9. In particular, the loss of national standards and the involved pieces of legislation.

10. For example: National Women's March process, FAFIA think tanks, Beijing plus-five processes, consultations with Status of Women Canada, rebuilding the left processes, World Social Forum processes, including Puerto Alegro, the Quebec anti-poverty bill processes, and Critical Resistance processes against the prison industrial complex.

11. CASAC convention in Ottawa, October 29-31, 2001. Minutes available at CASAC.

12. Women's Internet Conference proceedings, October 18-21, 1997, Ottawa: Canada. See online: <http://womenspace.ca/confer/>.

13. Rock had agreed to pay for several years of Internet access through the Access to Justice Network for those invited to the Justice consultations. That access permitted our early experimentation.

14. Women's Internet Conference proceedings, online: <http://womenspace.ca/confer/>.

15. METRAC was also experimenting and eventually built the OWJN, The Ontario Women's Justice Network website: <www.owjn.org>. The Hot Peach Pages had yet to launch its website: <www.hotpeachpages.net>.

16. Renting is promoted under the contract, but we suggested ways to buy and constantly trade-up to keep women abreast of the new technology.

17. CASAC policy requires communication in both official languages for all national meetings.

18. Fine, M., Weis, L., Weseen, S., and Wong, L. (2000). For Whom? Qualitative Research, Representations, and Social Responsibility. In Denzin, N. and Lincoln,Y. (Eds.), *Handbook of Qualitative Research*, Thousand Oaks: Sage Publications, pp. 107-131.

19. *Ibid.*

20. Until the LINKS project paid the rent and paid a half time worker.

21. Daytime advocacy is usually necessary to win those goods and services that are normally delivered by the government.

22. LINKS supplied one half-time salary for a worker who could fold the rest of her work into the LINKS project, and work the rest of a full-time job for free, until they could raise more money from the provincial government. We were hoping their work in the project would help them make the necessary connections to achieve that funding.

23. Fine, N., Weis, L., Wessen, S., and Wong, L. (2000).

24. Old debates about united approaches for battered women, raped women, harassed women, and prostituted women, as well as, debates about how to consider the work to protect children from the abuse of men in their families. But also debates as to whether sexual assaults in residential care should be considered within the incest paradigm, since the men were in surrogate father roles.

25. Coordinating bodies are often created by blackmail, cooperating in order to get funding, and are often comprised of low-level government officials, and take enormous amounts of time from frontline workers in a process that is more like "catch me if you can," using the failures of the system in individualized cases. Obviously it works to correct the treatment of some women, sometimes, but rarely.

26. Staff of CALACS (provincial association of anti-rape centres in Quebec) are also members of CASAC.

27. This worked well sometimes with members coming to translate, chair, observe, but gaining a sense of the movement and their national organization, as a by-product of giving the project that support.

28. There are as many as thirty ongoing women's service coalitions with offices and paid staff.

29. There is one rape crisis centre in Newfoundland, one in Nova Scotia, and one in New Brunswick. All under-funded and under-staffed. There are two rape crisis centres in Vancouver compared to several in Montreal and Toronto.

30. Except in the case of Ontario and Quebec, who have coalitions supported by federal funds, as well as, provincial, centres do not have the benefit of provincially funded coalitions of rape crisis centres. Victim services were quite another thing.

31. The Kenora centre hosted a meeting funded by Women's Programs in Winnipeg to construct a wide advisory committee that we kept informed through to the CASAC Women's Resistance Conference: from *Victimization to Criminalization*, October 1-3, 2001, in Ottawa. As well, members discussed in preparation for the convention, and criteria by which we could broaden our membership to include racialized groups, but not the new depoliticized victim assistance groups.

32. The reps agreed that the integration of service and politics was key, as was the continuum from consciouness raising to advocacy, and that we were not interested in intensifying the unity on counselling, for instance.

33. The problem we were facing in our communities is that of authority shifting to those groups who provide no service and, therefore, have no frontline sources of women's reality. Often they were paraprofessional and less working-class based.

34. The Quebec coalition in 2003 has assigned Diana Yaros to lead some internal education and access work for its centres.

35. In Australia: Flaskas, C., and Hounslow, B. (1980); and in the USA: Sullivan, G. (1982). See as well: Dobash, E., and Dobash, R. (1992).

36. Lakeman, L. (2000).

37. Senator Anne Cools' 1998 country-wide tour, For the Sake of The Children, sponsored by the Senate, provided a platform for men to complain about their support payment obligations as though they were custody and access issues.

38. An Act Respecting Victims of Crime, Victim's Bill of Rights, 1996, and the formation of the Office for Victims of Crime in Ontario under Scott Newark's leadership eventually assumed responsibility for overseeing women's rape centres, so that now women's equality issues are considered a sub-set of victim's rights according to the Ontario government.

39. The actual Vancouver Agreement among the governments of Canada, British Columbia, and the city of Vancouver, March 9, 2000.

40. For example, see online: <www.swc-cfc.gc.ca/resources/gba-research_e.html#gender>.

41. For example, see online: <http://herstory.womenspace.ca/timeline3.html>.

42. Ranging from lunch programs for school children to lack of long-term beds for elderly women.

43. Particularly women's well-paid jobs in the health, education, and welfare sectors.

44. Landsberg, M. (2003, September 28). Tories Waging a Sinister War on Women. *Toronto Star*; B.C. CEDAW group. (2003). *British Columbia Moves Backward on Women Equality*. (Submission to the United Nations Committee on the Elimination of Discrimination Against Women on the Occasion of The Committee's Review of Canada's Fifth Report).

45. Mary Lou McPhedran worked for years to hold accountable those doctors who abuse their patients. She is now facing a lawsuit from The Canadian Medical Association for naming doctors and other health professionals who rape in a *The Globe and Mail* article. See proceedings Women's Resistance at CASAC.

46. Kimberly Rogers paid with a lifetime ban from welfare for her transgressions and then with her life. See online: <http://www.elizabethfry.ca/rogers/3.htm>. The Coroners Inquest (began Oct. 15, 2002) inquired into the death of Kimberly Rogers, August 11, 2001.

R. versus Tyhurst and Gorman versus Tyhurst

Tamara Gorin

IN 1989, FOUR WOMEN came forward to the Vancouver RCMP and Vancouver Crown to report attacks on them by their psychiatrist, Dr. James Tyhurst. They described that over a period of twenty years, he conducted "treatment" on all of them that included signed contracts to participate in "master/slave" therapy. He required the women to undress and remain partially or completely naked throughout the therapy sessions. He escalated to sexual assaults, including rape, and physical assaults, including the use of sado-masochist paraphernalia, such as, whips and jewellery. These attacks occurred in his office, his home office, his home on Gabriola Island, and in the homes of the women.

At least one woman complained to the British Columbia College of Physicians and Surgeons in 1981, one woman informed the state (her parole officer), and another informed her therapist. Three of the women attended support groups with WAVAW (a rape crisis centre in Vancouver).

The RCMP did most of the job they were supposed to do in this case: they took the statements of the women and searched his home in Vancouver with a valid search warrant. They forwarded the appropriate charges to the Crown. After a gruelling and very public case in which the testimony of the women was luridly quoted daily in the local and national press, Tyhurst was initially convicted of five counts of indecent and sexual assault and sentenced to four years in jail.

At appeal, the defence argued the trial judge's answers to the jury's questions were confusing and not appropriate. The judge, Justice Whetmore, was accused of being drunk at the time. Had Justice Whetmore been sober, or, as he insisted, rested, when the criminal court jury asked him for further direction, the defence would have had little or no grounds for appeal. But the appeal was granted and, upon retrial, Tyhurst was acquitted of all charges. The Crown appealed to the B.C. Court of Appeal and was denied.

In 1991, at the same time as the criminal trial was proceeding, Jill Gorman, one of the complainants, filed civil charges. By the time the case came to court, it became clear that the defence would rest its case on the validity of similar fact evidence—that is, the admissibility of the evidence of other women who Tyhurst had attacked to support the complainant's case.

The court ruled in Ms. Gorman's favour in 2001. She was awarded just under $557,000 in damages. The defence immediately filed for appeal and the appeal was heard in May 2002. The Supreme Court of B.C. ruled in April 2003 that the judgement was sound and denied the appeal, ordering Tyhurst to pay Ms. Gorman the amount set at the first trial.

The criminal and civil cases brought against James Tyhurst by the Crown and Ms. Gorman are important for a number of reasons:

- The accountability of medical professionals for the treatment of their women patients, both at the time the original criminal charge was brought, and currently with the civil decision, remains contested;

- An examination of the criminal and civil court processes, including the treatment of women engaged in the court process, how the myths about rape pervade the judicial system to this day, and what prevents criminal convictions in cases of violence against women, what do women need to establish civil liability, and the frequency of the requirement of similar fact evidence to build both criminal and civil cases against violent men;

- The case exposes what the courts actually get to know, and, therefore, end up basing their judgements on, in violence against women cases. What ultimately becomes the court record of violence against women are not necessarily the violence and the crime that occurred.

The police did investigate, but they missed some key investigative procedures. If the police had obtained a warrant for Tyhurst's office at the hospital and for his property on Galiano Island, they may have found evidence to support the women's statements. As it was, any evidence found on Galiano Island was ruled inadmissible. Even so, a careful examination of the court record shows the evidence of the women, particularly Ms. Gorman, remains constant for the duration of the trials; it is Tyhurst's evidence that shifts and changes over time.

As for the civil cases, the Canadian Supreme Court decisions in June, and July, 2002, *R v. Handy* and *R v. Shearing*, each with distinct rulings on the admissibility of similar fact evidence, seems to have helped the B.C. Supreme Court settle on their findings in Ms. Gorman's case with more confidence.

The involvement of feminist therapists and the ongoing support and encouragement of first WAVAW, and then Vancouver Rape Relief and Women's Shelter, was crucial for the women involved and crucial in the public discussion. As the trial began, there was a groundswell of feminist support for the laying of these charges and calls for accountability.

The combination of the women coming forward, and the agitation of the women's groups, and women doctors, such as Dr. Susan Penfold and Dr. Judith McBride, provided forums for women to meet, take care of each other, and demand changes. Before these trials and the activism that accompanied them, doctors and other professionals seemed to be considered almost infallible and beyond reproach. The activism in both British Columbia and Ontario in 1990-1992 resulted in recommendations for change at both Colleges of Physicians and Surgeons by November of 1992. Now, women expect there will be accountability for the violence done to them by doctors.[1] The demand for the accountability of doctors and therapists in the last fifteen years could not have been accomplished without the work of the independent women's movement.

With Ms. Gorman's most recent achievement, the women Tyhurst attacked are finally vindicated: the courts are clear; he breached his duty of trust, his "fiduciary duty." The legal grounds for establishing this breach are laid out in the decision. While we cannot count on decisions of the court to last or remain constant for women over time, this ruling provides women the legal grounds for our complaints: violence against us by professionals is not only a breach of our trust, it is a breach of the law.

The personal toll on individual women, already damaged by violence against women, living through violence as fundamentally demeaning and oppressive as Tyhurst's, and then standing up to the scrutiny of the courts, withstanding the sexism of the defence councils and various commentators, is enormous. We have long heard women speak about the endurance they muster to withstand not only the violence itself but also the sexism imbedded in every step of the court process, which is directed at them personally. Ms. Gorman spent the last fifteen years working to hold this one doctor accountable, and there is still more to do.

All of the women were referred to Tyhurst because of suspected depression. By the end of the criminal trial, the Crown and the defence agreed to use the term "borderline personality disorder" to describe the illness. This diagnosis does not exist outside of the court record, but it persists through to the final judgement in Ms. Gorman's civil trial.[2] Ms. Gorman presented to Tyhurst and he did not ever treat her, either with therapy or medication, for the illnesses that she is described as having in the court record. These "symptoms" were only recognizable as such after years of violence against her at the hands of Dr. Tyhurst.

Many women exhibit varying degrees of poor self-esteem, self-hatred, eating-disorders, hyper-vigilance to their appearance, sadness after the birth of a child, loss of identity after marriage breakdown, loneliness caused by extreme isolation. These particular women walked into Tyhurst's office describing the feelings and thoughts associated with their oppression as women, and ended up fighting for their credibility in court. Yet at no time did anyone argue to any court that Tyhurst's attacks undermined their Charter Rights to equality and security of their person.

The cases brought against James Tyhurst are important to the average woman because average women are still pathologized and sent to medical professionals for therapy, medication, or treatment in response to their everyday lives.

Powerful men do not get to over-ride our rights; the courts seem to be our only way to ensure our Charter rights are upheld, though it becomes clear, even in Ms. Gorman's case, that the myths about violence against women persist to the highest level of the courts. For instance, in the B.C. Appeal Court judgement upholding the original civil judgement, the Judges state that particularly in cases where the attacks occurred several years in the past, both the victim and the attacker have reason to exaggerate the facts. In this case, and in similar cases, the medical reasons for which we are in the care of these men are used against us; depressed and damaged, our personal credibility is questioned, and as ordinary women, we have no standing before the courts. What is most often required is another woman complaining. But even then, as we see in the arguments to the appeal in the civil trial, the defence still can use women's individual testimony against each other.

At the end of the project, Ms. Gorman is waiting for the Supreme Court of Canada to decide whether they will hear the latest appeal launched by the defence. After conversations with me, we approached her lawyer who was preparing the response to the court to discuss how to include objections to the defence's continued characterizations of Ms. Gorman. It seemed to us that their insistence on using the psychiatric labels was undermining her Charter Rights. Also, there must be a way to include legal arguments about how Tyhurst's violating his fiduciary duty undermined her Charter Rights. The lawyer (who has not been paid and won't be until all is settled) responded that they had not made these points in the past and could not enter new arguments now, as they would constitute new information and, therefore, are not admissible. At that point, I went back and checked the judgements in the Handy and Shearing cases: no one seemed to have argued women's Charter Rights in those cases either. So there was no way to tuck anything in because the B.C. Court of Appeal referred to the cases in their decision.

Three very important cases dealing with violence against women and admissible evidence made it all the way to the Supreme Court of Canada, and not a single lawyer argued for any of the women's Charter Rights. With Ms. Gorman's case, we would hope this could be remedied with the rejection of the appeal, or with the acceptance of an intervener in the case should it proceed. Without access to federal money to do so, the latter seems unlikely.

Notes

1. So much so that the Canadian Medical Association is suing Mary-Lou McPhedran in Ontario for publicly naming doctors and other health professionals as rapists in a (2000) *The Globe and Mail* article. See: Women's Resistance: From Victimization to Criminalization Conference Workshop: *A Gender Analysis of Screwing Patients*, available online: <http://www.casac.ca/conference01/cd_order02.htm>.

2. And the diagnosis, of course, makes it into the defence's Statement of Facts in their application to appeal to the Supreme Court of Canada, June 2003, at paragraph 2.

Designing the Research:
Stepping into the River

It is the everyday experience of workers in sexual assault centres, women's centres, and transition houses that most events of male violence against women are not reported to the criminal justice system.[1] Of those reported, very few result in appropriate criminal sanctions. There are no charges recorded, for instance, that match the number of reports in government findings of attacks. *The 1993 Violence Against Women Survey* found that 51 percent of Canadian women had experienced at least one incident of physical or sexual violence since the age of sixteen, and of those women, almost 61 percent were the victim of more than one such incident.[2] Most are not taken beyond the initial reporting of the incident. Sometimes the incident does not even get recorded. It seems to us that the entire system, not just the courts, prevents cases from reaching conviction and/or any other appropriate resolution.

A better process would reveal and record violence against women as being the source of hateful, effective damage that it is. It would express community outrage. It would contain violent men, prevent future violent sexist incidents, impose community disapproval of men's violent oppression of women, and change collusive state practices that support male violence. It would reinforce women's dignity and freedom. It would *not* be an impossible task if the federal government chose to do so.

In this project, we connect the feminist women's centres, the women who use them, and the Charter of Rights and Freedoms, which promises all women in Canada equality under the law, and the actual, lived experience of women who engage the system after an incident of male violence. We examine what happened to the women who complained. We see some of the nature of and reasons for low conviction rates (as well as high attrition rates within the system) in these and other cases of violence against women. And we reveal the connections between these outcomes, with other facts of women's inequality.

Before the research and report design process began, we already knew some of the threads we hoped to weave together:

- A literature review of what was already documented that might support/challenge our understanding and that might result in a bibliography annotated for anti-violence workers;

- An examination by CASAC of the policies and procedures affecting local situations that would evaluate local consistency with the Charter of Rights and Freedoms;

- Interviews by CASAC with personnel in the criminal justice system to see what would be revealed of the barriers to Charter-promised justice;

- Interviews by CASAC with women who use the criminal justice system to learn from their subjective and objective experience and understanding;

- An examination of the high profile cases affecting public discourse and attitudes;

- Integration of the ongoing advocacy, discussion, and shared organizing work among CASAC women, so that we could bring thirty years of praxis to bear on the questions, and apply current, relevant feminist activity and analysis.

We began with books, and looked to the basics first: Del Martin and Diana Russell,[3] and Dobash and Dobash,[4] for instance, and, of course, Andrea Dworkin.[5] We were intent on focusing our discussion on Canadian experience and Canadian data as well as Canadian methodology. We were especially interested in documenting and theorizing about our own work. We engaged the professional and political assistance of Mary Crnkovitch and Linda Archibald, Ottawa-based feminist researchers.

What Do We Want to Know?

We focused our research inquiry on the question: How does the system prevent convictions in cases of violence against women?

We looked for 100 women who would tell us their story of using the justice system. We asked for the justice system's documents regarding policy and procedure at those same sites. That data was collected and analyzed across Canada at eleven local sites, and further collected, and analyzed, nationally. The study and its project considered the national situation, as seen by our member centres, and fifteen women, and as described to us by each of the eleven chosen sites as they interacted with the justice system at the following five points of contact: emergency response (911), police investigation, Crown Attorney (decision to proceed), court proceedings, sentencing We examined cases and situations that were reported no earlier than January 1, 1997. We located them within the context of some of the other events of those five years in Canada.

- CASAC LINKS researchers interviewed in their area and followed up with those local women. Researchers on-site analyzed the interviews according to an analysis template developed collectively;

- This first stage of analysis was further refined by the project coordinator and by the project director at the national office using the same tools;

- A tool for tracking charges as well as the application of policies was developed collectively among the researchers on site, the national staff, and research consultants;[6]
- The CASAC LINKS Director, who was also a Regional Representative, answered to the Regional Representative Committee as to the meshing of the project with CASAC's accumulated knowledge and current activity.

Qualitative Research: From the Point of View of Those Below Water

There might have been things to count or track in a study, but certainly there were stories that needed telling. We were interested in the stories themselves and with increasing the power of the voices that told them. We debated whether to simply repeat 100 stories. We knew that 100 women would produce many more than 100 incidents of criminal violence. We questioned whether to ask questions at all in interviews and, if not, how to compare narratives. We already know how to interview in order to plan our alliance with women and in order to advocate on their behalf. We built on our success with our confirmed, usual techniques of interviewing with very open-ended questions.[7]

We considered when to use collective voice/narrative and how not to reduce 100 interviewed women (or perhaps more accurately, 200 women's voices) to simple rhetoric.[8] We worried about how to reveal "the system" and the social and legal policy for what they actually are. It was a guiding principle that we wanted to "reveal up": that is, to tell more about the system and the process than about each individual woman. We worried, knowing those stories could over-reveal 200 women's resistances and lives to predictably harsh judgment and perhaps interference. We worried too about whether it would be safe or wise to reveal our feminist failures or even successes.[9]

The Money Story: Who Owns the Dam and Controls the Flow of the River

Research, especially research supporting government policy, is almost the only state-funded activity of national equality-seeking women's groups in Canada. We decided that the political economy of the project and of the research questions themselves should be something we considered and tried to incorporate into our analysis and report. Throughout the project and research we exposed and discussed:

- The federal budget decisions affecting violence against women;
- The current economic condition of women affecting violence against women;
- The Family Violence Initiative Fund;
- That interviewees were paid tiny honorariums and expenses such as childcare and transportation;
- A normal centre budget and rape crisis worker's pay;
- The economic state of other women's groups;

- Economic decisions dividing women, in particular, welfare, prostitution, and poverty policy affecting violence issues;
- Government's economic commitment nationally and internationally to women's organizations.

Action-Oriented and Participatory Research: Pulling One Another Out of the River…One by One

We planned our research so that, as much as possible, our actions advanced women's situation in that they: sustained and added to each woman's fight for equality, safety, and justice; and sustained and strengthened the centres and movements that we believe are the best tools in the struggle for legal improvements. We hoped to examine the awareness of and ability of women to invoke human rights, as promised by the Charter of Rights and Freedoms, in line with international human rights understandings. We hoped to understand the "right" being invoked by women choosing to use the justice system; we hoped to begin to explore an appropriate stance for CASAC regarding a human rights framework for resisting violence against women. And, we would be inclusive of all women speaking by accepting a colloquial understanding of women's expectations of government rather than requiring legal language. We would be using the sense common to women on the street and, only when necessary, interpret to a technically correct legal meaning or judgment. We decided that we would engage Canadian Charter debates which affect our work to end violence against women:

- Notions of formal vs. substantive equality;
- Notions of the need for protection from government intrusion vs. the need for positive obligation on the part of governments;
- Notions of collective vs. individual understandings of the condition of women and approaches to human rights;
- Notions of sexist violence, not interpersonal violence;
- Notions of a progressive debate between courts vs. parliament as democratic authority;
- Jurisdictional debates as to the application of the Charter;
- Notions of a resolvable contest between fighting for rights vs. economic control; that is, anti-globalization vs. world court, or UN processes, as well as, the contest between the authority of Canadian courts and the economic intentions of the government.

That women had contacted their government was our starting point. Each had called on the state voluntarily and from her judgment of both her rights and her situation. Our observations were always to be part of our overall plan of response to sexist violence, but also of her initial action, and call to us to act. Her attempt to use the system, as she saw it, was to be advanced with the help of the advocates whenever possible. We sought women to interview who intended to use the system and whose situation could be understood as a crime in terms of a best-case scenario for the legal system.

Equality Seeking: Let's Go Up the River and Get the Guys Who are Throwing Women In

CASAC used to simply identify ourselves as a women's group which was commonly understood to mean that we were pro-women and working for the advancement of the status of women. Once the federal government, under the Mulroney Conservatives, started to accept anti-feminist groups under the heading of "women's groups" within consultations and funding policies, it became necessary to identify ourselves as an "equality-seeking women's group." For many purposes, this term is fine. We used it ourselves when Richard Mosley of the Justice Department repeatedly included anti-feminists in meetings intended to shape an opinion requested from Justice Minister Campbell regarding a new Rape Shield Law.[10] Of course, any consensus of "women's groups" opinion was impossible under those conditions. Once we limited our group to "equality-seeking," the anti-feminist group were disqualified, and we could easily agree on how to respond.

We talk about violence against women in terms of a political category rather than limit ourselves to use only the social service delivery, mental health, or criminology categories of: battered wives, crime victims, women in counselling, family violence, intra family violence, child assault, children's rights, victim's rights, bad dates, clients, etc.

We apply a vision of women in pursuit of liberty, not one of vengeful retributive justice, or traditional "law and order," nor one of the "safety of slaves," or the agency of children, or the unable. We decided to emphasize equality over criminality. We decided there was no such thing as "an observer," no such thing as "value-free research." We would take responsibility to express our opinions from our unique position in the world. We decided to function within the authorized structure of CASAC to control the project: do the research, reduce hierarchy, and increase participation of the movement in the project. The structure emphasized the centre, instead of the individual researcher, so that both institutional and movement memory is maintained even when women come and go. Individuals led discussions in their centres and improved the overall discourse. The problem is systemic and not just individual. We decided not to reveal either the names or the identifying information of individuals working within the system, unless their behaviour was truly extraordinary in our collective opinion.

We expected to learn from each woman participating and for each woman to learn from the centre. We expected that reciprocity of communication and learning to be met at every level of interaction for the researchers/public educators/advocates. Our plan was to honour each woman's choice to act. We wanted to tell her story of purposeful resistance. She chose to use the system, and she also chose to use, or engage the local centre, and women's movement.

Identifiable Limits to the Methodology

We did not plan to bring every guilty man to justice. It was a failure of design. We could have decided ahead of time and announced publicly that CASAC would pursue every case as a national issue. That would have encouraged best practices on the part of the system and made it more possible to distinguish between personal and systemic failures.

We did not succeed in convincing every actor for the state to change a practice or propose a change of policy in some way that would increase convictions. We could have held individuals accountable for progress as well as the systems within which they functioned. Although we talked about this, we did not have a joint national action plan designed to aid this local, ongoing pressure for change; for example, we might have had mid-way reports of what we were finding publicly released nationally.

We did not design a tool to list and match the specific practices; particularly the specific polices that were most destructive in each case involved. We wanted and sought the overall view, but a step of also recording on site, identifying the specific failures to meet equality needs would have shown us more. Of course, it would have been enormously expensive. It would be better to have time and money to enable us to go back to the women to submit our versions of their stories as well as the whole collective story for their further comment. The learning could have multiplied many times over in both directions.

In seeking the cases that would endure in the system, we were in danger of painting a much rosier picture of what happens to women than is actually true. We abandoned the original plan of interviewing officials in the system because of time constraints. Workers met with the officials necessary to gain the documents they needed, and in some cases were able to access the information through the Privacy of Information Act, and web sites. We needed more discussion, ahead of settling on the design, to tease out the information about courts and sentencing. We underestimated our internal ignorance of what happens there, and so our follow up questions and probes were inadequate.

We failed to anticipate the ongoing attacks on the *Violence Against Women Survey*, and the likely attempts to reduce or counter the newly authorized statistical evidence of the existence of violence against women. We left ourselves dependent on the production of critiques, and supporting documents, and analysis by the Justice Department.[11]

Our research plan was modest and contained, but had some open-ended possibilities in that it was housed within the larger project of the *Canadian Association of Sexual Assault Centres*. We were not so much interested in the science of who has been attacked and who has been failed, as we were in the political science of how change can happen, including, but not limited to, criminal justice options. Our plan worked quite well to educate many and to inform many more. We hope it assisted 100 women to fight their attacker more effectively, to experience the solidarity of their community against the indignity they suffered, and to move toward a peaceful, egalitarian future.

We should have spent more time designing the research. We needed to pursue conversations with British, New Zealand, and Australian, or South African women, as to the implication of the erosion of the welfare state on frontline work, which had developed out of the welfare state.[12] We needed a meeting with an American expert regarding the loss of the ERA[13] momentum and the passing of the VAW bill; this could have included LEAF knowledge and NAWL[24] women. It would have been better if we could have interviewed academics and practitioners writing about criminal law and the Charter to pursue ideas they expressed, so we could jointly understand the implication of their judgment on the women, and so that they could be more aware of the practical implications and the Charter challenge possibilities. We did not plan to use one level of government against another: a traditional Canadian reform technique. In the preparation for research, we could have sought out the federal-provincial working group members relevant to our inquiries.

Notes

1. The Donner Foundation report that was eventually published as book. Clark, L., and Lewis, D. (1977). *Rape The Price of Coercive Sexuality*. Toronto: Women's Press. This was an early, if not first, of Canadian documentation of "unfounded cases," for instance. That work sprang from front line alliances between the Vancouver Status of Women (a women's centre) and the Vancouver anti-rape movement. More recently, Vancouver women complained for three days about policing to the Oppal Commission on Policing in B.C. Those proceedings are available at the Justice Institute of B.C.

2. Federal-Provincial-Territorial Ministers Responsible for the Status of Women. (2002). *Assessing Violence Against Women: A Statistical Profile*. Ottawa: Author, cat. SW21-101/2002E, p.10.

3. Martin, D. (1976). *Battered Wives*. San Francisco: Glide Publications. And Russell, D.& Van de Ven. (Eds). (1976). *Crimes Against Women: Proceedings of the International Tribunal*. California: Les Femmes.

4. Dobash, E., and Dobash, R. (1990). How Theoretical Definitions and Perspective Affect Research and Policy. In D.J. Besharov (Ed.). *Family Violence: Research and Policy Issues*. Washington: AEI Press, pp. 108-129; Dobash, E., & Dobash, R. (1992); Dobash, E., & Dobash, R. (Eds.) (1998). *Rethinking Violence Against Women*. Sage: Thousand Oaks.

5. Dworkin, A. (2003). Landscapes of the Ordinary: Violence Against Women. In Morgan, R. (Ed), *Sisterhood is Forever*. New York: Washington Square Press, pp. 58-69.

6. See Appendix: Tool for Tracking Charges.

7. See Appendix.: Interview questions of CASAC LINKS Report.

8. One hundred plus interviews, eleven LINKS workers, plus eighty centre workers, plus three national staff, and five regional representatives.

9. Fine, M., Weis, L., Weseen, S., and Wong, L. (2000).

10. Richard Mosley hosted those meetings and invited Gwen Landolt of REAL Women.

11. We were delighted to see Dawson, M. (2001, December) *Examination of Declining Intimate Partner Homicide Rates: A Literature Review*. Ottawa: Department of Justice Canada, cat. 2001-10e.

12. Department for Women. (1996). *Heroines of Fortitude: The Experiences of Women in Court as Victims of Sexual Assault*. New South Wales, Australia: Author, ISBN 073105204, was being produced at this same time from a very different starting point and using quantitative approaches. And the American women were working on books like Daniels, C., and Brooks, R., Eds. (2001). *Feminists Negotiate the State: The Politics of Domestic Violence*. Lanham, Maryland: University Press of America, as well as, internationally, Dobash, E., and Dobash, R. (Eds.) (1998). *Rethinking Violence Against Women*. Sage: Thousand Oaks, at the Rockerfeller Institute in Lake Como. Also see: Abused Women's Advocacy Project. (2000, February). *The Voices of Victims: Victim Accounts of Law Enforcement Response to Domestic Violence Data Report September 1998-1999*. Lewiston, Main: Author.

13. Equal Rights Amendment would have given American women some of what we have won.

14. Legal Education and Action Fund: see online <http://www.leaf.ca/> and The National Association of Women: see online <http://www.nawl.ca/>.

Nellie Nippard's Story

Louisa Russell

NELLIE NIPPARD KNOWS too well how the criminal justice system fails to protect women. That is why she was willing to come when I invited her to speak at the Women's Resistance conference, and to meet Jane Doe, and Bonnie Mooney.

> I automatically figured that if the time ever came that I would get the nerve or the courage to make the decision to go to the RCMP, I just took it for granted that everything would be taken care of, but I got no help...They told me it was a family dispute, we can't go in there. That was a big let down for me.[1]

Nellie's husband later stabbed her 33 times. He did it in spite of the fact the mother of six had gone to the police many, many times for help. It was her opinion that the officer had sided with her husband Lew and that they had become buddies.

One time she had gone to the police after he had threatened to shoot her in the woods near their house. He was taken to court for uttering threats. Like many women, she was feeling alone with the story and was looking forward to having the opportunity to tell it in court. Many people in the small town of Lewisporte did not want to talk about her experience so she had been alone with the problem until now.

On the day that they went to court, his lawyer took her aside and asked, "Do you really think that Lew would kill you?" She looked at him plainly, and said, "I know that he will."[2] But when she came to go to court they told her that it was not necessary for her to testify, as the lawyers had come to an agreement. The lawyers had told the Judge that the couple would like to reconcile and that she was not afraid of him.[3]

> I was too scared to say anything. No one explained what was going on. The defence attorney had lied, and said that I was not afraid, and the Crown, I guess, had believed him. Lew got off based on this.
>
> I moved to a house close to the police station and had been away from him for a year. He watched me constantly and phoned me nearly every day, counting down the days that I had left to live. Finally, the countdown was zero, and I was convinced he would try to kill me anytime now. I stayed at home.
>
> The following Tuesday I left to give a friend a ride and he attacked me on the lawn. I tried to keep him off with one hand. I felt something in my stomach—he sliced my liver three times, and stabbed me all over. I made a grab at him. I scratched his face. In the hospital the IV kept me alive. The stretcher was filled with blood. I fought to stay awake. I was scared if I slept I would die.[4]

Lew pleaded guilty to *attempted murder* in 1990 and he was sentenced to life in prison with no parole for twelve years. However, an appeal in 1993 concluded that the judge didn't have the authority to set an eligibility date, and he was, therefore, eligible to apply for full parole after serving seven years.[5]

Fortunately, for Nellie, Lew has not yet been granted parole. In 1995, the parole board decision stated that, "[Lew's] risk of causing serious harm to [his] ex-wife...is high." At the sentencing, two psychiatrists testified that the 47-year-old man was obsessed by a paranoid jealousy of his wife that led to unreasonable fits of anger and violence against her. The board went on to state "that [he] could act out violently, and of specific concern is [his] lack of understanding and minimization of [his] violence."[6]

Yet, Nellie still lives in fear that one day he will be released and come to finish her off. Part of her resistance has been to tell her story, so that she is not alone. Every two years Nellie travels to New Brunswick to tell the parole board in person what he did to her. Nellie established this practice. Before her, it was not allowed, and parole boards are prone to abandoning the judgments and monitoring to the abused women, imposing an impossible burden that belongs to the parole board and corrections.

Nellie has spoken at Take Back the Night, and at provincial conferences, such as Inquest of Justice, that looked at areas where women aren't getting what they need from the justice system.[7] Nellie and I shared a stage at the Women's Resistance from Victimization to Criminalization Conference. Her story, as told on television, is used as a training module in our rape crisis centre. Each time Nellie tells her story, she gathers feminist support; she continues to keep her story public for her own safety.

Notes

1. Nippard, N., personal communication (2001, October).
2. Nippard, N., Mooney, B., and Russell, L. (2001, October). From Victimization to Criminalization Conference Workshop: *How to hold the Police Accountable*. Available online: <www.casac.ca/conference01/ cd_order02.htm>.
3. *Ibid.*
4. *Ibid.*
5. Wife-Abuse Issues Subject of Conference (1993, October 25). Montreal: *The Gazette*, p. A8.
6. (1997) *Parole Board decision*, St John's, Nfld.
7. Wife-Abuse Issues Subject of Conference (1993, October 25).

Jane Doe and The Charter
from the CASAC Point of View

Jane Doe has told her story, we, as CASAC, feel freer to comment.[1] Jane Doe took full advantage of Canadian anti-rape centres. She walked into the Toronto Rape Crisis Centre already influenced by the feminist public education work done, by then, in that city for a decade. She was informed about the political nature of rape and her entitlement in law to police response. She was reinforced in her belief in a natural as well as legal right to complain about rape and be protected from rape. She was aware of and part of a political movement creating women's power. That knowledge informed her outrage at being used by the police as bait instead of being protected from the "balcony rapist."

She did her best to assist in the capture, trial, conviction, and imprisonment of that man and CASAC helped.[2] Then she went after the forces that contributed to her being attacked. When she wanted to officially complain, when she wanted to poster her neighbourhood to warn other women and find her rapist, when she wanted to organize a new temporary feminist action group, she used the resources of the Toronto centre. She asked for and got aid from phone numbers, to womanpower, paper and photocopier, meeting space, and library.[3]

She was the most difficult kind of woman caller for our centres: smart, angry, aggressive, working class, moderately well educated, opinionated, individualistic, and determined. She was not looking for a shoulder on which to cry, counselling about how it was not her fault, or basic facts about rape. She would not be satisfied with a lecture from anyone on how the system works. She wanted to know how to *make* it work. She hunched from the beginning that for her mental as well as social well being, whatever therapeutic aid she might need, had to be companioned with collective political action.[4] She was rarely grateful or satisfied since there was no real reason she should be satisfied or grateful for the way things are for raped women in the world or even in our centres.[5] She was the most difficult kind of caller, the most likely to survive the experience and effect social change.

Over the course of the next ten years, using the resources of the movement including LEAF, CASAC, and NAC, she fought for the right to sue the police, and won that right for all of us. Then she fought to hold the police accountable for their treatment of her for the sake of the next women raped.[6] She quietly criticized our members, at our request, as to how we could better assist rebellious women.[7] And finally, she tried to effect the reform of the very police force that had failed her in Toronto, by gathering together women's groups, and working with the city government to review the problems and propose solutions.[8]

She had to learn about rape law and the Charter. The only sources of information available to her to legitimize her equality-driven struggle with Charter law, were the women with whom she shared a support group for assaulted women,[9] feminist legal academics who followed and supported her case,[10] and two key women's groups committed to equality law: LEAF and CASAC.

During all those years, she received and called on the centre and members of CASAC for emotional, political, and concrete aid to support her insistence on access to justice. She has continued to insist on that support through the five years of producing the next level of her public education materials: speaking tours, the production of her made-for-TV movie, and her book.

The Jane Doe story is one of individual ingenuity, wit, and determination, but it is also the story of what Jane Doe has achieved for women raped, as part of the Canadian women's movement, particularly in partnership with CASAC. Jane Doe's story seems to be the best we can get so far: that failures of the justice system are met with outrage and work to change things for the next women. Jane Doe has worked more than a decade to hold accountable the justice system that failed her, and to make the struggle a little easier for the women who follow. She has succeeded. CASAC is grateful for her courage and her wilfulness. Our alliance with her has made all of us stronger, and angrier, and has increased women's expectations of law, especially, equality law for women in Canada.

Notes

1. Doe, J. (2003).

2. *Ibid.* Her poster campaign to warn others and identify him caused someone to suggest him to police and he was arrested.

3. *Ibid.*

4. Profitt, N. (2000, August).

5. CASAC invited Jane Doe to critique services and to suggest ideas for our conference planning at our Winnipeg meeting in 1998.

6. Jane Doe does not consider that fight successful. Personal communication, Winnipeg, 2001.

7. In her presentation at Winnipeg.

8. Bain, B. Plenary/Round Table, *Policing in Canada: Either They Won't Come, or They Won't Leave Us Alone.* Chair: Kim Pate, Beverly Bain, Anne Derrick, Julie McKay, Dr. Sherene Razack, Bonnie Morton, Tamara Gorin, Dianne Martin. Available online: <http://www.casac.ca/conference01/cd_order02.htm>.

9. They remain anonymous but are somewhat portrayed in the book and movie.

10. Notably, Law Professor Liz Sheehy, University of Ottawa.

An International Discussion: Violence and Equality

When and How Did CASAC Become Internationalist?

Canadian progress, the international promotion of Canadian law (for instance in South Africa and the Balkans), the use of rape in war, all focused attention on violence against women. But those were not the starting points for us. We have been aware for some time of the Canadian exporting of ideas regarding violence against women through both aid agencies and United Nations mechanisms. Too often we were confronted by the contradictions between what our government said abroad and what it did at home. Women from Russia, the Caribbean, India, Mexico, Latin America contacted us, convinced that the problems had been solved in Canada, and looking for the magic key we had found to win co-operation from our governments and enlightened responses from our politicians.

For CASAC women, the experience and understanding of the international consideration of violence against women has been very different across the country.

Quebec women dove into work on the International March of Women Against Poverty and Violence. It was thrilling for CASAC women to participate, and sometimes lead an international grassroots movement modelled on what they achieved inside Quebec with their anti-poverty march. As soon as the call became international, our members were delighted that the rallying cry included the call to end violence against women. These are the twin axis of women's oppression as the new century begins: poverty and violence. Quebec feminists not only organized women from around the world to speak to the United Nations special session, but marched us through the Streets of New York, spoke on our behalf to officials of the World Bank, and mobilized with others for the Social Forum in Puerto Allegro where we also spoke. Those same women came to report to us at our conference and convention.[1] All of this has resulted in fabulous opportunities for anti-violence activists to meet from around the world, and to discuss our shared understandings of our respective legal, social, and political situations.

Women in English-speaking Canada certainly participated in the Women's World March events, and national organizing, but had less of that consciousness-raising experience. We were shaped by other events. Ontario was the settlement site for many new immigrant populations who were taking their place in the political discussions. Toronto and southern Ontario are now more varied in cultures, more racially diverse, and more multi-lingual than most other major cities of the world. This dynamism is palpable and has pushed every public institution to new understandings of a world united. The whole country has been dramatically affected by swings in immigration and immigration policy. Proximity to New York, and the "security" issues pressed on us after the American response to World Trade Centre attacks, rocked Ontario women. The spectre of war both abroad and at home loomed over this period. We were suddenly connected to women in the Middle East in a new way. We struggled and found leadership in Star Hawk, and in Robin Morgan's, by then, dated book, *The Demon Lover* (a new edition has since been successfully called for; there hasn't been a war that didn't include rape).[2]

Women in Alberta were isolated from much of the international activism, but were, unfortunately, subject to the influence of American conservatism that was guiding local politics. The impact of this on anti-violence work was intense. Fewer women were focused on anti-violence work, and there was a lot of pressure for them to focus the work on victimology. There were, of course, fine exceptions like the coalition work to build the Mills case.

The women and children so desperate to enter Canada that they would take to the life-threatening waters off our coast, challenged B.C. women. At the same time, we had to contend with both the missing women of Ciudad Juarez, and the missing women of the Vancouver downtown east side. A campaign began to grow for the missing aboriginal women of the north coast; this has since become a national issue. B.C. women were the most engaged in challenging the Canadian government's fifth report to the United Nations CEDAW committee, perhaps because the recent change in provincial government propelled our understandings of the links between international and local policy, and perhaps because the leadership of aboriginal women dramatized the plight of the women most affected in this country.

CASAC, as an organization, had been involved in international work for some time. Not only had we sent a delegate to the UN Conference in Nairobi and to the Commonwealth Women's Conference in Toronto, we also sent a delegate at the invitation of Russian women to Moscow for the first all-Russia meeting of women to fight violence against women. For a week we trained those women who would be opening the first rape crisis centres and shelters, and contributed a foreword to their manual on how to open such centres. It is still in use and has been updated with a new message from us. We also attended a week-long seminar at the women's university in Bombay, SNDT, to compare strategies, and tactics on ending violence against women with women activists from across India.

Discussion of Equality and Sexist Violence in the UN, Post Beijing

For CASAC members, the push toward internationalism began with Beijing, and the alternate conference held there of women's NGO's (non-government organisations actually registered by the United Nations). Women began to imagine the possibility of the United Nations' reinforcement of their aspirations. Every state was being challenged by its citizens and residents to come to the aid of women. We were convinced that such aspirations are normal, and universal, and that the experience of sexist violence is everywhere understood by women to be an impediment to women's freedom and well being.

CASAC women watched with interest over several UN meetings, the discussions between states about violence against women. "Watch" is a bit of an understatement. The CASAC Regional Representative from the Prairies, Unide Johnson, represented us in Nairobi, CASAC representative from B.C. and Yukon, represented us in Cairo, as well as, the NGO planning meetings for Beijing, and Beijing plus five. CASAC also attended in New York for the discussions of the Optional Protocol to CEDAW. CASAC participated as a member of FAFIA in the Vienna meetings, and in the CEDAW Alternate Report Committee, both at the national and B.C. provincial levels.[3]

In this book, we are examining the application of Canadian law by state officials responding to violence against women (with particular reference to the five-year period of this report), so we thought it best to review for ourselves Canada's legal responsibilities to women, as they are understood internationally.

In May of 2003 when the Minister Responsible for the Status of Women sent us the report *Assessing Violence*, we were a little surprised. This wasn't our first reading of the federal *Assessing Violence Report*.[4] In January 2003, it had been considered by a UN Committee working with and between national governments to improve the lives of women.[5] Many states had agreed on CEDAW's[6] policy and platform. Canada, to her credit, had also signed on to The Optional Protocol, an important implementation mechanism that women's groups, including CASAC, had promoted.[7] The Canadian government delegation had used the Statistical Report as part of the argument for how well Canada was doing in her compliance with this international commitment, the purpose of which was to end sexist discrimination. As part of this process, Canada reports every five years to an international group overseeing CEDAW.[8] Those states that signed the agreement are to account for what efforts (in this case, Canada) have been made and how successful they have been in improving the status of women.

Women's groups independent of government can also report to the Committee to provide an alternate source of information. CASAC, as part of a coalition of women, prepared an alternate report, and sent a delegate to attend the New York session in which Canada made its fifth periodic report. Our version, which varied considerably from the government's version of the situation in Canada, was written and delivered in alliance with other women's groups.[9] The facts and stories had been gathered by feminist frontline workers in both specific regions, like B.C. (where things were changing even more quickly for the worse), and Canada-wide.[10]

Reading and hearing Canada's official presentation, including the Statistical Report on Violence, was a caution. From our point of view, the official report didn't begin to describe the extent of the crisis being endured by women in Canada. And, it set the example for official obfuscation, instead of revelation, of what is commonly known of the problem. In any case, even allowing for such differences in worldview, and attitude to accountability, and social change, we were astounded by this use of the Violence Report.

How could the nature and numbers of violent crimes committed against women in Canada be reassuring?[11] How could the understanding of the relationship between social policy, social programs, and their impact on violence against women be reassuring? How could one avoid facing the impact of the loss of women's right to welfare on the violence situation? How could one accept the hiding of the class and race divisions that so profoundly affect any understanding of violence against women? How could the loss of national standards in health, education, and welfare be made to appear unrelated to the devastating violence figures? How could the loss of any of the commitments to gender-specific initiatives, from stand-alone ministries, to the funding of shelters and centres for women being diminished, allow any hope of solving the problems of violence against women and women's equality?[12]

While we prepared our alternate report to the UN, anti-violence workers could hardly bear the compounding of our understanding about the conditions of many women in Canada. Every meeting with other feminist groups meant new realizations of how bad it was and how much worse it was getting. For us, it was painfully discouraging and sometimes overwhelming. For battered, abused, raped, and harassed women it was desperate and sometimes hopeless. Every voice in those meetings increased the depth of understanding between us and strengthened our hand but added terrible new interlocking data and analyses. Certainly, all the groups and their delegates shared the burden. We had excellent professional advice and counsel and, more importantly, excellent leadership in composing our unity and in arguing our joint positions in New York.[13]

To CASAC it was and is clear that if any progress is being made in Canada at reducing violence against women and its impacts, it is unacceptably and unnecessarily slow and shallow. Furthermore, it was and is clear that women are suffering terrible set backs in policy that will affect both the aftermath of violence against women in each life and community and will surely increase the levels and severity of individual incidents of violence against women.

Sometimes we could see that politicians were even using violence against women cynically to excuse a "law and order" approach to governance, a gated community approach to nation interests, which we know and they know is contrary to any advance for women.[14]

The international committee considered all these sources of information and expressed its opinion in its recommendations and concluding remarks.[15]

Even at this state-controlled UN level of removal from our lives and from the women who talked to us, the Committee concluded that women in Canada could and should be much better served by government at all levels. Indeed, we all agree that law and international agreement have promised women in Canada better. In its recommendations, the Committee agreed with us on many points. But certainly even without the UN women and before the movement-wide meetings, antiviolence workers had our own frontline understanding of the inseparability of criminal law and equality law and social policy.

Peers in the UN body reviewing compliance with this agreement have criticized Canada. In the "concluding comments" the committee points out Canada's several failures to meet international obligations.[16] These comments include criticism for the lack of funding for feminist service/advocacy organizations fighting sexist violence as well as for the failure to hold provinces to their obligations to equality. The comments particularly focus on the needs of aboriginal women and the particularly dire situation in B.C. Now we take up the work of pressing the government in Canada for compliance.

We are also engaged in discussions about the human rights abuse that is violence against women and we are beginning to partner with several Canadian and international NGO formations regarding this approach.

At the official UN conference in Beijing, China, Canada endorsed the Beijing Platform for Action that calls governments to "seek to ensure that before policy decisions are taken, an analysis of their impact on women and men, respectively is carried out."[17] It calls on governments to "review policies and programmes from a gender perspective" and to "promote a gender perspective in all legislation and policies."[18]

Canada also endorsed Further Actions and Initiatives to Implement the Beijing Declaration and Platform for Action that was adopted by the Special General Assembly of the United Nations on June 10, 2000. In it the UN calls on governments "to ensure that national and legislative reform processes…promote women's rights,"[19] and it states that governments must "as a matter of priority, review and revise legislation, where appropriate, with a view to introducing effective legislation, including on violence against women, and take other necessary measures to ensure that all women and girls are protected against all forms of physical, psychological and sexual violence, and are provided recourse to justice."[20]

In 1992, the United Nations Committee on the Elimination of Discrimination Against Women (CEDAW), in the General Recommendation 19 framed during its eleventh session, viewed "gender-based violence" as a form of discrimination that seriously inhibits women's ability to enjoy rights and freedoms on a basis of equality with men.

It clarifies that "discrimination against women" under Article 2 of the Women's Convention includes:

...gender-based violence. That is violence that is directed against a woman because she is a woman or that affects women disproportionately. It includes acts that inflict physical, mental, or sexual harm or suffering, threats of such acts, coercion and other deprivations of liberty. Gender based violence may breach specific provisions of the Convention, regardless of whether those provisions expressly mention violence.[21]

Gender based violence impairs or nullifies the enjoyment by women of human rights and fundamental freedoms under general international law and it circumscribes women's ability to function as full citizens in society.

Those rights and freedoms of women that are implicated in gender-based violence include:

The right to life.

The right not to be subject to torture or to cruel, inhuman, or degrading treatment or punishment.

The right to equal protection according to humanitarian norms in times of international or internal warfare.

The right to liberty and security of the person.

The right to equal protection under the law.

The right to equality in the family.

The right to the highest standard attainable of physical and mental health.

The right to just and favourable conditions of work.

The CEDAW General Recommendation 19 also emphasizes that while gender-based violence under the Women's Convention applies to violence perpetrated by public authorities, states may also be responsible for private acts, under general international law and specific human rights covenants, if they fail to act with due diligence to prevent violations of rights or to investigate and punish acts of violence and for providing compensation.

Acts of violence directly committed by the State and its personnel are breaches of State obligations under general international human rights laws and under other conventions, including the Women's Convention. It further emphasizes that discrimination under the Convention is not restricted to action by or on behalf of Governments: it calls on State parties to take all appropriate measures to eliminate discrimination against women by any person, organization, or enterprise.

The initiative taken by CEDAW through its General Recommendation 19 was groundbreaking. It became the normative basis for the UN Declaration of the Elimination of Violence Against Women (UNDEVAW)[22] the year after and the creation of the mandate for a UN Special Rapporteur on Violence Against Women (UNSRVAW). While not itself legally binding, the Declaration represents an authoritative international consensus between states on government obligations, including Canada's, to eliminate violence against women. It affirms norms that are legally binding, either under specific human rights treaties or as customary international law.

The UNDEVAW defines violence against women as "any act of gender-based violence that results in, or is likely to result in, physical, sexual or psychological harm or suffering of women, including threats such as acts, coercion or arbitrary deprivation of liberty, whether occurring in public or private life."[23] This definition emphasizes that acts of violence against women are rooted in gender inequality. The adoption of the same text in the 1995 Beijing Platform for Action (under Strategic Objective D on violence against women) strengthens the normative basis of this definition.

In our minds, violence against women in armed conflict and in peacetime conditions are not distinct phenomena but form part of the same spectrum of behaviour. They are both products of systemic relations of male power and domination.

The 1998 Rome Statute of the International Criminal Court (ICC), which explicitly recognizes rape, sexual slavery, enforced prostitution, forced pregnancy, enforced sterilization, and sexual violence as war crimes and crimes against humanity, builds on earlier developments in international law and signals another important addition to the human rights system that promises accountability for gender-based violations of human rights.

Violence, according to the UN, can be physical, psychological, or sexual and may take the form of deprivation or neglect. In her first report in 1993, Radhika Coomaraswamy of the UNSRVAW considered various forms of violence against women under three principle categories:

- Violence in the Family: domestic violence, including battering, marital rape, incest; traditional practices, including female genital mutilation, son preference, early marriage, dowry-related violence, and penalties such as stoning or floggings under religious customary laws;

- Violence in the Community: rape and sexual assault; sexual harassment in the workplace, educational institutions and elsewhere; forced prostitution,[24] trafficking for purposes of prostitution or domestic labour; violence against women migrant workers; and pornography which is linked to violence against women;

- Violence Perpetrated or Condoned by the State: custodial violence, including rape and other forms of sexual assault and beatings; violence against women in situations of armed conflict; and violence against refugee and internally displaced women.

CASAC agrees with what seems to be clear at this level of inter-state discussion that a continuum exists across the various forms and locations of violence against women mainly because they share common roots found in deeply embedded discriminatory behaviours, values, and practices toward women that are still prevalent in many societies, including Canada. These roots perpetuate the cycle of discrimination and violence against women.

Oftentimes, the different forms of violence are inter-connected. For example, numerous studies indicate that physical violence by an intimate partner is often accompanied by sexual abuse and even rape. Incest, while always coercive, sometimes includes child rape. All human rights are connected.[25] Violence against women can be understood to violate many forms of human rights. CASAC understands that freedom from sexist violence cannot intelligently be separated from any or all other women's human rights.

International human rights standards such as the UDHR affirm the equal rights of men and women and claim that everyone should enjoy human rights without discrimination on the ground of sex. However, women's rights activists, including CASAC, have only recently explored the application of this statement of principle to our own state. We have pointed out that women's enjoyment of their rights is not only affected by the will of their states to uphold human rights, but by their gender as well as class and race.

In practice, human rights theorists and actors (never mind the limited application by states) have not usually properly analyzed the gendered nature of women's oppression and violence. There has been virtually no understanding of racialized or class-based gendering. Until recent years, very little feminist awareness and analysis has been applied by anyone, other than the international non-governmental women's movement, to the many forms of violence that primarily affect women, such as "domestic" violence, date rape, sexual harassment, prostitution, or incest. A "gender blind" international human rights framework has ignored all.

However partial the UN discussion (between states, human rights experts, etc) was, it is important to note it has also been threatened with foreclosure. In our fourth year of this project, war was declared by the American state on the Middle East. Canada was asked to support the American military force. The bombing of the World Trade Centre in New York happened.[26] Violence against women and women's oppression was a big part of the American rhetoric used to justify obstructing and defying UN peace processes and even bombing and invasion.

Does Trade Trump Rights? World Trade Organization (WTO) and the UN

At the time, CASAC was hosting more than six hundred women at a conference in Ottawa: Women's Resistance from Victimization to Criminalization.[27] The women on the opening panel of the conference were well known for their integrated activism and as women who would not avoid the challenge of the day. Each in turn, from Susie Rojtman who had just addressed World Bank executives, to Sunera Thobani, past president of the National Action Committee on the Status of Women, to Kim Pate, prisoners' rights activist, joined us in denouncing war as an alternative.[28] They addressed, among other things, the relationship between the behaviour of the UN and its member states and the violence done to Afghani, Palestinian, and aboriginal women in Canada.

Over and over again we were confronted with the reality of corporate interests, including the WTO, World Bank, and World Monetary Fund in restructuring states for the sake of profit making. They also addressed the impact that the structural adjustment drive was having in Canada: the elimination of the public sector and the imposition of a very gendered "law and order" agenda.[29]

CASAC does not argue for abandoning the work at the UN level, but we are cautious with our energy and focus. At best, we see we are dealing with a definition of human rights agreed to by states and a comprehension and compliance only as useful as the uprising of women within each state. Calling on the state to enforce women's rights is always problematic. There is no state in which women have full democratic access to power. No state upholds women's rights fully. No state has the full confidence of its women citizens. How wise is it to call for the criminalization of violence against women in all states, when women do not have economic and social equality, and when there is no parallel initiative to enforce those rights?

Women carry yet another burden when regimes do not uphold the right of accused persons or the rights of prisoners to vote or even to eat. States may use violence against women to attack innocent or even progressive men and women.[30] How valuable is a civil or political right when one is starving or facing indentured slavery?[31] These topics were opened up at the conference. One of the achievements of this project is our cooperation with the conference presenters to gradually post all proceedings on our web site.[32] All plenary proceedings are now available; the 100 workshops are being added.

In any case, appealing to the UN as a kind of super government will rarely be useful for the women who call on us in CASAC centres. But we do note that it was useful for the women of Tobique.[33] There is no power of enforcement and who could trust it if there was? At least the uneven power of states and the hegemony of the American state would often sabotage us. Feminists, including CASAC, successfully lobbied Canada to sign CEDAW's Optional Protocol. But we know that so far, women have had to fight their government in court, usually without funding, all the way to the Supreme Court before even approaching the UN. The women who call CASAC seeking justice will rarely struggle through such processes.

We don't underestimate the importance of the UN as a forum for world discussion. And we will probably continue to participate, intermittently, in lobbying at that level. And we are aware of several dramatic, positive highlights of activity in the UN over these past few years. Kofi Annan's (Secretary General of the United Nations) recognition of the role the unequal status of women plays in the international AID's epidemic, and the necessity to fight for the liberty, and autonomy including sexual liberty and sexual autonomy of women for the sake of world health.

> We need a deep social revolution that will give more power to women, and transform relations between women and men at all levels of society. It is only when women can speak up, and have a full say in decisions affecting their

lives, that they will be able to truly protect themselves-and their children against HIV.[34]

This clear reference to rape and sexual coercion was helpful.

The delivery of the message of our coalition, the World March of Women, by Francoise Davide, to the assembled states of the United Nations.[35] The World March activities engaged us all in 2000, but especially the women at both ends of the country, and in Quebec. B.C. was awestruck by the organizing of the Fraser River Journey of the Aboriginal Women's Action Network. They gathered partners from the anti-violence groups and set off down the mighty Fraser River in a two-week rafting trip that took them through some ten communities. In each they stopped and held a focus group to gather the opinions and outrage of the aboriginal women in those communities about restorative justice. It was a dramatic and effective action to denounce the sexist violence in their communities and identify the problems with restorative justice. On the East coast women rallied, trucked, marched, and met in large and colourful numbers connecting their economic plight and their lack of services to deal with poverty and violence. But the women of Quebec were amazing in their province-wide engagement in this international action. There is no doubt that the March 2000 activities internationalized and advanced the consciousness and effectiveness of the entire women's movement in Quebec. The speech at the UN and at the World Bank became symbols of the understanding of many women new to the movement that rights could be enlivened by our own organizing of political power outside of the circle of authorities and not just those bestowed by the authorities. They also effectively united the struggle for an end to violence against women and the struggle to end women's poverty in a unity that promised to sacrifice neither.

The refocusing of many actors within the UN systems on the indivisibility of rights and the necessity to attend to the economic rights of women in our efforts to end violence against women. From the achievements in Vienna to the new expressions of traditional human rights groups, like Amnesty International to the Charter cases proceeding through the Canadian courts, hundreds of women both within Canada and within the UN network are reconstituting a struggle to reintegrate the efforts to give meaning to equality by meshing women's international poverty and the international phenomenon of sexist violence against women.

We value the possibilities of the United Nations, especially as a forum for the examination and development of human rights. We also have seen the value of the Social Forum processes. We, along with the world's youth, have also had to turn our attention to the multi-nationals that are over powering and replacing our governments. And we have had to attend to the refusal of our governments to buffer us from that unrestrained greed. The World Trade Organization (WTO) was formed in 1995, the same year that the Beijing Platform for Action was adopted. The WTO "battle in Seattle," the Puerto Allegro and New Delhi fora, and the changing tide in the Third World have all caught our imagination and hope. CASAC has taken its place on the international violence committee of the World March of Women as the elected delegate from the pan-Canadian March Committee.

International exchanges and perspectives are affecting those working in professional disciplines as well. The 1998 publication of *Rethinking Violence* edited by Dobash and Dobash crosses professional as well as political boundaries in updating the discussion of what can be documented and understood, at least across the industrialized west and north, as violence against women and its function in the repression of women's rights. Soon the literature available in Canada will encompass a more global understanding.

In a similar vein, we have become active members in international electronic networks linking frontline women's activists around the world. We have been inspired by the work of Japanese women to confront the sex tourism launched from inside their borders by their alliances with women in the hosting/invaded countries, for instance, Thailand. And we have modelled projects on that cross-border work. The international communication is awkward and truncated still but never the less revolutionary. Nothing has replaced or diminished our hope in and commitment to the growth of an independent, democratic, international women's movement and, within it, the development of collaboration and mutual aid possibilities among grassroots frontline women's groups committed to ending violence against women.

Notes

1. Women's Resistance from Victimization to Criminalization, October 1-3, 2001.

2. Morgan, R. (1990, c1989). *The Demon Lover: On the Sexuality of Terrorism*. New York: Norton.

3. Canada has played a significant role in that discussion, for instance: Canada led the resolution at the fiftieth session on the Commission on Human Rights in 1994, to appoint the special Rapporteur on Violence Against Women, to obtain information on violence against women, and to recommend measures to eliminate such violence.

4. Federal-Provincial-Territorial Ministers Responsible for the Status of Women (2002).

5. Convention on the Elimination of All Forms of Discrimination Against Women (CEDAW), Review committee of the United Nations.

6. See Appendix: Convention on the Elimination of All Forms of Discrimination Against Women.

7. This mechanism is designed to allow, under very limited circumstances, women to appeal to the CEDAW committee when our national governments have failed us. See: Accession to the Optional Protocol to the Convention on the Elimination of All Forms of Discrimination against Women (2002, October).

8. Canada's Fifth Report, for the Convention on the Elimination of All Forms of Discrimination Against Women. Available online at <http://rapereliefshelter.bc.ca/issues/cedaw_Jan2003.pdf>.

9. Feminist Alliance for International Action (FAFIA), a coalition of women's groups, including CASAC, are autonomous from government, and independent of other political forces and formations.

10. Feminist Alliance for International Action (FAFIA) (2003). *Canada's Failure to Act: Women's Inequality Deepens*. Submission to the United Nations Committee on the Elimination of Discrimination Against Women on the Occasion of the Committee's Review of Canada's Fifth Report. Also B.C.

CEDAW Group (2003). *British Columbia Moves Backwards on Women's Equality*. Submission to the UN CEDAW on the Occasion of the Committee's Review of Canada's Fifth Report).

11. The 1993 VAWS found: "Grouped together 45 percent of all women had experienced violence by men" known to them," Federal-Provincial-Territorial Ministers Responsible for the Status of Women (2002), p 10.

12. World March of Women demands federal funding to feminist anti-violence services. This Canadian agreement was adapted from a demand worked out at the National Action Committee of the Status of Women (NAC) and led by CASAC. The federal government has a responsibility to the equality-seeking nature of these organizations. They are not just services, but combine service with advocacy through which women could collectively achieve equal treatment toward equal participation in Canada. They had been initially partially funded through the women's programme department of the Secretary of State as a matter of establishing women's equal citizenship. The reversal of that policy is still challenged. And a proposal to win support for a fifty million dollar initial budget has begun.

13. Shelagh Day, Professor Margo Young, and Sharon McIvor.

14. Lakeman, L. (2000).

15. CEDAW Committee Concluding Remarks available online at

<www.un.org/womenwatch/daw/cedaw/28sess. htm#report>.

16. See Appendix, also online: <http://www.casac.ca/allies/cedaw_recommendations2003.htm>.

17. Available online at

<http://ods-dds-ny.un.org/doc/UNDOC/GEN/N96/01/pdf/N9627301.pdf? OpenElement>.

18. *Ibid.*, para.204.

19. *Ibid.*, para.68.

20. *Ibid.*, para.69.

21. CEDAW, Article 2.

22. Available online at: <http://www.genderandpeacekeeping.org/resources/5_DEVAW.pdf>.

23. UN Declaration of the Elimination of Violence Against Women (UNDEVAW), Article 1.

24. As far as we are concerned, this inclusion of "forced" is discriminatory in itself.

25. See UNDHR: <http://www.un.org/Overview/rights.html>.

26. "9/11" (September 11, 2001). We are grateful for the correspondence with Robin Morgan and the pre-existing version of her book, (1989) *Demon Lover*, which allowed to us live this moment with more intelligence. And we encouraged a just peace with a joint statement of conference participants available in the conference proceedings.

27. Women's Resistance Conference proceedings, October 1-3, 2001, Ottawa, Canada. See online: <www.casac.ca>.

28. Women's Resistance: From Victimization to Criminalization. Opening Plenary. Locating this Conference in the Wider World – 2001. Chair: Diana Yaros, Tina Beads, Senator Landon Pearson, Dr. Hedy Fry, Dr. Sunera Thobani, Dr. Julia Sudbury, Suzy Rojtman, Kim Pate, Lee Lakeman. The panel presentations are available on CD and also on the web site: <http://www.casac.ca>.

29. Lakeman, L. (2000).

30. For example, in Canada, see: the Marshall case, online at: <www.casac.ca>.

31. Lee, A. (2000). Working With Refugee. *Canadian Women Studies*, 20 (3), 105-107.

32. CASAC online at: <www.casac.ca>.

33. Silman, J. (1987).

34. Annan, K. (2001). Annan Calls For Global Trust Fund to Fight HIV/Aids. Speech at OAU Aids Summit, April 26 2001. Retrieved online Jan. 15, 2002, from United States Information Service Web Site: <www.Aegis.com/ news/usis/2001/us010408.html>.

35. David, F. (2000, June 9). Speech delivered at General Assembly. Available online: <www.ffq.qc.ca/marche2000/commun-2000-06-09.html>.

The Trafficked Chinese Boat Women of Fujian Province

Alice Lee

EVER SINCE JULY 20, 1999 when the first boat from China arrived on the shores of B.C. with 123 Chinese refugees, Vancouver Rape Relief and Women's Shelter has been grappling daily with the issue of trafficking.[1] In the months following that summer, three more decrepit boats arrived depositing a total of 599 refugees into B.C. Traffickers from the second boat had dumped its passengers in the cold waters of the North Pacific near Vancouver Island as they fled from authorities. We were all horrified to hear about the conditions the refugees had endured trying to get here and, along with other women, we struggled for an effective response. Although at that time our collective was not as clear, we soon confirmed that trafficked women are subjugated to indentured labour, including prostitution.

People arriving in Canada as refugees are not a new thing. But the arrival of several boatloads in a row gave many people in B.C. a sense of urgency. People wanted to materially aid the women, men, and children.

Canada engaged in a systematic and purposive response to the refugees. With the end goal of deportation, the government encouraged a racist media campaign, introduced incarceration as an appropriate immigration policy, and actively suppressed the legal rights that are the entitlement of all persons who come to Canada.

Upon arrival on B.C. shores, the refugees were "welcomed" by local police. They were immediately detained under military guard and checked by doctors for disease and general health. Most of them were strip-searched, finger printed, and handcuffed. After the first boatload, many were automatically detained and remained in jail until their deportation (some were jailed for more then a year and a half). Children under eighteen were apprehended and placed in government group homes. Out of the 599 refugees, 90 of them were women, and 96 were under the age of eighteen.

Because Zhen was nineteen, she was jailed with the women. Solitary confinement was a common punishment. She and other refugee women, who eventually lived in our shelter, told us they were held in solitary confinement and Zhen herself was isolated there for crying. She was in confinement for days and, feeling unable to cope any more, Zhen attempted suicide by jumping and hitting her head on the concrete.

In response to the first boat, the Immigration Department designated the Canadian Forces Base at Esquimalt as a port of entry to process them. The Fujians were confronted with a process that jeopardised the likelihood that they would be rightly recognized as political refugees. They were detained illegally and denied legal counsel during their initial interviews with Immigration Canada. This made them extremely vulnerable because the interviews became part of their refugee application. It was under those circumstances that they were processed and, as a result, many exclusion orders (legal determinations that individuals could not apply for refugee status) were issued.[2] Denied access to counsel, the claimants were unaware that they could assert refugee status and, under B.C. law, engage legal aid to assist them with the immigration process.

A media that branded and isolated them supported the government strategy. Messages carried in local and national media embodied predictable, negative judgments that prevented humanization of the people. We were not informed of the conditions of their lives and the reasons why they would take such dangerous risks. We were directed and encouraged to participate in the construction of racist and classist stereotypes. As the boats arrived, the media continued to sensationalize the story, evoking strong racist anger causing a split in my Asian community as well as the general public.

The distancing of the refugees was enhanced by the structure of current immigration laws that have opened the borders to those who are wealthy or hold professional standing. Headlines such as *Go Home*³ fuelled the debate, distorting the public discussion in terms of a matter of costs, the "relaxed" Canadian immigration laws, and the illegal refugees "jumping queue." A demand for deportation, without legal process, was loudly and repeatedly expressed in the media. There was no discussion of why the people had been illegally detained or reasons for a substantive shift in legal criteria whereby group profiling was utilized as a just reason for detention. They were deemed guilty without a fair hearing.

Women around us were outraged and rallied against the detention on International Women's Day, March 2000. That summer, women's groups at a Legal Education Action Fund (LEAF) conference heard Direct Action Against Refugee Exploitation (DAARE) recount the plight of the refugee women who were jailed. We called for their immediate release and challenged the argument that the government was only protecting them from dangerous traffickers and that there was no place for them to go.

My shelter collective quickly offered space and a welcome to the community. We joined with DAARE. Our efforts aided in the release of several Fujians and created opportunities for them to group with other women to share and plan for their survival. Zhen was released to us from prison, pending her refugee hearing. The Fujians were eventually allowed legal representation, either through legal aid, or individual lawyers paid by the province. Providing inadequate translation services, insufficient and overworked legal counsel, the government ensured that most refugees would lose their claim for refugee status. Since that time, even our own justice system has recognized the unfair treatment the Fujians received and has acted to overturn many of the exclusion orders in court. Of course, some of those people will not benefit. Justice delayed.

In the process of offering what we hoped would be useful and appropriate aid, we were confronted with many challenges, some successfully resolved, others regrettably not.

The primary difficulty we faced was the collection of useful information regarding the trafficking of women. During the months that followed the arrival of the first boat, it was almost impossible to get any accurate information regarding how many refugees there were, why they chose to take this incredible risk, who had trafficked them, and who benefited from the trafficking of women.

Zhen knew very little about her traffickers. She had contact with one person and only knew his alias. He told her not to bring any belongings as everything she needed would be provided for her and that she would be traveling for only a few days. He had assured her the ship was fully equipped, including her own private room and bed. Zhen was on the ship for over a month. She did not want to talk much about it.

Zhen came from a poor family and had no opportunity for higher education. Her mother had remarried, but her stepfather was in jail, and she could barely keep up with the living expenses of Zhen and her brother. One day a stranger asked Zhen if she would like the opportunity to come to Canada. It would cost her 35,000 USD. She was not required to make a deposit but had the understanding that work would be set up for her when she arrived to repay that debt. She had no idea what kind of work she would be doing but decided to come since she had always heard that Canada was a land of opportunity and freedom. When I asked what made her take such a risk, she replied that she was her family's only hope for any future.

Zhen lived in Fujian province, China and lacked formal educational training, characteristics shared with many of the refugees trafficked by boat. Almost all were either escaping political repression or extreme poverty. Women are subjected to severe birth control measures under China's one child policy. Forced abortions or sterilization continue to be common enforcement methods. The pressure and push for globalization in the West is an impetus for China's change in economic policy, resulting in extreme poverty and massive unemployment. It is estimated that by 2002, over twenty million public sector workers will lose their jobs as China moves toward privatization. It is said that China's "floating population" is around 70 to 100 million people.[4]

Many people migrate to the cities in search of work. Both women and men end up working for little pay at exploitive jobs as day labourers, factory workers, restaurant cooks and servers, and for many women, as prostitutes. Although prostitution is not legal in China, it is rampant, very much a part of the local economy.

In Jinan, China, people I talked to noted that change in municipal government policies have greatly encouraged the growth of "night entertainment." "Night entertainment," restaurants and bars has been accompanied by a tremendous increase in prostitution. Some believe this is deliberately overlooked as part of the government's plan for increased tourism and investment. With no social safety net, women are forced to service men. Canada, along with other Western countries, actively promotes such conditions by aggressively pressing for economic trade agreements that are only beneficial to the wealthy few. By moving their businesses to the developing world and demanding outrageously low wages and poor working conditions, the businesses not only control the world resources but they have succeeded in commodifying human lives and migration opportunities.

Even the Criminal Intelligence Service of Canada acknowledges that international migrants are highly extorted and women are often gang raped and sold into prostitution. Zhen was unaware that she was a likely young candidate. The federal government, however, is aware of the presence of various gangs in Vancouver trafficking women like Zhen. To close the borders more and more, and then to jail the trafficked women, seems the least effective way to manage the situation. Often women like Zhen are sent on to Toronto and New York.[6] Both of these destinations have a high Fujianese population. Many remain there without status. They are very much a part of the economy providing cheap, illegal labour in the sweatshop industry and prostitution. Without legal standing in our country or the US, trafficked refugees are intimidated and controlled by real threats to them and/or their families back home.

Helping, in this environment, is difficult. Women are suspicious of services offered for their aid. In China, women's services are often controlled and operated by the state, not an independent women's movement. These realities, in conjunction with the women's treatment by the Canadian government, created barriers that made it difficult for them to trust in the possibilities. A guarantee of Landed Immigrant status would increase the willingness of at least some to testify against their abusers. Obeying our own laws might help to make us trustworthy.

Zhen told me that she had no idea what the journey would be like and would never have imagined being put in jail by the Canadian government. If she had known, she might not have come. Having women visit in jail was a great encouragement and having a place to stay at Rape Relief was a tremendous relief for her. After staying at our shelter, along with DAARE, we found her more permanent housing while she waited for her hearing.

Zhen grew more and more restless as she waited. She grew increasingly scared of being deported, as she knew prison would be waiting for her in China. Any future that she might have had back home would no longer be an option. The media was full of stories of other refugees' deportations, and, in the end, Zhen disappeared.

Our collective found that the individual experiences of the Fujianese women were not so different from other battered women staying in our transition house but they had the extra burden of language barriers, cultural differences, and global positioning. Isolation is a primary factor in all of these women's lives. Extreme poverty makes women even more susceptible to male violence. Both the traffickers and the State acted to isolate these women from each other and from the community—that is, they created and sustained conditions where women remain desperate and can be duped by promises of a "better life." In such an environment, there is little wonder why women are apprehensive and find it difficult to navigate their way toward autonomy and freedom. We regret that we could not offer Zhen any guarantee that staying in Canada for her hearing would mean a fair chance to achieve a "better life" and her autonomy.

Notes

1. Lee, A. (2000).
2. Direct Action Against Refugee Exploitation (DAARE) (2001). *Movement Across Borders: Chinese Women Migrants in Canada.* Vancouver: Author.
3. Harnett, C. (1999, August 15). Go Home: We asked you to have your say about the latest wave of migrants to reach our shores. Your response was huge, the message was clear: send them back immediately. *Times Colonist*, p. A1.
4. James, A. and Price, J. (1999, November). *No Safe Harbour: Confronting the Backlash against Fujian Migrant Workers* (Working Paper Series-Series #1, Working Paper #2). Vancouver: Canada Asia Pacific Research Networks.
5. Canadian Intelligence Service Canada (1998). National Organized Crimes Priorities, online: <www.cisc.gc.ca/AnnualReport1998/Cisc1998en/asian98.htm>.

Restructuring Canada
at the Beginning of the New Century

On May 28, 2003, roughly a week after Sherry Heron's death, the Canadian government sent CASAC a letter signed by the Hon. Jean Augustine, Minister Responsible for the Status of Women.[1] It accompanied the publication called *Assessing Violence Against Women: A Statistical Profile*.[2]

That publication confirmed that, at least for the moment, we were not, as frontline workers, in a struggle with our national government about the existence of the violence done to women. After thirty years, some things had been accepted. The data sources listed in the government publication: Assessing Violence Against Women: A Statistical Profile included the Canadian Criminal Victimization reports and surveys of 1998 and 1999, including the Statistics Canada General Social Survey (GSS) and the Violence Against Women Survey of 1993.[3] Based on the source of the report and accompanying letter, it seemed clear that the government understood the situation to be a critical infringement on the status of women.[4] Obviously too, the Status of Women staff and Minister were aware of the value of the Violence Against Women Survey created by Holly Johnson and now recognized by scholars internationally and were protecting it from the predictable ideological challenges: questioning its outcomes by challenging its methods.

Maybe, as we hoped, it is no longer necessary to repeat to government the basic numbers or basic definitions.[5] Of course, our point of view—that of rape crisis centres, transition houses, and women's centres—both allows and compels a more detailed and encompassing view of the landscape of women's lives. From where we stand, it is more possible to see the extent and function of sexist violence being committed by men in Canada.

Some Effects of Restructuring on the Nature, Severity and Incidence of Violence Against Women

"The poor will always be with us," "prostitution is the oldest profession," and "men are just naturally that way." These essentialist positions or attitudes are not promoted in CASAC centres.[6] Rather, we see that among other things, each corporate move, social policy, and interaction of the state and its subjects moves us toward or away from the desired future. Class, race, and gender division and domination are social and economic constructions always in the making. As is equality.[7]

There are those who see it differently. We have had to defend our positions rather rigorously in the last few years. The government has applied only formal equality when attending to equality at all. It has sometimes ignored both the Supreme Court rulings against formal equality and the reverse impact of the application of these polices. Huge economic and political forces have been mounted to oppose any government role beyond armies and prisons. Sometimes we have found ourselves reeling from many simultaneous blows.

Sometimes both progressive prison abolitionists[8] and capitalist privatization promoters challenge us to consider whether the adversarial justice system (either criminal or civil) is an appropriate vehicle for women to use. They apparently agree with each other that the state is suspect on the issues of freedom and oppression. One side fears direct repression by the state and the other fears wasteful expenses and "social engineering." Others challenged that this was a time of the "shrinking of the state" and our worries about the imposition of the law and order agenda and victim's rights approaches were ill placed. Our insistence on the positive obligations of government, they claim, are dated and doomed. But some of the same people support aggressive federal government intervention in urban redevelopment in the name of health or so-called "harm reduction strategies." Some do not see the government intervention and impositions involved when, in divorce settlements of property, mobility, custody, and access, the government falsely claims gender neutrality while upholding the apparently perpetual, paternal, social, and economic interests in the family.

The end of the welfare state provided the backdrop for all of this legislative intervention, and so we found we had to reconsider welfare. Funding to national women's groups was essentially gone. The funding that had been available to women's services through the provinces because of CAP arrangements was gone.[9] At the same time, there was a big push, supported by government, to promote the rights of victims, even a possible new national victim's association. The government promotion of the notion of "victim" as a legal policy category plus the changes to community policing, sentencing changes to confinement in the home rather than jails, and the promotion of prostitution, opened questions within criminal justice of who defines community and how? And who is considered part of the community? What is the relationship between the state and the community? We were interested in those conversations that might affect our understanding of our options as the nature of the Canadian state changed.[10]

The end of social welfare and the welfare state is part of the globalization process in which Canada has played a role and that has engulfed women living in Canada. We have rarely had the opportunity to express, in our own way, the connections we live daily between those international economic forces, federal laws, and policies, and what is happening in anti-rape centres. Rare indeed is our opportunity to express the LINK between global/federal forces and our advocacy supporting women, especially those violated women trying to engage the state against abusing men.

The autonomous member centres of CASAC have come together, exposing what is commonly happening to women who call us from across Canada. We share a joint vision at the national and international level. Initially, we stated our agreements in our constitution.[11] We renewed and tailored those agreements in an internal evaluation completed in 1981.[12] In response to the government mandate of the "Blue Ribbon Panel on Violence Against Women," we again captured and advanced our common understanding in *99 Federal Steps to End Violence Against Women*.[13]

The CASAC LINKS project offered possibilities for renewal and speaking out about the lives of women; we were compelled to do so by the changes in our daily work brought by the changes in Canadian society.

We learned early in our herstory, as we understood and discussed our lived experiences, a critique of the welfare state as social control.[14] And we share with many a critique of the dismantling of the welfare state and the social safety net that it sometimes provided.[15] The documentation and criticism of the imposition of the neo-liberal agenda is formidable. Those sometimes overlapping understandings have found widespread agreement among our members, and, in fact, among second and third wave feminists.[16]

Women working in the anti-rape area of advancing women's interests also have observations and analyses from our distinct and discreet points of view: our class and race composition, geographic locations, day-to-day advocacy work, consciousness-raising methods, and from the positions we took previously regarding disability, lesbianism, and immigration, for instance.[17] We have also been shaped in our opinions and polices by our herstory of alliances.[18]

We are not the best ones to articulate and there isn't space here to fully express the loss to the women of Canada of public sector jobs and services.[19] But from our point of view, there are few women who have not been made more vulnerable to criminal sexual assault. There is no incident of criminal violence against women in Canada that has not been negatively affected. There is no libratory and/or ameliorative process affecting violated women that has not been negatively affected.

CASAC's economic target of a social economy that values women's labour and shares wealth with women has been moved back drastically. The trajectory of reforms toward those ends that had been won by our grandmothers, mothers, and ourselves…from the vote to unemployment insurance, pensions to childcare, self determination to settling land claims, welfare to more humane immigration policies, criminalizing sexist violence to the inclusion of women in a living Charter of Rights and Freedoms, has been reversed in the service of grotesque individualism and corporate wealth.

CASAC wishes to express our understanding of those impacts which we have encountered most often in our crisis work and which affect anti-violence work most profoundly: the loss of women's right to welfare, the promotion of prostitution, the use of the Divorce Act in such a way as to uphold the permanence of the patriarchal family, the restructuring of Canada from the shape of the justice system to the shape of the community, with neither offering a diligent application of the current knowledge of the condition of women's oppression nor an appropriate commitment to women's advancement. It remains to be seen whether the Social Union Framework can and will substantially improve the future situation. It does of course improve the prospects that loomed under the Meech Lake Accord. Certainly the process so far has limited Canadian non-government involvement in the planning and consideration.[20] We have seen no reassurance that either our particular identities will be recognized or that our collective and universal needs and entitlements will be met.[21] While there seems to be a consensus that the framework can be adjusted to serve us as citizens, and specifically as women, we should not be satisfied with less than language that encodes those promises in enforceable national standards and oversight mechanisms.

The Bottom Line: The Loss of the Women's Welfare

Most voters, citizens, and members of the community realize that we are contending with mean-spirited welfare reductions and restrictions that make life more difficult for the poor. Although it is difficult to keep track of the specifics, some have been publicized. In B.C., for instance, we know that "women with children will lose one hundred dollars a month from their already inadequate cheques by April 1, 2004."[22]

No government declared honestly to its citizens before election either the nature of welfare cuts it intended or the further gendering of poverty that would be imposed by those welfare cuts. It is simply not true that Canadians voted for those attacks on the poor. And no government within Canada has been given a mandate to end welfare. Any such mandate would be legally questionable in any case given the Charter and human rights law and conventions. This is perhaps why no government makes public those it is refusing subsistence. But CASAC women are witness to the fact that women across the country have no guaranteed, or even likely, access to a promised minimum standard of living. No matter how poor, women have no guarantee of welfare in any form. As women consider their options for improving their lives they/we certainly learn it.

We have lost a small but significant recognition of the historically disadvantaged economic condition of women's lives. But as predicted in feminist accounts of the end of CAP funding[23] and as recorded in our alternate reports to CEDAW, women in Canada have lost what application we had of this encoded economic human right.[24]

CASAC is most concerned that we are losing this benchmarked redistribution of income toward equality.

In each province and community the attacks and erosion have been different: from workfare to "man in the house" rules, age limitations, rate decreases, time limited access, life time bans, immigration and settlement restrictions, punishment bans after and through criminalization, to bans based on health requirements. Not only has the formal policy been degraded, but the positive discretionary power in procedures and regulations has also been curtailed. Management and sometimes the remaining staff too often interpret rules with the same anti-entitlement attitudes.

The abdication of the federal role in assuring women and others who need a guaranteed dignified income is plain and Canada wide. This includes the downward pressure of shrinking transfer payments and block funding without national standards.[25] That abdication encourages provinces to set welfare, education, and health needs against the needs of business for roads and bridges, to ship goods, and transport tourists.

Transition houses in Canada emerged partly to deal with the limits that existed in the welfare policy of the 1970s. Welfare departments would refuse to grant women a welfare cheque when she came to the state for assistance in dealing with an abusing husband. Welfare workers were directed to tell women that the state could not be responsible "for the break-up of families."[26] If she left and established residency on her own, then welfare might be granted since it was an assumed economic right of Canadians to not starve or be homeless. Since they usually had no money, women moved to transition houses, where they didn't need rent or deposits, not only for immediate safety, but to establish a separate residence to prove to the state that they had left the marriage/family/couple. During their stay with us, they qualified for welfare.[27]

Women still come. Transition houses are full. Shelters for the homeless or other emergency facilities are also full. But now these women "qualify" for welfare less and less often, and they do not ordinarily receive benefits without aggressive advocacy from someone independent of government. They are told constantly that it is not a right and cannot be relied on. Welfare, she is told, can be reduced, withdrawn, and denied temporarily. She could be banned for life.[28]

Women, especially poor women, have always had to make extra legal deals with the men in their lives. When ex-husbands or lovers are taking responsibility by sliding women money under the table for childcare we are all glad. But in a position of extra dependence, created by the state withdrawal, sometimes those deals are dangerous underground contracts, which the women cannot enforce, and which subjugate them to the very men they are trying to leave for the sake of themselves and their children.

Any welfare granted currently is so inadequate and insecure as to force the women into subsidizing it with an informal economy: house work for others, childcare for others, personal health care for others, food preparation and production for others, drug sales, and prostitution.[29]

Poverty is criminalized.

Women who complain to the state of rape, sexual harassment, incest, sexual exploitation, and trafficking, face the denial of security: no exercisable right to welfare. If by some cleverness, accident, or kindness she gets welfare and is subsidizing it to get by, she is vulnerable to blackmail by her attacker. If she reports criminal sexual abuse, she will quickly be threatened (directly and indirectly) by the defence bar. Exposure can cause either a loss of informal income or the loss of credibility as a complainant. She can and will be painted as a liar, thief, con, drug dealer, prostitute, unworthy of the protection of the law.

The fourteen or eighteen year old incest victim leaving home, the worker on minimum wage, or making her way in the informal economy, the dislocated women pulled from small towns or reserves into the city for work or education, the immigrant women struggling to survive or trying to transition into lawful citizenship and a reasonable life, are all frustrated. If the normalcy of male violence against women were not known, one might think this was something other than state collusion with violence against women.[30] Access to the rule of law and equal protection under the law become meaningless.

Predictable access to welfare was a power used by more than the destitute. It was a power in the hands of all women: the knowledge that we could (in a very modest amount) pay for food and shelter for ourselves and our kids by right. It was a power used to fend off attackers and to take advantage of opportunities. It was a basis on which to build one's self respect: the community had declared, in the organizing of the 1930s and legislated in welfare rights, that everyone in Canada was entitled to at least this minimal share in the common wealth.

We have no romantic memories of the days when welfare was great. In all social welfare schemes, there was always too much emphasis on social control, especially of women. We needed much more income redistribution and much less regulation of the lives of women.[31]

In anti-rape centres we now face daily many women who judge that they simply cannot leave or escape men who criminally abuse them: husbands, fathers, bosses, pimps, johns, landlords, and sometimes social or welfare workers.[32] Since they cannot afford to actually leave, they cannot afford to effectively stand up to them either. Those that do leave these economic positions are on their own with their children and they know it.

Canadians have been deceived and manipulated to achieve this reversal of social policy. Clearly national standards are necessary as are achievable protections for women across the country. When we redesign "welfare," as we surely will, we must revive and improve the Guaranteed Annual Income concepts that generated the welfare reforms from the 1930s to1975. Feminists will not tolerate going back to notions of family income, the worthy and unworthy poor, disentitling immigrant workers, divisions of minimum wages from disability rights, disassociated child poverty, or mother's allowances, aboriginal disentitlement, forced work camps, age restrictions, or entitlements. We will certainly not tolerate going back to the intrusive state supervision of the private lives of women.

In this desperate time for so many women, perhaps we should take heart that most Canadians have not yet realized our loss of welfare and will surely rise to the occasion.

A Global Economy: The Promotion of Prostitution

Can anyone still believe that there is no connection between the economic redistributive functions of the state, including within the social safety net, and the staggering increase in the informal economy? Are we meant to say the emperor is clothed? The economic division of the peoples of the world is staggering. The economic division between Canadians is growing exponentially.

Racism infused much of the violence against aboriginal women in Canada since earliest colonial time. Organizing against racist violence has accelerated in the last five years to match the threat. Not only the Ontario Aboriginal Women and the AWAN collective have led the way, but so have women of colour formations both permanent and ad hoc. India Mahila persisted through thirty years of support work, but smaller situational coalitions also formed to deal with moments of violence. In Vancouver one such group responded to a number of violent street assaults against Asian women by calling a press conference and asserting their observations of how the media and officials were handling the events and refusing to see the racism that connected them. They wanted to provide a strong image of Asian women in resistance and they did.[33]

Child and street level prostitution and the so-called "adult entertainment" industry are booming. This is globalization being brought to Canada. Drug trafficking and prostitution are replacing welfare, health care, and education as the hope of the destitute.

Professor Dara Culhane at SFU describes it as "a process that moves women farther and farther out from under whatever small protections working people and women have been able to construct within the state."[34] They are moving out past the imposition of the law and order agenda to the no woman's land of the urban and suburban informal, illegal economies. Aboriginal women have been talking about this for years as a factor in violence against women on and off reserve. We remember Teresa Nahanee at an Ottawa LEAF conference in the early 1990s describing the condition of aboriginal women in many parts of Canada as having to live without any basic rule of law. Now these are the conditions for many women in every major Canadian settlement.

Many women are being driven into the hands of global traders in labour, flesh, and drugs. They are trafficked into and throughout Canada, on the one hand, by those global traders and, on the other, within Canada by Canadian gangs, particularly the motorcycle gangs.[35] As protection we are offered racist immigration practices that jail the people trafficked and legalization of the prostitution industry. Of course, we don't want the criminalization of the victims, including all those at the bottom of these rigid hierarchies.[36] But surely we are all aware now that this multi-billion dollar prostitution industry is actively involved not only in the trade itself, but also in the promotion of the legalization of the trade in women and drugs.[37]

As with our struggles against the rest of the inhumane multinational trade agenda, we must expose, confront, and interfere with the managers, owners, and profiteers. The leadership of Sweden in this matter of human rights and women's rights is impressive and hopeful.[38] Sweden has criminalized the traffickers, pimps, and buyers, and begun to protect the women and chidren. It regards prostitution as violence against women. It is no accident that Sweden is not building an economy on tourism or the sex tourism that goes with it.

To ignore women's equality aspirations and the current unequal status of women in Canada and in the world will undermine any progressive efforts to protect prostituted women from criminalization. Naive good intentions to protect the individual women should not be used to tolerate the development of this grotesque industry. In our efforts to address the needs of women trafficked into and throughout Canada, CASAC has come to the conclusion that we can only serve them by protecting their gender rights, their status as women, and the status of all women. No one is disposable or worthy of any lesser rights.

In our centres we are contending with women trafficked from abroad as indentured labour, mail order brides, domestic workers, and street level prostitutes. Sometimes we are asked to support beaten and raped exotic dancers, women in "escort" services, and "massage" parlours. Daily we are dealing with women dislocated from remote territories within Canada and trying to make their way in the cities. We are taking calls and housing and referring women who have been supplementing their incomes with prostitution and who want protection, both legal and political, from their pimps, johns, boyfriends, lovers, fathers, and sometimes government officials to whom they try to report incidents of violence.

The public provision of exit services to women is inadequate. From our centres in the early 1980s we supported the development of both the ASP (the Alliance for the Safety of Prostitutes), and POWER (Prostitutes and Other Women for Equal Rights) networks.[39] Both were spin-offs of the membership and politics of anti-rape centres that wanted to specialize in serving women prostituted.

We participated in Direct Action Against Refugee Exploitation (DAARE)[40] and have supported financially and politically Justice for Girls[41] and many other initiatives across the country. But we remain convinced that to use the easier provision of services as an argument for legalization is misguided. As Cherry Kingsley says:

> If we want to set up areas to protect women, to give women dignity and police
> protection, appropriate childcare, housing, and job training, and so on, then
> we should do that. Why should women have to service men sexually to be offered those things needed by all women?[42]

Certainly among the women who call us and come to us, most do not choose prostitution except as a highly available way to survive. We speculate that the few women in the world who do choose it are short-time participants with privileges that allow them to leave. The provision of services specific to women trapped in or wanting to leave prostitution is inadequate everywhere. But to think that such services alone will curtail the offence of prostitution in the midst of this economic agenda is ridiculous. And for the federal government to refuse to try to curtail the domestic and international prostitution of women is barbarous.

The recognition of the so-called "rights of prostitutes" or the new talk of decriminalization (meaning legalization) is a self-serving policy ploy.[43] It legitimizes men's right to abuse women and also legitimizes Canada's refusal to redistribute income to women, some of whom are the most needy women, both within her borders and in the international community.

Men who buy women on the streets of Canadian cities and in the third world are almost always situated in higher class and race designations.[44] Sex tourism is surely a cash cow for many a government (national and city). "The sex industry now accounts for five percent of the Netherland's economy."[45] "Prostitution has become an accepted side line of the tourism and casino boom in Victoria, Australia, with government sponsored casino's authorizing the redeeming of casino chips and wheel of fortune bonuses at local brothels."[46] Is it any wonder that Canadian rape crisis centres protested the mega tourism plans as far back as Expo and up to the current Olympic plans?[47] Before both those tourism events, there was a heightened promotion of prostitution in the city.

In Canada, most of the men buying the sex services of women on the street for use there or in their cars, could afford to purchase sex in more comfortable surroundings, but prefer the street trade where the degradation, humiliation, and violence are part of the purchase.[48] CASAC and many others have discredited the ineffective and silly use of John Schools to divert these men from the consequences of criminal activity.[49] The illusion that this trade will simply move indoors and be tamed by the legalization of prostitution is ridiculous. It hasn't worked anywhere else in the world and it won't work here.[50] Women who are so trapped as to be part of that disastrous practice will not be incorporated into the imagined self-organized bawdy house or the call girl trade of the Pretty Woman propaganda. More than 50 percent are aboriginal women raised in poverty and racism who are dislocated from their communities to the urban ghettos.

In any case, the phoney division in law and practice between the attitudes and approaches to innocents (the adolescents, survival trade women, "forced" trafficking of mentally handicapped women), victimized by sexual exploiters, and women somehow deemed complicit in their own victimization, is reminiscent of the traditional virgin/whore dichotomy used to divide and conquer each group of women who tried to use law on all other violence issues: the raped, the beaten, the impoverished, the racialized, the disabled, the designated lesbians.

Nor will their dignity, body integrity, or human right to a life without violence and a life with a reasonable standard of living be assured by legalizing prostitution. Pretending to accept prostitution as a viable option for our sisters and daughters, including the protection of men from criminal sanctions for buying and selling women and sex, presents us with a grim version of women's equality under the law. To use a woman in this state of desperation as the example of protecting women's agency is to make a mockery of the concept.[51]

CASAC women fear that we are facing an era when women will be designated, numbered, and regulated by city health departments as prostitutes. They will cooperate in order to evade immediate and punitive criminalization.[52] That designation will remain with them for life and will affect every aspect of their lives and futures. Those who are sick, drug addicted, or rebellious to this trade regulation will be further forced into the illegal informal economy and will simply be the "bad" prostitutes and "bad" drug addicts who have refused the "harm reduction" model and therefore are even less worthy of the protection of law.

The current public policy debate of adult prostitution is constructed around the wishes of men, and the needs of the big city interest in real estate development, and the international interests in migrant labour, and international capital. In those debates, pro-prostitution voices use the women subject to prostitution in their rhetoric. They try to box us into a discussion limited to the anecdotes about individual women and their individual adaptation to a horrible situation: choices. It is as though political concepts of disadvantaged groups are silenced. The public is confined in the debates to giving our approval, or not, of how women, and their children live in the belly of the beast of international trade.

City officials notably in Ottawa, Toronto, Montreal, and Vancouver trot out urban decay, including the debauchery of the informal economy in the sale of drugs and flesh, as a rationale for a new government relationship at the federal and city levels.[53] In the Vancouver Agreement, money-short services are bribed so obviously that local people refer to them as "poverty pimps" and the "poverty industry." But so far those negotiations do not invite or even tolerate participation from equality-seeking groups (those committed to redistribution not just services) and are not in any meaningful way public processes. The misery of the people on the streets is cynically used to justify new and questionable, if not bad, governance processes.

This is further weakening women's access to Charter rights. A federal legal and social policy approach is needed to address the plight of prostituted women and girls, which must be based on an equality-driven attack on the beast that is prostitution: a hugely profitable form of violence against women.

The Basic Social Unit: Enforcing the Private Domain and Upholding the Patriarchal Family After Divorce

It is questionable what privatizing public roads, rails, and airlines may be doing to Canada, but it seems now obvious to us that there are devastating equality losses with privatizing criminal and civil law, legal assistance to individuals, and consultative processes of law reform, as well as what we normally understand as "cops, courts and corrections."

Many Canadians are not yet aware that we are experimenting with privately-owned and run jails. And most are not aware that for a decade, policing has become more and more a matter of private companies guarding private property and private interests. Although, we are all getting inured to the image of security guards in shopping malls and building lobbies who are armed with handcuffs, clubs, stun wands, sometimes guns, and never the Charter.

When we began this work we were worried by the imposition through public police of the "law and order" agenda, the promotion of insubstantial and false restorative justice as an alternative to that, the funding cuts to already inadequate legal aid and legal services, and the pressure to label and categorize our work as victim assistance rather than as initiatives toward the equality of women and the prevention of women's sexualized victimization.[54] These past five years has dramatically changed the picture. To take the example of the divorce law now under consideration by Parliament, we can see a different use of the state emerging.

This newly adjusted state carries with it the danger of further reinforcing the patriarchal family, including the violent ones. Most violence against women that enters the courts does so at family court level. This is not only because much of violence done to women is committed in the family, but also because of the history of law and policing, and because those designing the justice system prefer it that way. It is important to remember here that civil law contends with struggles between individuals or private parties, and criminal law was developed to deal with offences against the community/state.

CASAC claims that violence against women is not simply or best understood as a crime against one woman but as an individuated incident or stream of incidents in the campaign of sexist violence that terrorizes and contains most women. It has some of the character of hate crime against a minority, racialized group, and some of the character of violence that we categorize as terrorism. That is, it affects all women and all women's freedom. And this is no less true when the violence is committed in the family.

All through the 1970s feminists interfering with sexist violence negotiated with the welfare state. We were funded by it. We relied on it to guarantee income to women leaving abusive men. We referred women by the thousands to legal services. As assistants to women beaten (especially by their husbands) we were in constant contact with the courts.

Those of us who worked with women raped by strangers were constantly aware of the differences in criminal justice offered to wives. We always debated the acceptability of diversion of wife assault and child incest from criminal court rooms to civil law, mediation, and counseling rooms. We sometimes agreed that it was a solution women could sensibly try when police offered no court at all.[55] One side protested the acceptance of this diversion. The other side argued that it was useful to women and children that they be spared the rigors of criminal court, including the burden of proof of violence, and that relaxed and specialized methods could be applied in family courts, which might serve women well.

But we agreed then and agree now that mediation and counseling must never be mandatory. Sometimes the existence of the specialized courts for a year or more improved the criminal conviction rate and the response to women's complaints. In the early days, the concentration of professionals particularly interested in the problem and the coordination of their energy paid off.

The current Yukon Domestic Violence Treatment Option Court is a good example of such concentration. As long as the original personnel are present the conviction improvements are likely to hold. This option of course is built on the belief that women do not want their abusive marriages to end and that the court can reduce violence against women by intervening early with a conviction and treatment option. We applaud the conviction and question the promotion of these families.

Too often these specialized courts became job ghettos and policy pockets. They faced the lack of respect for women and carried that contempt into a lack of respect for woman-identified legal venues and proceedings.[56] However, isolated from the criminal justice norms, these venues and processes did replicate the racism and class biases of the wider legal movement. Men of colour and aboriginal men were much more likely to be tried and convicted of wife and incest assault than their white neighbours.

Generally, the Specialized and Unified Family Courts suffered a lack of financing from both federal and provincial budgets. On the whole, they failed to grapple with the many problems and any initial success was usually sabotaged. Whatever the motivation for its creation, family court, including specialized family courts, and unified family courts, often seemed to those of us working on the violent cases to be torture chambers for battered, and raped wives, and children sexually assaulted by their fathers. The problems ranged from nowhere to sit or stand that wasn't vulnerable to his gaze, view, harassment, following, verbal assault, silent intimidation, all the way to no way, and no assistance, to make her message understood to staff and professionals because of language, culture, and class, but mostly because of gender biases.

We do not hold out much more hope for the Domestic Violence Courts being instituted in Ontario. The 56 courts funded with some 24 million dollars claim to respond to the May/Iles and Hadley inquest jury demands.[57] Of course, the public outcry after those wife murders and after the investigative journalist series called *Hitting Home* in the *Toronto Star* in 1996 that examined the murder of wives, will not be silenced by these adaptations. Certainly, we hope that some practices may improve, at last.

As one example of the faulty practices in family courts, women, when they had lawyers through legal aid, were told to be careful not to breach the "friendly parent" or "maximum contact" rule for fear of appearing uncooperative with the court. It was unwise to raise violent incidents against either the wife or the child unless women and girls had winnable criminal cases of violence. And who did! Alternatively, they might be heard as truthful in this family court if the women and children had professional authorization of their voice as the officially raped and battered. That authority could only be attached by a medical or social work professional. Their lawyers were not free to assert it, and there was no police or crown function for checking out the criminal activity, even if there was abundant evidence still available.

In fact, in family courts most decisions were made by professionals other than legal ones and were then confirmed by the judge. In our minds, there was always a problem of the equality issues. Even after the Charter and the discussions fostered by it, the staff, and professionals, including the few who were legally trained, didn't see themselves as being guided, much less bound, by the Charter, Human Rights law, or any other legal concept of equality. And their personal or collectively held view of equality was never declared or open to challenge or review.

These rooms were (and are still) finally technically answerable to the criminal justice accountability systems. With expert legal counsel, or a topnotch advocate, or highly trained and committed family court staff, some women could make their way. But that is rarely the situation. And like many other "special" venues offered to women, it could and often did turn out to be a ghetto or dead end in the search for assistance to assert a right to be free of violence.

Making her way through a custody and access agreement that protected her children from abuse, or protected them from helplessly watching and being trained by abuse, often seemed the best trade available. If the professionals believed women, they might get a separation settlement that protected both mother and children but no criminal procedure against the abuser. Criminal immunity for him in return for autonomy and or safety for her. Otherwise, women were better to remain silent about such criminal abuse and to fight for custody and access, supervised visits, and autonomy as though it had never happened. That was of course a difficult case to make once she had to leave out of her story the most important facts.

To do otherwise was considered by some professionals within the system and by the law an unfair use of the police and courts. It might well cost a mother sole custody of her children or an access order that eliminated the safety plan of the protesting ex-wife. There were always many pitfalls, even for those women granted custody. The victory might be limited to having the abusive husband or father ordered to see the child only under supervised conditions. But supervision was privatized and most of the time in most of the country had to be bought. Often men would claim inability to pay, but the legal order stood and had been hard won by women, so usually the abused wife paid. Even then the supervisor was neither under her contractual control nor ordered by the court to secure her safety or her equality interests.

Not every marriage break up is the end of an abusive, battering, or incestuous relationship of course. But of the ones that go before the state, most are troubled if not abusive. Otherwise, they would just resolve things themselves with less bother and expense for both of them. And the trouble is usually between two who are unlikely to be equally positioned, resourced, or of equal status in the world. In any case, shaping the policy law and procedure, applying our knowledge of the current unequal status of women, and the current level of violence in marriage is the most useful way to proceed.

Most women in family court do not choose to be there in the sense of asking for mediation in a struggle between two individuals. Many have called on the state because they are told by welfare departments and sometimes by legislation that they will not receive welfare unless they do. Staff of child protection agencies do blackmail abused women, often aboriginal women, with threats of apprehension of their children if they do not sever violent marriages formally. They are motivated often by the knowledge that men who abuse their wives often also abuse their children.[58]

The co-opting pressure on us introduced through protocols, coordination models, and funding standardization to screen or monitor the mothering of women who come to shelters, and the destructive pressure on our relationship with battered women by social workers bullying women into shelters for the sake of the children is short sighted and counter productive and an infringement on women's equality. The autonomy of these women is essential to the safety of their children and the voluntary relationship of trust between us and the women who call us is an essential ingredient of the children's safety and women's autonomy. For many reasons, usually less noble than the interests of the safety and freedom of the women and children, state officials demand that women formally settle child custody and access agreements. Police almost automatically press women to engage civil restraining orders and other family law processes. The poorest and racialized women, those most vulnerable to state apprehension of their children and those who have tried to involve police and criminal law are often those who enter the family courts.

Others who don't distinguish between civil and criminal law but understand themselves to be completely over powered and unfairly treated join them. They seek fairness and security and they think and are instructed that family court is the appropriate place to invoke the protection of the state for their children and themselves from inequality and sexist domination by their intimate enemy. They have no idea that, practically speaking, it could mean they are dependent on convincing some untrained person, who may well be empathetic or kind, but who is not Charter literate, never mind equality literate, to see the danger or unfairness in her situation.

This family court process shirks state responsibility to equality and to enforcing criminal law against violence even as it forces women to accept more and more state intrusion and imposition of inequality.

Sometimes what has been missing is the intervention that can be made in criminal court to assert the social interests of women as a group. The domestic violence courts in Ontario and the Yukon conceive of women's groups only as low cost service delivery systems for women's emergency housing and comfort. The court development incorporates the knowledge that the programs to counsel men (out of illegal abusive behaviour) that are tied to these courts as diversions from jail, require the ongoing assistance of the escaping wives. Men lie about the criminal violence they do even in these diversion programs promising them criminal evasion. The presence of the wives and ex-wives is essential to the therapeutic diversion plan. Both courts plan to spend inordinate amounts of time and money on these therapeutic approaches, which so far have very limited results, and which do not in any way address the equality issues of the women. And both courts reduce women's groups to advisory committees outside the formal processes and do not guarantee even their operating expenses never mind their core funding. We might expect then that for a while these courts will improve some women's safety, but in the long run will fail. The independence of the women's services, which came from their connection to the wider independent women's movement, will be compromised and weakened. Their embodiment as a kind of women's auxiliary to the courts will render them as victim service providers directly under the control of the courts. The chance of women's groups advocating for Charter rights from that position and maintaining enough independence to do so is not very good. If not us, then who?

This year, CASAC women and all other anti-violence workers have had to examine the proposed amendments to the Divorce Act, Bill C-22, for their implications for women raped and battered by their husbands, and women mothering children who have been incestuously attacked by their fathers. Coalitions formed all across Canada to look at the issues from an equality perspective and to prepare proposals for the Standing Committee on Justice this fall.

The resentment about this is high. We have been forced into this work by the government pandering to the agitation of the fathers' rights groups in response to the small victory of the changes Allan Rock, then Minister of Justice, introduced to the Child Support guidelines in 1997. Senator Anne Cools traded her vote in support of those changes for a promise of control over and financing for The Special Joint Committee on Child Custody and Access and its attendant fathers' rights dog and pony show.[59] Our resentment and criticism centres on the repeated refusal of the Canadian government, in all its parts, to consider seriously how to respond to this political situation.

And then there is the refusal of the government to redress women's equality up to and including violence against women, in the proposals of law change to the current Divorce Act. There can be no need for education of state personnel on this matter. The same needs and the same issues have been illuminated in reports of women's experience and in women's groups' presentations on criminal and family law since 1973. Any ignorance of equality interests here is wilful.

Allowing a few right wing men and one Senator to front this irresponsibility is pretty transparent. These are not forces that could not have been handled. At least one reading is that women and our safety and freedom are being sacrificed as unimportant chattel in the negotiations for the imagined right wing votes. This is a strategy that will be destructive to everyone. The Charter and gender mainstreaming were supposed to side-step such banal politicizing.

In May 1995, the Federal and Territorial Minister Responsible for the Status of Women agreed "on the importance of gender-based analysis undertaken as an integral part of the policy process of government"; later that year, Status of Women Canada published *Setting the Stage for the Next Century: The Federal Plan for Gender Equality*,[60] which says that "the federal government will where appropriate ensure that critical issues and policy options take gender into account." Elsewhere, we have reminded ourselves of the international expressions of the same promise to women.

No one could reasonably assert either that divorce law is an occasion where it is inappropriate to consider women's unequal status or that this proposed law has dealt with the risks to women. In this democracy we should be able to rely on implementations of the heart of the decisions of parliament in declaring the Charter, the Supreme Court adjudication of cases that interpreted it, and the legal precedents set in cases women have brought. Surely "mainstreaming gender" meant something to someone. That should have guaranteed at least due diligence and attention regarding equality and violence in the drafting of the amendments to the Divorce Act.

It is simply not credible to CASAC that competent state officials and politicians forgot, or are unaware of their equality obligations in the course of their work. But there it is! The unequal status of women in the family and the prevalence of violence in the family, which enforces that inequality, has been left intact. No one, no one group, no Justice Minister interfered with this sexist backlash when conducting the hearings of the Joint Committee in 1997, preparing the critique of the current legal practice and law, preparing the *For The Sake of The Children Report* in 1998,[61] preparing Justice Minister Anne McLellan's research and drafting in the next year, preparing the Federal/Provincial Territorial Family Law Committee report released in 2001, or the new report in November 2002 and in the work of the drafting staff that proposed the amendments announced in December of 2002. It must have been discussed yet still:

- This draft refuses to name gendered inequality;
- Acknowledges violence but not who does what to whom, including by stating the obvious: that men commit the violence in the family and they use the family structure to do it;
- Does not assure or attempt to assure women's equality at the time of divorce;
- Does not allow women to be assured that divorce ends the patriarchal relationship; in fact the amendments could keep her more married;
- Does not assure women of safety and security in divorce proceedings;
- Does not contribute to women's ability to plan for safety and security in the months after separation/divorce, which we know are potentially dangerous for women in tense or abusive relationships;
- Does not assure legal representation in legal processes that require representation to assure equality interests;
- Is not consistent with Charter obligations;
- Is not consistent with Canadian positions taken and promoted internationally;
- Is not consistent with election promises;
- Is not consistent with common sense versions of equality and safety.

Having parliamentary intent stated in a preamble just so that we can all now go about suing or intervening in court cases to accomplish that intent, is too silly for words. Twenty or thirty years ago we might have understood that differently. In this new era of government it is an example of the unlawful and unconscionable abdication of the state responsibility to protect women and children with the rule of law (in this case both criminal and civil law). At the same time, it imposes the state upon women in laws and legal processes that, by refusing to meet substantive equality standards, enforces the individual and collective rights of men over women.

The proposals in the draft to assert, exempt, screen, identify, or isolate violence against women cases and treat them differently are unworkable. Officials know it and therefore there is a cynical recognition of the violent reality. There is no workable plan to redress the violence or redistribute power. The government proposed draft leaves unchecked the power of violence to enforce inequality and the male held power of that inequality on which that violent behaviour is based.

It is still very unevenly wise for women to reveal to the state or the community the violence committed against them by husbands and fathers. They get blamed for the violence, labeled as attackable women, discredited in the story telling of their own lives, and belittled with facile advice about how they could or should have protected themselves. They may well be abandoned by the state to a more angry man. The justice system still grossly underconvicts violence against women reported to it. It is therefore unreasonable to base access to equality interests of women divorcing on whether a woman can prove or convince others about violence in her life. Women should not have to prove violence or even expose violence against them or their children in order to secure their right to safety and autonomy. The process and law should assure that universally.

Nor should they be invited to relinquish privacy and autonomy in a search for safety and security from sexual violence. We have not achieved any reasonable level of proving violence in any court yet. The draft, like all new family law initiatives, proposes to step even further back from equality law. It and all new law implements ADR approaches with no plan for how they will meet equality obligations to women, even as determined by the Charter law and rulings.[62]

"But don't worry," says the draft: First we accept inadequate universal entitlement to the rule of law, then we build in an exception designed to deal with violence. So now we easily and often could be put in the position of having to prove violence in order to apply for equality.

Two things are likely: One is the temptation on the part of non-feminists and humanists to widen and soften the definitions of violence in hopes more women can qualify for equality practices, whether or not they have suffered violence, and then there will be backlash against that tactic which uses that widening as a further excuse for the withdrawal of the state from assisting women against violence at all. The other is a gradual realization that because there is no money, no legal initiative, or incentive, women will still get pushed through the screen that was supposed to catch their stories of violence because no one believes them, and anyway, all women continue to get unequal application of the law at divorce. In those cases where women are believed to be victims by the screeners, they will lose control over decisions of how to proceed by virtue of being victims. That is, they will predictably and too often face unwanted state intervention. Some women stand to lose even more agency, privacy, and dignity, and sometimes, security.

There are many practices of law applied to the family in which we could demonstrate the same degrading and sometimes lethal mix of abandonment and over-powering of women and children. The withdrawal of aid to the oppressed and simultaneously the insistence on intrusion into and control over the lives of the oppressed are practices that move away from the responsibilities of welfare and redistributive justice (for individuals and groups of individuals) within the state. They also move away from any equality-seeking protection of individuals (including the most historically disadvantaged) from the unfair intrusions of the state.

This is obvious to CASAC in the flip-flop application and reversal of the "mandatory" arrest practices as well as in the abandonment of any useful contextualizing policy such as the Violence Against Women policy in B.C.[63] It is clear in the apprehension of adolescents from the streets under "secure care acts"[64] and the failure to protect young women in the care of child welfare authorities from the prostitute training that is now well documented.[65] It is clear in the continued disproportionate acts of apprehension of the children of aboriginal women and the consequent damage to both women and children while maintaining an economic program that assures those women, on and off reserve, destitution, and impossible parenting conditions. Offering identity and recognition in place of legal entitlements and redistribution.

Recognition of Our Identity as Victims in Trade for Our Right to Equality

It is the overall policy framework of the new Justice department that sets the tone for all this. When we protested the changes to the sentencing bill that brought us conditional sentencing we only hunched that we were facing a new leviathan. Protest as we did, we got nowhere. Nor did anyone else. Judges complained that there was no probation staff at the provincial level to exercise any control or offer any support to achieve compliance with the conditions ordered.[66] Anti-prison activists complained that the set up for failure on conditions meant men habitually breached the conditions and were then jailed for longer terms.[67] Women found themselves dealing with men ordered to house arrest after assaults. That is, ordered to the community-based jail keeping of the very women and children who had sought assistance from the state to deal with a dangerous bully.

We could see that the legal aid system was being very quickly shrunk to a useless size and shape. Women had never had much access anyway so although we were alarmed for the rights of the accused we did not see the full implications for women. Women violated were usually not accused but complainants wanting promised equality. Over these last five or seven years we noted the increase in criminalization of women, especially for self defence, poverty crimes, prostitution, and low level drug offences.[68]

We added that need for legal aid in the criminal law to the need that had never been filled for legal representation for women in the civil system.[69] Our hopes of funding for representation and intervention in Charter Challenge cases at the provincial level simply evaporated. Alternate Dispute Resolution had hardly begun to surface.

This new construction of the state was more apparent as women were encouraged to assume their victimization as an identity. Women were invited to trade recognition of that identity for their rights. Nothing has changed in that women are still largely unassisted by the state in their attempt to prove, document, censure, prevent, reduce, or ameliorate the crimes of violence committed against them. But as compensation, on the basis of an extra-legal status as victims, they were listened to and invited to participate in all manner of quasi-democratic, quasi-judicial, or administrative law practices affecting their lives:

- Parole hearings of men who attacked them in which they are asked their opinions on community safety and other sentencing principles as though they could take responsibility; often women were left with the impression of affecting sentence;

- Victim impact statements at sentencing hearings; women were invited to describe and convince judges of the seriousness of the crime in terms of the destruction of their physical and mental well being;

- Family group conferencing under the RCMP where their children might escape harsher threats if they and/or the mothers would be judged and sentenced without counsel;

- Mediation by nonlegal professionals with their abusers in family court;

- Requests that they participate co-operatively in discussions to inform and advise those doing court mandated counseling of abusive men evading criminal sanctions;

- Mandatory counseling for them and/or the men who abused them;

- Circle sentencing, sometimes of the criminally convicted and sometimes replacing criminal conviction;

- Victim offender reconciliation in and out of jail, including criminally raped victims;

- Restorative justice initiatives of many kinds usually falsely claiming to be based on aboriginal concepts;

- Privatized compulsory health programs like methadone administration as criminal sanctions in the name of "harm reduction" to the community;

- Privatized health programs that removed criminal sanctions, as in the diversion of violent men from conviction to anger management counseling, regardless of the low success rates of those programs;

- The "John schools" to divert, even from arrest, the men buying street women;
- Snitch lines paying for citizens to spy on each other;
- Programs which invite women to self-identify and be legally licensed and registered as prostitutes for brothels and massage parlours;
- Offering services only to licensed prostitutes which all poor women need;
- Diversion to privatized services delivered by religious leaders including Christian, Jewish and Moslem patriarchs.

At stake is every version of human rights and women's rights outlined in the Charter and the Charter cases, as well as the international human rights concepts of equality.

Women cannot always evade these legal processes and procedures. Often they feel that they are coerced into them by their security needs for the good will of the state officials observing or involved. Sometimes women are entering the processes in a purposeful but ill-advised search for equality. They don't realize which of these services are extensions of the state, which are privatized. We must at least suspect that a state evasion of equality obligations is part of why they are privatized. Which of these have no obligation to public interest or in meeting humane standards of privacy, security of the person, dignity?

We know that in some situations one could appeal or sue and women are preparing such cases but to do that requires legal information, safety from one's attacker, and legal aid of a whole new sort. Not to mention years of litigation work that could be avoided.

We first heard of the "victim-centred" approach to rape as a justice policy from Thea Herman in 1997. It was, she explained, "time for a victim-centred approach" in which we would improve on the old version of law, when rape was a crime against the state, by now seeing that it was in fact a crime against the victim (only). This is the shame of ADR applied to rape.

Women have not been struggling for thirty years to be told again that we are on our own with our rapists! The point of criminalization was to bring the power of the community, through the state, mediated by the Charter, to bear on the bullying: to put power on the side of the historically disadvantaged, the oppressed.

Of course that should include sensitivity and information sharing and other simple courtesies to complainants, but it does not mean that we want sexist violence to be privatized. If women could subdue these men on their/our own they would have already done so.

While the Minister Allan Rock was assuring us in the Members Lounge of the House of Parliament that he would approach provincial attorney generals to insure that conditional sentences would not be applied to violence against women, the Alternate Dispute Resolution policy was in fact over-riding everything. So much for a gender reviewed analysis and a commitment to equality. So much for the argument that there is no way to apply national standards. The state again proves its ability to shrink and expand at the same moment.

Restructuring Civil Society and the Community: Social Engineering

Some current practices have roots belonging to the previous government and can be best explained by looking back. Mulroney convened a conference too: the Family Violence Conference held in the government conference centre across the street from the House of Commons.[70] If we remember correctly, it was the occasion of the announcement of the fund from which this project got the last dregs and the first enactment of "gender mainstreaming."

We experienced it as the first occasion in which anti-violence workers and feminists in total were rendered a small caucus among a thousand "stakeholders" on violence against women. All were invited to celebrate Mulroney's Conservative approach to women's equality and new methods of consultation with civil society.

We were in the post-Montreal Massacre era. The year previously the public had amply displayed its understanding and displeasure with violence against women and with government responses to it. There was a surge in anti-violence organizing, including gun control, pro-woman organizing (including calls for a second Royal Commission), and demands for many layers of effective government action. In hindsight, we see how important it was for the new government to control the public discussion.

A never to be forgotten hour of that conference was spent listening to the YWCA national executive director usher in the new era. The YWCA had just been granted a million dollars to prepare a public education campaign on violence against women as though public ignorance was the problem. Looking back, we see that the problem was quite the opposite. After twenty years of successful frontline public education, women and many men were speaking the same message. Women deserve equality and violence prevents it. The state must act.

The YWCA spokeswoman was invited to address the conference not on violence but on the wonders of partnership with business as a key component of mainstreaming. Women's groups, in front of the assembled authorities from government, business, and the professions, were told we did not "own" the problem. While we might find this concept challenging, we were told to buck up and share the "power." The "community," meaning business and men had to participate (and take control) for progress to be made. "Violence is not a woman's problem but everyone's problem." And "everyone" had to be involved. Funding, we were told, could be politicizing for everyone. By partnering with business, they claimed we would all advance.

Since its inception, CASAC had been public in its opinion that, indeed, funding was a political issue.[71] We advised our members against being so dependent on government funds that they could not do the appropriate challenging and correcting of government at all levels for which we had been formed. We advised each other to cultivate community support for our explicit viewpoints and for the importance of expressing them.

We also advised and encouraged our membership to avoid corporate entanglements that promoted businesses, especially large ones, or that could compromise the independence of these small political/service/community/women's groups. But CASAC was not aware, until that speech, and perhaps neither was the YWCA, that the Conservative government was paying them to Judas goat us all on a new trail to the future of government funding and consultation policy.

The YWCA executive director explained that the Y had developed a business partnership. That partnership was "mutually beneficial beyond the dreams" of the YWCA boss. She and her executive had been invited "into the boardroom" of their partners to have their say in affecting "business culture" and they had "invited their business partners" to their boardroom. They had been lent corporate staff and expertise and resources. A marriage made in heaven. It was all working very well apparently.

Then she introduced the CEO of AVON Canada, her business partner in the enterprise of women's equality and coping with violence against women. From the back of the room, through the stunned silence of our caucus and past the cheery applause of the invited stakeholders, the CASAC delegate shouted, "how about you just pay the Avon lady."[72] In the intervening years, Avon has left Canada and the YWCA has been offered federal money over three years to restructure the anti-violence coalitions by gathering, "uniting and harmonizing" those groups who operate on an anti-feminist model of family violence with those who operate on an equality model.

In 2003, we face a more devious and sophisticated version of this reorganization of Canadian society through Social Entrepreneur initiatives. Universities, professional marketers, and professional social organizers vie for the proffered government contracts and corporate dollars to set up meetings of and manage systems of networking Social Entrepreneurs. Some of these new funding and control mechanisms link the power of the federal state with corporate control to contain, manage, and steer the non government groups, and the self-organizing of the oppressed. For several months, representatives of the federal, provincial, and municipal governments convened meetings under the Vancouver Agreement to get private industry to pay for a van for prostitute services in Vancouver. The money was to come from the private sector. The service was to be staffed and organized by two non-government groups. But they had not been searching to fund such a program; they had other priorities. The government supplied nothing yet controlled the exchange and the outcome.

This is not a shrinking of government but a shirking of government social responsibility to democracy and civil society. Business does not support all comers. Even United Way funding over the years has not been without strings and controls antithetical to women's equality (or anti-racist organizing or even to unions). Major battles had to be fought and won, for instance, to keep the United Way from imposing anti-abortion conditions on anti-violence groups.

Few in government seem to be concerned by or working against the loss of government support to women's groups (or other equality-seeking groups) or the effect of that on community development or on future government policy. Groups need money. The current policy of funding only through the Voluntary Sector Initiative compels groups to serve pre-stated government department policy intentions.

So, community groups or non-government groups are formed and sustained and directed in the name of community organizing, which have no base in the community and no political legitimacy to the claim as groups of the self-organizing oppressed. Existing women's groups twist themselves inside out to meet the criteria of serving government agenda's, not their own. Not only does this mean that groups who remain true to their own agenda lose funding, but it also means that groups disappear for lack of funding and the community is reorganized in the service of current government policy initiatives.[73]

Nor is this government intervention in the community restricted to funding the basic operations and organizing of lobby and advocacy groups. Current research funding can be skewed and close off intelligent consideration of issues. The funding for most violence against women matters is through the federal government and requires not only that the research complement government's agenda but also that the mandatory community partners be those that are approved by government.

In another reshaping phenomena, the federal government altogether reversed its policy of funding the independent women's movement. During the Trudeau years, a policy held that the government should be self-correcting by moving toward formal equality.[74] The leadership of the Cabinet, including Trudeau, accepted that women were on the rise, did not have equal citizenship, and should.[75]

Funding was established and programs developed through the Status of Women Canada. One expression of the policy within that department was to "spread seed money around and see what equality-seeking leadership emerged within that movement of the community and then follow it."[76] Through that policy, among others like the CYC (Company of Young Canadians), and LIP (Local Initiatives Grants), community organizing flourished.[77] That provided the start up funds for the first wave of women centres, transition houses, and anti-rape centres.[78] They then qualified for federal funds on the understanding that they helped to rectify the unequal status of women. The federal government policy was to assist in the development of women's access to equal citizenship.

Women's groups always had to battle intrusion and meddling and manipulation by Status of Women but on the whole those funding policies were at least honourable, if still inadequate. They have utterly disappeared.

Women centre funding was foisted off on the provinces. They had to re-invent themselves as social service delivery vehicles to meet provincial funding criteria. They had once been local organizing bases from which women designed and executed all manner of equality-seeking campaigns. By this funding shift, they were forced to rebuild as deliverers of low cost social services to individual women. They built soup kitchens, anti-violence counseling programs; job training programs, assertiveness training work-shops, and all manner of such things. They gradually were pushed away from equal-ity-rights promotion for the collective good of women. Now each province, in turn, has increased the standardization of service delivery to shape them into traditional, if cheap, social services, or has cut off their funding entirely.[79] This process has had devastating re-sults in terms of the interference in women's self-organizing in our own communities.

This policy shift has silenced our own version of integrated equality, and it has damaged women's capacity for participation in each nation-wide debate of social, politi-cal, and economic policy. A very similar process has been applied to anti-violence groups and indeed has reshaped the national women's movement. There is no doubt that this restructuring of women's self-organized formations has reinforced the capacity of the right wing to repress progressive political organizing. It may be a result of the swing to the right, but it is also a guarantee of the force of the right to control legislated unfairness. This too is a Charter issue.

Once we could come together as a movement with the breadth of the consulting group that met to inform the rape shield law and the depth of CASAC, which works with and learns from individual women on the frontline, but also sustains a national and in-ternational network of thinkers and actors committed to civil society, to work toward the equality desires of women, and an end to sexist violence. Such configurations as this movement advance democracy as well as women's equality. Such groups as this equality movement are essential to equality policy development.

For now, some groups like CASAC are finding ways to fund their activity and put for-ward their positions, but it is unlikely this can be sustained. We will be left with the Vir-ginia Slim version of the equality network, or the Body Shop version, or the Ford Foundation version, or the Tampax version, or the Avon version, or the Marriott Hotel ver-sion.[80] Government funding used to be at least a little under the control of the electorate.

The uprising of the community during the last thirty years did push the government to the point of Red Book promises to support rape crisis services and transition houses and to create special funds to address sexist violence.[81]

But if we are expected to fund equality-seeking groups with corporate donations, how are citizens supposed to control international corporate agents in their manipulation of Canadian equality debates? What regulation can we fight for that can make it past WTO and World Bank scrutiny to control the behaviour of those corporate agents and their charitable foundations within our borders? Who will stand up to the corporate pres-sure to change immigration, labour, marriage, criminal law, citizenship, and governance if the equality-seeking groups continue to be delivered to them as dependent "partners?"

We have only begun to see the effects of this entrepreneurial approach to social and community development and to human rights. The American example is far from encouraging. While huge amounts of charitable dollars become available and great experimentation is possible, there is no standardized support for the advance of equality.

The constant undermining of collective and community initiatives shows up at the local level in racism, poor-bashing, and public, as well as, private violence against women and children, all of which are on the rise. People are in need of the leadership that their community figures should display in government policy.

It is still possible in Canada to resist corporate control of governance, dialogue, and consultations even in the exercise of liberal democratic state obligations. But it is highly unlikely without positive government relations with equality seeking women's groups.

Notes

1. Letter dated May 28, 2003, from the Office of the Secretary of State (Multiculturalism) (Status of Women) is available at CASAC office.

2. Federal-Provincial-Territorial Ministers Responsible for the Status of Women (2002).

3. Johnson, H. (1993). *Violence Against Women Survey*. Ottawa: Statistics Canada. See also (2002), p. 53.

4. At least some parts of governments did. Jean Augustine signed this letter on behalf of those federal-provincial ministers responsible for the Status of Women. In fact, such ministries if they existed as stand alone ministries, and perhaps none still did, all had been greatly reduced in power and influence, which indicated at least a contrary point of view from other powerful parts of government.

5. Federal-Provincial-Territorial Ministers Responsible for the Status of Women (2002), p. 49.

6. We are saying that there is nothing different or intrinsic in the women and children who end up poor or violated. And the men who violate them are not biologically compelled; they make choices to do so.

7. Professor Dorothy Smith's work has helped us to keeping seeing this. Her early analysis of the United Way struggle in Vancouver from the 1970s to 1990s was followed by conversations about class and the women's movement over the years.

8. See Julia Sudbury in the proceedings of Women's Resistance: From Victimization to Criminalization. Opening Plenary. Locating this Conference in the Wider World–2001. And, for an example of a corporation profiting from mediation, see online: <http://www.mediate.ca>.

9. Brodsky, G., and Day, S.

10. The "State Public Policy and Social Change" discussion is best introduced in Dobash, E., and Dobash, R. (1992).

11. See online: <http://www.casac.ca/about/constitution.htm>.

12. Available at CASAC.

13. For panel results, see Health Canada online: <http://www.hc-sc.gc.ca>. For CASAC positions, see Lakeman, L. (1993).

14. See CASAC newsletters (1978-1982) available at Vancouver Rape Relief library.

15. For Alternate CEDAW report, see Appendix: Canada's Failure to Act: Women's Equality Deepens.

16. Such as the member groups of FAFIA and the B.C. CEDAW group.

17. The women who founded and work in our centres are largely from working class backgrounds. Most centres would have one or less women with university degree, for instance. Our structures are still largely cooperative, if not collective: Montreal, Toronto, and Vancouver are all collectives. There has always been about a third of the labour pool identifying as lesbian, and there have been women of colour in leadership within major centres for fifteen years at least. Our delegate to the UN Conference on Women, in Nairobi in 1985, for instance was chosen on an affirmative action strategy.

18. With Canadian equality-seeking women's groups like: BCFW (now closed), NAC, see online: <www.nac-cca.ca>, FAFIA, see online: <http://www.fafia-afai.org/>, FFQ, see CATW online: <www.catwinternational.org>, and Marche Mondiale des Femmes, see online: <www.ffq.qc.ca/marche2000/en/index.html>, but also with anti-racist formations, labour formations, and welfare rights organizing.

19. We have learned a lot from Penni Richmond, Madelaine Parent, Sharon Yandel, and Linda Shuto, and suggest their work as a source of that history and the importance to women.

20. Cameron, B. (1997, December). *Rethinking The Social Union: National Identities and Social Citizenship.* Ottawa: The Canadian Centre for Policy Alternatives.

21. Cameron, D. (1999, September 02). The Social Union Pact is Not a Backward Step for Quebec. *The Globe and Mail.*

22. Duncan, C. (2003, October). Raging Women: Fighting the Cutbacks in B.C. Paper presented at the Raging Women's Conference by Vancouver Women's Health Collective. Vancouver, Canada.

23. Brodsky, G., and Day, S. (1998).

24. *Ibid.*

25. Brodsky, G., and Day, S.

26. Lakeman, L. (1993).

27. Between 1975-1995 it was rare for women to have trouble getting welfare after living in a transition house.

28. In both B.C. and Ontario lifetime bans have been imposed. Temporary refusals have been instituted. Time limits, for instance, of only being eligible for two years out of five have been imposed. Health criteria have been imposed. Rate reductions have been imposed.

29. All welfare rates as well as minimum wage rates in the country are below the poverty line.

30. Federal-Provincial-Territorial Ministers Responsible for The Status of Women. (2002).

31. Sidel, R. (1996). *Keeping Women and Children Last: America's War on the Poor.* New York: Penguin.

32. Welfare workers and social workers are sometimes reported to us as abusers of their clients. They have much more power to do so if the women know they have no enforceable right to welfare: they are dependent on the discretion in his hands.

33. Asian Women Stand Together to Speak Out Against Violence, <http://www.rapereliefshelter.bc.ca/issues/asian_women_sJay.html>.

34. Personal communication, October 2001.

35. In our work we have become aware of the ownership and prostitution dealings of, at least the Hell's Angels in every province except the Maritimes, Big Circle Boys gang, the Lotus gang, Fukienese, the Russians, the Mafia related gangs, and the Vietnamese gangs.

36. Most of the Canadian women's movement has agreed that prostitutes and low level drug dealers should not be jailed or even criminalized. We have also agreed that those women trafficked as indentured labour or sex slaves should not be criminalized or deported. Our debates are about how to deal with the men and how to interfere with the trade.

37. Gunilla Eckberg, personal communication, September 2003. She is special advisor to the government of Sweden on prostitution.

38. See online <http://www.naring.regeringin.se/fragor/jamstadlldhet/aktuellt/trafficking.htm>.

39. See online: <http://www.rapereliefshelter.bc.ca/herstory/rr_files86.html>.

40. For those who wonder the extra A is because the cookie company DARE threatened us with law suits if we used their trademarked name.

41. A group focusing on feminist intervention against the exploitation of young women.

42. Kingsley, C., personal communication, October 2001. Cherry Kingsley works in the International Centre to Combat Exploitation of Children.

43. Decriminalization used to mean preventing charges against the women. Now it short hands the legitimating of the trade. We continue to stand with the women and against the trade.

44. Professor Dara Culhane, personal communication, October 2001. Some of our version of the situation in the street prostitution in Canada is being documented and analyzed by Professor Dara Culhane's projects in the Downtown Eastside of Vancouver.

45. Daley, S. (2001, August 12). New Rights for Dutch Prostitutes, but No Gain *New York Times*, pp. A1, 4.

46. Sullivan, M., and Jeffreys, S. (2001). *Legalising Prostitution is Not the Answer: The Example of Victoria, Australia*. Coalition Against Trafficking in Women, Australia and USA. Retrieved online October 2002 from CATW Web Site: <http://www.catwinternational.org>.

47. Lakeman, L. (1985 February 27). Who killed Linda Tatrai? A speech delivered in Vancouver available online: <www.rapereliefshelter.bc.ca/herstory/rr_files85_linda.html#02>, and at the meeting, October 2002, between women's groups and COPE candidates for Vancouver city election.

48. Dara Culhane, personal communication, January 2003, in conversation about the research she was conducting in the Downtown Eastside of Vancouver.

49. Lowman, J. (Ed.) (1998). Prostitution Law Reform in Canada. In *Toward Comparative Law in the 21st Century*. Institute of Comparative Law in Japan, Tokyo: Chuo University Press, pp. 919-946.

50. Amsterdam's Street Prostitution Zone to Close. (2003, October 21). *Expatica News*.

51. CASAC women note that the most destitute and violated are always invoked as a reason we should accept legalization: to save their lives and then the most uncommon and privileged are invoked as the proof of agency. We say we should look at the common and real.

52. We imagine them charged with nuisance charges or other offences. So far the regulating processes of Harm Reduction are not made to answer even indirectly to Charter rights. How for instance would we keep the records of past sexual history out of the case of sexual assault against a registered prostitute when the state already would own those health records and the legal practice would make those records vulnerable to disclosure obligation claims.

53. "Municipalities urge Martin to give Cities a Fair Share of Funds: Heads of Municipal Organization Tours Downtown Eastside and Calls It's Problems A Canadian Issue, Not a Vancouver Issue." (2003, September 24). *The Vancouver Sun*, p. B5.

54. Lakeman, L. (2000).

55. By not arresting and or laying criminal charges.

56. For the lack of respect for women in the profession see: Wilson, B. (1993) *Touchstones for Change: Equality Diversity and Accountability*. Ottawa: Canadian Bar Association.

57. May/Iles and Hadley Jury recommendations from the coroner's inquests, See Appendix.

58. Edelson, J. (2003). Should Childhood Exposure to Adult Domestic Violence be Defined as Child Maltreatment Under The Law? An essay, from (in part) Jaffe, P.G., Baker, L.L., and Cunningham, A. (Eds). *Ending Domestic Violence in the Lives of Children and Parents: Promising Practices for Safety, Healing and Prevention*. New York, NY: Guilford Press (in press).

59. The Joint committee of Senate and Commons held hearings across the country in 1998 that were noted for their inflamed hostility to women, especially to mothers, and most especially to women's advocates. Women's groups across the country complained of the indignity of these government proceedings.

60. Status of Women in Canada. (1995). *Setting the Stage for the Next Century: The Federal Plan for Gender Equality*. Ottawa: Author, cat. SW21-15/1995.

61. Special Joint Committee on Child Custody and Access. (1998). *For the Sake of the Children*: Report of the Special Joint Committee on Child Custody and Access. Ottawa: Author.

62. Alternate Dispute Resolution has been the over arching policy of the Department of Justice at least since George Thompson was deputy minister in Allan Rock's administration.

63. Gulyas, M. (2002, December 31). Proposed Abuse Policy Changes Worry Chiefs: Amendment Would No Longer Make Charge Automatic. *Delta Optimist*, p.11.

64. Justice for Girls. (2001). Statement of Opposition To The Secure Care Act, see online: <www.justiceforgirls.org/publicactions/pos_securecareact.html>.

65. Cherry Kingsley, personal communication, October 2001, in discussion of children in care.

66. Once, while attending court in Vancouver, I heard Judge Kitchener address a young man convicted of a drug offence, apologize to the young man that he, judge Kitchener, had been tricked by the two levels of government into supporting conditional sentences because he had been led to believe there would be supporting and monitoring services and without them, he implied, the young man was set up to fail.

67. Pate, K., personal communication, October 1996.

68. *Ibid.* (October 1-3, 2001). Opening Plenary Locating This Conference in the Wider World 2001. Women's Resistance: From Victimization to Criminalization. Canadian Association of Elizabeth Fry Societies and Canadian Association of Sexual Assault Centres.

69. Addario, L. (1998). *Getting A Foot In The Door: Women, Civil Legal Aid and Access to Justice*. Ottawa: Status of Women Canada.

70. The same space in which we later held the Women's Resistance conference in 2001.

71. CASAC newsletters are available at Vancouver Rape Relief Library.

72. Avon women were generally housewives who sold cosmetics door to door on a strictly commission basis and had few to no employee rights and protections since they were essentially private contractors.

73. The end of NAC was announced by Miriam Abou-Dib of the executive at the meeting of the Canadian Women's March Committee, September 19, 2003, in Ottawa.

74. Personal communication with Carol Assiz, at the end of June 1999, after she retired from field work of Status of Women Canada. I also spoke with Maude Barlow at the anniversary of the Royal Commission on the Status of Women, held at Kingston University, as to her role in the PMO circa 1973, personal communication, 2000.

75. Maude Barlow was hired in the PMO with a mandate to design what the Liberal government could use in the next election as a platform that would win the women's vote. Barlow, M., personal communication, 2000, Kingston.

76. Assiz, C., personal communication, 1999.

77. Kostash, M. (1980). *Long Way Home: The Stories of The Sixties Generation in Canada*. Toronto: J.Lorimer and Co.

78. Lakeman, L. (1999, June 22). Address on the Occasion of the Anniversary of the founding of Woodstock Women's Emergency Centre, Woodstock, Ontario.

79. The B.C. government cut 100 percent of every women centre's provincial funding on April 1, 2004.

80. Virginia Slim was a cigarette producer that used to advertise with a slogan: "You have come a long way baby." The Body Shop marketed environmentally friendly makeup and bath products; the Ford foundation has funded both imperialistic and pro democracy projects around the world; Tampax produces feminine hygiene products and at one point was accused of damaging women's health in search of profit; Avon was explained earlier; and Marriott Hotels profit from prison labour and are deeply implicated in the privatization of prisons.

81. Red Book was a listing of Liberal election promises, which included funding to women's anti-violence services, and funds to the Crime Prevention Fund, and the discussed Family Violence Initiative Fund.

The Charter of Rights and Freedoms

E*quality and The Charter* records the ten years of shared work between CASAC and the Women's Legal Education and Action Fund (LEAF) in arguments applying the Charter before the Supreme Court. In its forward, Bertha Wilson says,

> Most judges have a thorough knowledge of the law and an extensive familiarity with the adjudicative process: it is in the achievement of the proper balance between citizen and state that we falter. Legislators may find the balance through their political ideologies: citizens may perceive it in their own self interest; but how do judges find it in their mandated stance of impartiality and neutrality (ix)?[1]

Too many Canadian legislators have learned to use the courts (cynically) to avoid revealing their ideologies. In so doing, they undermine democracy. If people don't know government and political positions clearly, their votes are of little value. The current situation regarding the same sex marriage debate is the latest case in point. This approach to governing hides the necessary value decisions in a democracy. It also upholds a pretence that human rights either do, or do not exist in some contractual or "scientific" way that courts can adjudicate. Responsibility to govern openly is evaded. The responsibility to develop rights is abandonned. We argue that it is a discredit to democracy to leave matters to the process of court cases that could and should be legislated in the interest of minority or equality rights. Moreover, with respect to sexist violence and equality issues, we are concerned with rights of a majority and rights to which the community has repeatedly given agreement.

Of course, the courts, too, are full of invisible ideology. The male supremacy, racism, and class bias is obvious to our callers and us. While we are not quick to dismiss liberal law or the possible protections available thereunder, we do look forward to the promised neutrality! We do agree with Bertha Wilson that part of the appropriate role for equality-seeking anti-violence groups is to bring that bigger picture to the courts and legal processes. Who else will?

CASAC women heard Bertha Wilson speak at her retirement address at a LEAF conference in Vancouver. She was guiding us as to what might be possible under the court considerations of security of the person. It was an inspiring and moving experience to hear a Supreme Court judge address the question of Women's Liberation, especially the role the courts could play in liberating women from sexist violence. It was exciting to hear that speech in the company of feminist legal scholars and practitioners, including aboriginal leaders Sharon McIvor, and Theresa Nahanee, Anne Derrick (defender of the wrongfully convicted Donald Marshall), and intellectual feminist pioneers like Sheila McIntyre. It was the sort of occasion that raises expectations and engenders hope. It raised our expectations of law and of the implementation of the equality promised in the Charter.

When we undertook this work, we still had that speech in mind. We wanted to explore and examine for ourselves the nature of our call to the state on our own behalf and on behalf of the women who call CASAC. It is our understanding as CASAC that while we may not have been fully schooled, in a formal legal sense, in women's Charter rights, we are fully aware of the community understanding of those rights. We, as well as the Canadian community, express indignation at the unfairness of women's situation. CASAC members organize based on an explicit expectation that women in Canada should be treated better by their government and by the law. In an ordinary sense of the words, we express a belief that women's claims to government assistance against the inequality imposed by violence are righteous claims.

We wanted to replicate, for a new group of CASAC members, some of the enriching experiences that CASAC Regional Representatives had in participating in the Charter discussions that had occurred in the earlier national coalition and consultation work, particularly in the O'Connor case and in the development and protection of the Rape Law.

In the early eighties, CASAC and our member centres were barely involved in the lobby to enshrine the Charter and women's equality within it.[2] There was a battle to enshrine women's rights. It was largely middle class women, many with professional credentials as journalists, lawyers, and academics who waged that battle.[3] They were privileged to have the political information and connections to understand the situation and the opportunity created by Trudeau's attachment to the development of a Charter of Rights and Freedoms. They put that privilege to work for the rest of us.

There was a danger of women's rights being omitted in this process. Their personal contacts, positions, and professional judgments convinced these women of the importance of the new Charter of Rights and Freedoms and the importance of fighting to enshrine women's equality within it. They were matched, of course, by Doris Anderson, and others who researched the issue from other positions, both within and outside the government, including the Canadian Advisory Council on the Status of Women (CACSW), and the National Action Committee on the Status of Women (NAC).[4]

Of course, these women had more to gain from a formal equality approach: equality with the men of their class and race. Equal access to the privileges of their husbands, brothers, and classmates was essential to their advancement in their own professions and personal lives. Yet their commitment was to far more than their own gain, even from the beginning, and for some, this has grown to include all women and to mean substantive equality. They knew that the construction of LEAF as an organization was also necessary so that they could act strategically to shape the meaning given to rights legally encoded in the Charter.

CASAC women of the time saw very little connection between this and our lives or work. We did not struggle to be included. There was no formal record of discussion, within CASAC, of any debate or position. Apparently, however, there were discussions among LEAF's founding leadership of the importance of the violence cases and issues.

LEAF made early efforts to solicit the data, connections, and intelligence of many parts of the anti-violence movement, including the frontline workers. There were consultations in which CASAC members participated across the country to prepare for early cases, for instance, Seaboyer and Gayme.[5] To be fair to us, the style of consultation was weak in its understanding of how to engage the frontline. In those days, we CASAC women were likely to defer to feminist lawyers and legal authority as though law was a foreign science. And feminist lawyers were likely to think of us as a source of raw data but not of political/legal theory or strategy born of a different point of view.

Even the work of supporting Jane Doe that connected LEAF and CASAC was not understood by us to be creating law from the ground up or as using and developing the Charter. Only in hindsight is that so clear. To add to that, most CASAC workers were properly sceptical of the possibility of achieving anything through law because of our frontline experience and understanding of the state. We were ignorant of what reform strategies and tactics might be possible and necessary in these forums, and we had very little opportunity to discuss what legal actions were consistent with our knowledge and goals.

But men like Seaboyer and Gayme attacked rape law and the women's movement achievements using the Charter! CASAC was dragged into court and constitutional debate to defend what little we had.[6]

We closed ranks with our feminist allies across class and race lines and began, occasionally, to assess and sometimes use Charter language and processes as we fought to hang on to the criminalization of violence against women and the rest of the legal imperative to resist the enforcement of women's inequality.

Our expectations for a living Charter have grown since then. Now we think it necessary, lawful, and righteous, albeit difficult, to call on the federal government as well as the courts to provide real and meaningful assistance in the achievement of women's substantial equality.

From our explorations, we understand that legally the Charter must be read together with CEDAW and the other international agreements and conventions signed by Canada. We understand the Charter to promise women dignity and the equality that springs from a fundamental belief in the dignity of every person. We understand that our rights spring not from government but from our humanity. We understand women to be promised protection in Canadian as well as international law. We understand that the membership of all women in a historically disadvantaged group—women—has been established in law. And that that law has been enshrined in the constitution to protect it from shallow political considerations. We know that our recognized disadvantage entitles us to call on special redistributive action of the government to protect our interests in achieving the social, political, and economic equality that dignity requires. We understand that the law has understood that for any woman to experience fair treatment, government actions are required to move Canadian society toward human equality, especially in relation to all rights, including social, economic, civil, and political rights. We understand that no level of government, and no third party within Canada or affecting Canada, is exempt from that Canadian promise to all women.

We understand that these rights exist before law and before the Charter and it is not only these rights, but also the appropriate actions of others toward these rights, that are in debate. Those legal rights are the political achievement of people worldwide.

We wanted to use this research to advance the ongoing work of CASAC members: by selecting, supporting, and responding to Charter issues and cases; and, by building intelligent alliances based on those legal and political cases where our callers require it.

Current government policy makes Charter interventions on the part of CASAC, even within coalitions of groups, extremely difficult. Canadian rape crisis centres have never had the funding to employ lawyers. As far as we know, not one lawyer has been hired by a CASAC centre. Since the law is not fully or fairly applied, our work frequently requires challenging, if not defying, the law. CASAC is, therefore, not usually considered to be much of a placement opportunity for law students.[7]

CASAC women don't plan to study law in order to do our jobs as anti-violence workers and organizers. We manage by working with and learning from many of the women who have spearheaded the violence against women legal strategies. We have learned much from NAWL and LEAF.

Since CASAC has begun to initiate our own legal strategies, we have received the counsel of many of Canada's most outstanding feminist legal scholars, including Christine Boyle, Shelagh Day, Gwen Brodsky, Mary Eberts, Marilyn McCrimmon, Teresa Nahanee, Sheila McIntyre, Sharon McIvor, Mary Eaton, Joanne St. Lewis, Elizabeth Sheehy, Mary Lou McPhedran, Andrée Côté, Diane Olescieu, Kim Pate, Anne Derrick, and Elizabeth Pickett to name a few.

We began to identify and meet with these women through our coalition work with LEAF as well as in the parliamentary hearings that resulted in the *The War Against Women* report, the Kim Campbell conference, the meetings to confront the Canadian Panel on Violence Against Women, the C-49 hearings, and so on. It was our assessment then, as now, that we were fortunate to have a critical mass of feminist lawyers available and committed to Charter work in the years between 1980 and the turn of the century.

We gathered as many of these women as we could for the CASAC conference, *Critical Resistance: From Victimization to Criminalization*, in hopes of reviving some of the best energy of that feminist legal force. Most of these women have served in consultative roles with CASAC in the last five years and continue to be a source of strength (especially in the form of legal opinion) to our frontline women.

There are many others who work with us in specific regions or on specific cases or legal issues. For at least a decade, this cross-class alliance has been good for us all. But the pressure of the neo-liberal agenda, and specifically the changes to eliminate national funding to equality initiatives, is threatening this alliance.

It has become more and more difficult to keep lawyers under the direction of, or in, cooperative coalitions with frontline women's organizations. The class and race divide is being imposed on us all. The end of the federal funding of NAC is key to that loss. CASAC never received federal funding for its operations. Now no national women's organization receives sustaining core funding other than the Feminist Alliance for International Action (FAFIA) for work to see to it that international agreements are met domestically, and the Canadian Association of Elizabeth Fry Societies (CAEFS) for work with women in prison and the National Association of Women and the Law (NAWL). While these organizations merit support and contribute enormously to the movement, they cannot constitute the movement.

Even at the best of times, we quickly learned that we were disabled by a lack of funds in our attempt to use the Charter "in our own interests."[8] The women who complain to us about Charter violations often don't have money for their survival needs much less to hire legal help.

Our first concern, is why is this litigation necessary? Since the rights clearly exist in law, why must we chase them in the courts? Secondly, when an obvious breach of women's dignity occurs, and a woman challenges that breach in the courts, why is it that each woman is put in the position of having to fight the entire government to secure what the Charter and violence legislation already has promised her? Too often, the government spends a fortune defending a mistake of policy or practice. Why does the government itself not assume responsibility for that fight for equality? Bonnie Mooney and Jane Doe's cases are two clear examples.[9]

Why is there no ongoing internal process of self-correction within the justice system to uphold the standard set in the Charter and in the most recent cases? Even without a formal process, why is it that so many justice system players seem to be compliant, if not complicit, in accepting the ongoing enforcement of inequality?

Most women's cases of criminal violence, complete with the documentation of the infringements of their rights, disappear at the level of policing and the lower courts. No one at that level of the state mentions her equality rights.[10] In the rare exception, when someone has noted unfairness in the system, there is no correction offered. Too often, the criminal justice representative will blame some other branch of the justice system. In our experience, there is often no correction even when advocates bring to the attention of authorities that an injustice has occurred.[11]

The system is not incapable of these reforming corrections, but it does require the active equality-seeking engagement of more than a few state functionaries. It requires that they believe in the Charter rights of women and act upon them or that their superiors at least not punish them for doing so. It also apparently requires the monitoring and political pressure created by an independent women's movement.

There is little or no access to funding for a legal case to assert a woman's rights. The lack of legal aid for civil cases, the lack of provincial test case litigation funds, Charter challenge funds federally and provincially, the government's move to mediation (ADR) effectively unsupervised by legal professionals accountable to the Charter, all compound the problem. We must at least promote the recording of lower court decisions so that processes of observing the application of the Charter can be noted. We can and do predict more situations where women's rights are trampled.

At this time, there is no way, at the bottom levels of the court hierarchy, for a complainant to meet with other women affected or to seek the advice of feminist legal scholars. Currently, women rely on hope that the rape crisis centre, transition house, anti-poverty group, or anti-racist formation, including the local LEAF office, can sustain not only their own ongoing under-funded work but can also take on her individual struggle until it reaches the national level. The closing of NAC and women's centres across the country make that much less likely. NAC's annual meeting and lobby provided an opportunity to note the on the ground situations we experienced in common from one end of the country to the other. It was also an opportunity to identify where there was new energy and leadership to fight a particular wrong. It was the only regular cross-class, cross-race, cross-region, and cross-issue meeting of the women's movement.

The cutting of rape crisis centres and transition houses from federal women's equality-based funding and the pressure to conform to provincial "service only" criteria, impairs women tremendously in our attempt to keep a legal complaint alive. Often, having an intervener case requires some advocate risking quite a lot. Sometimes individual lawyers spot a good opportunity, and so they advance the expenses, but this is not the normal case and not a desirable relationship for a woman to have with her counsel.[12]

Along the way to Supreme Court, it seems governments feel the need to fight every woman to the breaking point. Why not accept responsibility for the unequal application of law and welcome the opportunities for change created by women's complaints? Still, women have not been stopped. Jane Doe and the civil suits following her are only the tip of the iceberg. The Bonnie Mooney case seems an obvious one in which all three levels of government are engaged in proving that there is no consequence for inadequate and sloppy policing in the lives of battered women.

How can this be in the interest of the public? By the time the court case is complete, the dollars spent in proving an absurdity will be enormous; the settlement with Bonnie Mooney's family could have been easily absorbed while justice was done and been seen to be done. While policing may be more an issue for the Department of the Solicitor General to correct through the RCMP, the legal strategy to fight against Bonnie Mooney was directed by the federal Justice Department. There seems to be much more government interest in using the courts to fight women in ways that maintain pockets of inequality or routes to escape accountability, than in assisting women to fight sexist violence in the courts.[13]

We fear that as the effects of restructuring settle in and public legal funds available to women are more and more restricted, it will become more and more the case that only those already privileged will be able to use the Charter and to prevent the advance of the dispossessed.

We, as centres or as a national association, also face these economic effects on Charter law. We did join with other women to defend the Charter Challenge Fund. But there has never been a fund for Charter litigation in all of the provinces where things begin and of course, even the national fund is limited and never fully pays the costs of a struggle. Nor has it paid for the costs of a woman being in charge of her own case and actually directing counsel. For Supreme Court interventions we, as advocates, are not paid for our staff time or full expenses to participate in the legal strategy. It is enormously time consuming. The Court Challenge Fund does pay lawyers and court costs, to a large degree, when a case is accepted for subsidy. Sometimes it pays the meeting expenses to develop the preliminary ideas for a national case's court preparation. But equality-seeking interveners still have to be willing to raise huge sums and because of the importance of the case, risk core funds.

What is more menacing is the combination of these pressures: the restructuring (or neo-liberal structural adjustment) of Canada and the abandonment of equality as enshrined and possible through Charter implementation. Together, they eliminate the context in which all the state's achievements of criminalizing violence and assisting women violated were secured.[14] Without that context, it is not clear how any of it will be maintained, much less developed.

We have been on the defensive to hold on to any of that interactive network of law and policy. Initially, LEAF secured and controlled what funding and feminist labour was available. CASAC forged alliances several times with LEAF to build coalitions that could intervene in cases already launched by others. LEAF had organized itself to accomplish this. In the jointly constructed factum, LEAF usually had all the responsibility for the administrative work and held final say over counsel and legal tactics and much of the public strategy, but as the years passed, they yielded more and more influence to their coalition partners on the substance and nuance of the arguments and the political battle outside the court. We could more effectively bring our frontline and working-class understanding to the table. And we were joined there by groups of aboriginal and other racialized women and by formations such as the Disabled Women's Network (DAWN). At its best, we all participated in learning some equality-based thinking and action.[15] There is an entire body of work to be examined from those cross-class alliances and the leadership role that CASAC played in coalition and theory building. There is much to be recorded of the sophistication of the coalition politics from which we all gained. LEAF, with CASAC's permission, has published the factum, which emerged from the first ten years of Charter cases, including those cases affecting violence issues in which we were key participants:[16]

Canadian Newspapers v Canada

Seaboyer and Gayme v The Queen

R v Thibaudeau

O'Connor v The Queen

But more recent cases have also required and received less of the attention and involvement of front line anti-violence centres. The nature and integration of national coalition politics and the voice of the frontline has been substantially weakened, compared to our earlier work. This is not because of the wilful withdrawal of CASAC or other anti-violence coalitions from such work; it is the outcome of the financial impoverishment of the movement at the national level and also of the frontline organizations and our own national associations. No one could pick up the slack.

While the political agreements accumulated among equality-seeking women's groups during the earlier consultation work has held, there has been a sea change, after the work of the rape law and the years of the justice consultations, imposed on the women's movement by the legislated agenda.[17] This area too requires further study. The consequences are already visible in the conducting of casework. More and more, Canada is creating the public misunderstanding that the practice of litigation alone can be a route to the advancement of women. Surely no one believes litigation strategies can win much without the existence of the frontline community education, public agitation, and political organizing that must support and inform each case:

A.(L.L.)v Baharriell (1995)

Ewanchuck (1998)

Mills (1999)

Darrach (2000)

These recent cases defended against notions of "implied consent" and called the court to uphold statutory restrictions on the disclosure of confidential records and sexual history restrictions, all ideas that had been formulated and expressed in the C-49 consultations. The coalition building to create those legal notions of what was possible and necessary had already been done. The legislated impoverishment of Canada-wide coalitions of the women's movement and anti-violence casework has yet to be fully felt in working through the next development of ideas. And even with the consensus established, a huge political initiative has been necessary to propel each of these cases forward.

The CASAC LINKS project improved the ability of frontline workers to follow, understand, and assist the progress of these cases through the courts to the Supreme Court. It allowed women in their communities to respond to and develop the community consensus. LINKS gave quick electronic and digital access to the decisions once made. It allowed us to follow and affect the critiques and media considerations of those decisions.

As CASAC, we have now heard three Supreme Court judges speak to us on the question of intervener status and the importance of the role we play. At our conference Women's Resistance from Victimization to Criminalization, Madame Justice Louise Arbour spoke about her attitude toward interveners and effectively cautioned us about the loss of respect for that role and work.[18] Claire L'Heureux-Dubé discussed the importance of interveners providing context, in her address to NAWL at the announcement of her retirement.[19] Perhaps Bertha Wilson put it most optimistically in her foreword to LEAF's book of joint facta saying:

> Enter the intervener whose proper role, I believe, is to distance him or herself
> from the narrow facts of the case, to paint a broader picture and to assist the
> court by hypothesizing a wide range of contexts in which the section might be
> invoked, all with a view to discerning its purpose and delineating and defining its contours.[20]

But unless our groups continue to exist and are properly funded, such intervention will be impossible. Already, intervention is so impaired that we may not be able to defend equality initiatives we had believed secured in the will of parliament and the decisions of the Supreme Court.

CASAC thought we might be able to achieve something for women with the 1992 Criminal Code reforms. The federal government in reaction to the Supreme Court on Seaboyer, the demands from women's groups and the public, initiated them. The Charter was in place. The level of agreement among women's groups was very high and had been identified by CASAC in the parliamentary hearings leading to the *The War Against Women* report and in the feminist caucus of the conference Women, the Law, and the Administration of Justice.

CASAC advised the government on most of the provisions in new law by leading to consensus an unprecedented series of consultations between Canadian women's equality-seeking organizations. We remain solid in our opinion that the coalition work to prepare for advising the government was the most important element of the C-49 work. It was the theory, solidarity, and political consensus that were our best achievements. We were never naive enough to think that the law would be fully implemented. Nonetheless, we hoped. Even the consensus within the movement was a compromise for anti-rape workers.[21] But still, we hoped. Having applied ourselves to criminal law reform, we had expectations. Bill C-49 (Canada, 1992) was a well-crafted bill that introduced a set of procedures and criteria to govern admissibility of sexual history evidence and a codification of a statutory definition of consent. Consent was defined as the voluntary agreement of the complainant to engage in the sexual activity in question and specified situations which ruled out consent including where agreement is expressed by other persons, where the complainant is incapable of consenting, where submission is introduced by abuse of authority, and where the complainant expresses a lack of agreement to continue. The bill also sought to limit the use of the defence of mistaken belief in consent, restricting it to circumstances where the accused has taken "reasonable steps, in the circumstances" to ascertain consent, and excluding "self induced intoxication" and "reckless or wilful blindness" as basis for claiming the belief that they had consent. It has been necessary for us to defend the sense of the law in all settings, including the courts.

Those who try to use criminal law in cases of violence against women are learning that we will more and more have to contend with men defending themselves from criminal charges by using the Charter. But so few men are charged and fewer still convicted and that made us begin to examine the other criminal law practices that prevent actual criminalization of violence against women. That defence, sometimes of patriarchal power against women's equality interests, is coming not only from the individual attackers but also from the commonplace behaviour of police, criminal defence bar, judges, and too many offices of the justice system.

As soon as we started to pay attention to Charter-based equality expectations, we learned that "Charter arguments" and "Charter rights" were most often colloquial expressions used (mostly by men) in the legal community to mean the rights of the accused. They are rarely understood to mean women's rights to autonomy, security, privacy, agency, dignity, or well being. They are rarely understood to mean the right of the complainant to a fair trial or the right of women to access the rule of law. If the state actors (police, victim assistance, crown, judge) even mentioned women's equality rights in any of the cases in which we have been involved, it was never in the context of advancing a complaint of violence against women. It was only in the construction of a limit to those rights such as "he has rights too" or yes, she has a right to…but we must "balance those rights" said by someone other than a judge and meaning something less than achieving her rights or any version of balance.

To have any progressive use, Charter rights will have to be understood to always mean some version of the right to substantive and meaningful equality. We need the legal community colloquialism to be the language of the aspirations of the historically disadvantaged; the oppressed. They should not just legally arm aggressors against the state. A fair trial is not one laced with indignity and bigotry.[22] The full defence, of even those unfairly targeted by the state for criminalization, does not need to resort to bigotry. And no amount of bigotry will produce a fair trial or protection from unfairness. Obviously such processes and attitudes dignify no one.

State functionaries regularly ask questions and solicit opinions of CASAC members as though there is a finite quantity of rights available to Canadians. We, including the women we represent, are in some competition for them with all other groups of people wanting rights. This is not CASAC's analysis. Our understanding is that rights, entitlements, and obligations, even in the sense of rights within a liberal democracy, build on and compliment each other. We don't imagine a pie of rights to be divided. We imagine a democratic harmony in which each person's right, entitlement, or obligation is a voice, sometimes combining with groups of others, to create a fuller, more sophisticated, and refined sound of justice. We hope for a time when women's voices, individual and collective, will be heard above the sexist, racist, classist din. It is in the speaking, listening, recording, and upholding of everyone's rights that democratic liberty can be conducted.

In part, we saw C-49 as an aid to limit (through the Charter) the discretion of individual men within the system to collude with or assist attackers in their application of the power of the state against women. We were particularly interested in the state power exercised through decisions made by police, prosecutors, the governance of the defence bar, and judges. Feminists, including CASAC, have continued to attempt to limit that discretion, and the limits continue to be contested by one branch of justice or another and often by one branch of justice undermining another.

The mandatory arrest policy was an example. Women's groups have been very clear, over the years, that police discretion in handling wife assault has been used against women too often, too normally. While "mandatory arrest" was not the invention of CASAC or any part of the women's movement, we did not unite to oppose it. We understood it as an effort to curtail police discretion: to press them to arrest when they could indicate that men had probably assaulted. It has never worked. It has never been fully applied. Police are obviously told one way or another by their bosses not to follow it, as they were directed by their bosses previously not to respond to the crimes of violence against women. The policy was not and is not the only problem. Often police increased the arrests of the already targeted populations of men and consistently continued to refuse to respond to the calls of women for assistance from any, but especially from the same disadvantaged communities that they targeted for men's arrests.

Increasingly, women were aware of this and told us that they thought the equality rights of the men were being abused. Men in their lives were being arrested essentially for being aboriginal or black or, at best, for being drug dealers or thieves, when women complained of violence, but the rights of the violated women are also violated. Men would not be arrested for wife assault, or sexual assault, or incest simply because they had committed criminal acts of wife assault, sexual assault, or incest.

In B.C., the provincial government authorities had been substantially won over to the need for an over-arching provincial policy on the responses to wife assault and the need to include in that policy the encouragement to err on the side of arresting men who seemed to have beaten their wives. The RCMP fought tooth and nail in the name of their independence to reject the provincial policy. After the Vernon Massacre and the political inquiry that followed, they created their own policy.[23] But the defence by all levels of government of the police behaviour toward Bonnie Mooney continues to the present. The RCMP continued to attempt to split any equality-seeking forces within the system regarding the necessity for the provincial policy and finally, they added to crown resistance contributing to the Liberal and B.C. provincial government reversal of the policy in 2002. Bonnie Mooney and CASAC continue to fight them in court.

Everywhere in the country, CASAC women see huge expenditures of public money and time on training and education of police prosecutors and judges with too little positive impact. Ongoing education within any profession is important. But this model of social change is clearly not working as a way to win compliance with the law or the best equality efforts of women. Why not apply more strict job performance requirements that these professionals meet the Charter standards?

In spite of twenty years of demands for accountability processes like civilian review bodies over police and judges, public inquiries, inquests into deaths of women, and the governments that were implicated, not to mention costly and long civil suits against public officials, these generalizable results are ignored or undermined.[24] Increasingly, these political processes (coroners inquiries, public reviews, etc.) are disqualifying equality seekers or the interventions based on equality that they wish to make as irrelevant to the issue before them.[25]

"Coordinating" bodies[26] at the local and provincial levels have become roadblocks to effective reforms against sexist violence. They are not structured or funded to advance cases that could change the landscape nor are they neutral in their orientation. In fact, they play a significant role in exposing possible "problem" cases to the system for papering over. The committees are over-run, by design, with "systems" employees at the lowest levels of power and influence who are not required to demonstrate a commitment to equality and who, instead, are invited to window-dress inequalities with coordination rhetoric.[27] As though each incident of inequality was isolated and unusual and could be solved by communication and intra-professional courtesies. Aggressive, urgent equality seekers are either sandbagged or leave. Hamilton and Vancouver coordinating committees are prime examples. Ontario is now the most vivid example of province-wide pressure to pre-empt the independent critique of women's anti-violence centres. Domestic Assault Review Teams (DART), Children's Aid Society protocols, police departments, hospital-based victim services, and new Domestic Violence Courts embed women's groups and services within the current services and inadequate legal options in each community in a way that reinforces the status quo. It threatens to bury their advocacy on behalf of women and their knowledge of what is actually happening in much the same way that embedding journalists in military troops buries the truth of war by forcing journalists to see themselves as part of the military equipment and personnel. In this case it is the army of forces of the status quo.

Victim's Rights groups, including both those with a restorative justice orientation and those covering a more obvious right wing "law and order" agenda, oppose and interfere with women's equality-seeking initiatives.[28] In the last five years, they have succeeded in grabbing the public dollar and winning the cooperation of politicians without interference from those attached to Charter concepts. Every province has introduced mechanisms to fund police-based victim assistance and contributed to blurring, for the public, the difference between a non-government organization offering advocacy against government actions and inaction and a police-based or state-based one answerable at best to the state and usually to a current government. The Ontario Harris government created the Victims of Crime Office and tried to herd women's services and advocacy under it. The federal government, through the Department of Justice, assigned a victim file complete with a bi-annual victims conference, largely devoting its attention to inter-governmental plans to limit the services and roles of victims. It has, however, given rise to a national association of victims and a public debate about enshrining the "rights" of victims in the constitution. During these same years, both provincial and federal governments discontinued funding to many women's groups concerned with women's legal rights, especially those women victimized by sexist violence. How is this a Charter-based or "gender mainstreaming" perspective?

CASAC and other women's groups were quite vocal in our anticipation of this impact on equality-seeking groups and liberal justice concepts such as the role of the state versus the role of the individual complainant.[29] But there has been no Charter-based examination of these issues by the bureaucracy. Since its formation, CASAC has debated the possibilities and problems of relying on law, especially criminal law. These debates and examinations of positions and orientations continued at our recent Women's Resistance Conference and at the CASAC convention in 2001. As the list of speakers and workshops would indicate, we have had to discuss prison abolition, restorative justice initiatives, the making of monsters like Bernardo, Lepine, and Olsen. We have debated and reconsidered the racializing and classing that persists in the targeting of those arrested.

The victim rights voices argue with us that we should abandon men's civil liberties, call for increased police power and increased prison sentences for all crimes including violence. We do not agree that undermining civil liberties is ever in our interest. We are also aware that the increased criminalization of women for poverty crimes and self-defence would be ill served by such a solution to the crimes of violence committed against women.

Some, though not all, prison abolitionists argue that we should immediately and entirely reject criminalization. Using the current justice system, they say, moves away from democracy and economic justice. We are pressed to abandon any call for increased criminalization of violence against women to save our community from the imposition of unfair and undemocratic policing and jailing. We have had to consider whether race and class targeting compels us to advise women against cooperating with the criminal justice system at all.

But CASAC women have come again to the conclusion that, in Canada, we must press for the application of criminal sanctions against violence against women. We are aware and appalled that the law, especially criminal law, is selectively applied. The theft and wrong doing of the privileged is handled completely differently than the theft and the wrong doing of the poor and racialized. Drug taking and selling are obvious examples. Theft is even more obvious. But it is true too that this selective criminalization affects women violated in a specific way: the refusal of the justice system, as a whole, to use the resources of the police, crown, courts, and other parts of government, to effectively protect women and hold men to account. We believe that progressive forces should join us, locally and nationally, in defending women by demanding the shift of priorities for the use of public resources from managing the interests of men, however privileged, to protecting equality rights.

Not the least of our reasons for this reform demand is the fact that most women cannot escape the reach of law, including criminal law. When they are sexually violated, they are under the eye of the state already. Women asking for medical assistance in response to a rape or assault, women seeking economic assistance from the state, women who are institutionalized in any public institution, including marriages, cannot just hide their attack.

Increasingly, women cannot leave abusive marriages without state authorized mobility permission from their husbands in formal custody arrangements. To get such arrangements, women often tell someone of the violence. If that someone is a professional representing her legally, mediating the end of the marriage, teaching her child, counselling her or her children, managing her housing, day care or her immigration, she may well be pressured to report. Women are ordered to pursue charges of violence to protect custody of our children. A live-in caregiver faces similar pressure. She cannot voluntarily choose to change her employer without penalty, and she cannot report her employer as violent without facing pressure to report to police. A prostitute numbered by the health department wanting to escape a violent john will be similarly pressured.

Women who call police in the heat of an emergency, for instant protection from a punch or a gun, can be and are selectively pressed into formal report giving, whether they like it or not, by threats of mischief charges, or the accusation that if they do not proceed, they are effectively recanting and should be punished for wasting the time of the state.

The least able to escape the wishes of the state's actors, are those pushed out of social protections that used to be available from the state and the voluntary sector. That push comes from the economic and social changes described earlier and is experienced in the forced migrations of the poor of the world from one part of Canada or the world, to another, and out of welfare and marriages into the informal economy. Ex-wives managing on women's depressed incomes receiving under the table child support, aboriginal women on reserves subject to unprincipled band council decisions about how to handle the violence, First Nations women forced into the informal economy of the urban ghettos, poor women cheating because of too little (if any) welfare, immigrants without adequate settlement services, students working under the table to supplement smaller student loans, older women on insufficient pensions, disabled women (those that qualify at all) working to supplement their meagre aid, all live in a permanent state of illegality.

Unless we force the redistribution of policing and other criminal justice to their aid, they are left to face both the targeted criminalization for their adaptations to violence and poverty, and the withholding of legal protections and services on the basis of their status as women and their therefore unworthiness of the legal services and protections of their community. How can women cope with the ever present reality of harassing and stalking husbands prepared to murder, drug merchants selling date rape drugs in bars, raping and pimping motorcycle gangs, multinational traffickers, raping priests and murderous, armed prison guards without the aid of criminal law?

It seems to us that the women in Mission who called on us to "speak to the bigger picture" in the wife murder described in our Preface, are calling upon CASAC to collect the stories of all the women who call and make the solutions proposed suit as many of us as possible. That role can and should be played both in and out of court. Canadians need women's groups who are informed by work against violence to give time and attention to the larger picture and the predictable scenarios. We need to meet, discuss, write, and otherwise give voice to and act as equality advocates. This is the role we wish to play using the Charter, and Charter cases, as part of the fight to end violence against women as we "remember the dignity of womanhood, take courage, and stand with us."[30]

Notes

1. Wilson, B. (1996). In *Women's Legal Education and Action Fund* (LEAF). Toronto: Emond Montgomery Press.

2. In 1982, The Charter was enacted, and in 1985, Equality provisions came into effect.

3. There were labour leaders, as well, for instance, Kathleen O'Neil of the women of the Women Teachers Federation; for an account of the Charter gang see: Razack, S. (1991). *Canadian Feminism and the Law: The Women's Legal Education Fund and the Pursuit of Equality. Toronto*: Second Story Press.

4. Doris Anderson, former editor of *Chatelaine*, who headed the Canadian Advisory Council on the Status of Women (CACSW), is a well-known feminist and Liberal. She organized for the conference on the constitution, and NAC declared constitutional reform would be its priority for the year.

5. Marilyn McLean, Toronto Rape Crisis Centre participated as CASAC in on-going consultations, too.

6. LEAF acknowledges too in its book of Facta "it has spent much of its time defending existing provisions for equality that have been threatened." See: Women's Legal Education and Action Fund. (1996) *Equality and the Charter: Ten Years of Feminist Advocacy before the Supreme Court of Canada*. Introduction. (p. xii). Toronto: Emond Montgomery Publications.

7. This is explained in the tribute to L'Heureux Dubé delivered at the University of Ottawa event on her retirement, See: Lakeman, L. (2002) *Farewell Address to Madame Justice L'Heureux-Dubé* available online: <www.casac.ca/ issues/fairwell_heureux-dube.htm>.

8. "In our own interests" in the sense that Bertha Wilson used the expression above.

9. Both of these stories are included in this report as high profile cases.

10. Frontline workers have been frustrated in almost every city trying to deal with these situations in Coordinating meetings and Coordinating Committees.

11. See, for example, Bonnie Mooney's case or Jane Doe's case.

12. Jane Doe, Bonnie Mooney, and the women fighting Bishop O'Connor all suffered for lack of money to control the case. Without the intervention of women's groups it is arguable that none of them would have proceeded.

13. In the Bonnie Mooney case, federal government lawyers led the defence of all levels of government irresponsibility. After the original police officer was proved guilty, the government should have accepted responsibility.

14. That context included state funding for women's groups and services, funds to compensate victims of crime, consultations with women's group's on policy and law reform, court and police policy changes to aid women and children complainants.

15. For an assessment of the case success see: McIntyre, S. (1996). Feminist Movement in Law: Beyond Privileged and Privileging Theory. In Jhappan, R. (Ed.), *Women's Legal Strategies in Canada*. Toronto: University of Toronto Press, pp.42-98.

16. LEAF. (1996) *Equality and the Charter*.

17. The national women's groups meeting in Ottawa at the invitation of NAWL and CRIAW (Canadian Research Institute for The Advancement of Women), in September 20 and 21, 2003, constructed this analysis.

18. Women's Resistance: From Victimization to Criminalization plenary: Can Law Deliver for All Women? Chair: Dawn McBride, Madam Justice Louise Arbour, Supreme Court of Canada, Former War Crimes Prosecutor and Commissioner for the Inquiry Into Certain Events at the Prison for Women, Kingston. Plenary proceedings, see: <http//www.casac.ca/conference01/cd_order02.htm>.

19. National Association of Women and the Law Conference, March 7-10, 2002, "Hats Off" event.

20. Women''s Legal Education and Action Fund. (1996). *Equality and the Charter: Ten Years of Feminist Advocacy Before the Supreme Court of Canada*. Forward (p.ix). Toronto: Emond Montgomery Publications.

21. Our political position as CASAC was that our records and women's personal sexual history were never necessary evidence in court cases of violence.

22. This idea was raised repeatedly by both by Sheila McIntyre and by Christine Boyle during our deliberations in planning the O'Connor facta and the struggle to protect the confidentiality of records of complainants (1992) Vancouver.

23. RCMP policy E division was adjusted after the inquiry in 1998 by Josiah Wood into the Vernon Massacre.

24. See the May/Iles and Hadley cases in this report. Hadley raises the horror of the failure to apply the inquest recommendations from May/Iles.

25. Ontario Inquiry into the death of Kim Roger's for what was ruled out, see the DisAbled Women's Network of Ontario (DAWN) *Kimberly Rogers Inquest Alerts: Judicial review decision in CAEFS vs. Dr David Eden, coroner* available online: <http://dawn.thot.net/kimberly_rogers/judicial_review.html>.

26. Usually comprised of the paid staff of some service organizations and the lowest levels tolerated by them of the police and crown office.

27. Selecting representatives for instance that are half from government systems and half from the community is a complete sham. All should be based in equality-seeking work and the self-organized groups of the oppressed must have pride of place even for this tiny reform to have meaning. Otherwise, it just steals the time and energy of the equality-seeking groups to no good end.

28. Lakeman, L. (2000).

29. See the record of the Justice consultations and presentations to Minister Allan Rock available from Justice Canada and on file at CASAC.

30. Nellie McLung: "Remember the dignity of your womanhood; take courage and stand with us."

Bonnie Mooney's Story

Louisa Russell

BONNIE MOONEY'S story begins with a police officer saying, "I am sorry there is nothing we can do." Those were the words of Constable Craig Andrichuk as he responded to Bonnie's desperate plea for help in dealing with her ex-common -law husband, Roland Kruska. The police knew Kruska to be armed and dangerous (he had previous convictions, including manslaughter, sexual assault, and forcible confinement, and had been imprisoned numerous times).[1] Kruska beat Bonnie time and again from 1991 to 1995, three of which resulted in her being hospitalized. Each time the violence escalated, until he choked her unconsciousness, and battered her with a stick in November 1995.

Kruska was subsequently charged with *attempted murder* but was sentenced to 21 days for *assault using a weapon causing bodily harm*—after the charge was reduced.[2] While on bail, Kruska told Bonnie that he would sign over the house to her if she concocted a story to the courts. Terrified for her life, and convinced that the criminal justice system wouldn't protect her; she agreed to tell the courts that her police statement was "bullshit."[3] The Judge relied solely on Bonnie's "testimony" and did not believe hospital records, previous records of his violence, nor the witness statements to the contrary. Consequently Kruska was soon roaming freely.[4]

Kruska reneged on the deal; he called Bonnie frequently, threatening to kill her. "I was feeling like his eyes were on me and he could hear and see everything I was doing. Like I said, this man had so much power over me."[5] The attacks continued to escalate. Bonnie drove to the RCMP detachment and begged for help. She told the Constable everything that had happened in the past and why she was so fearful now. Andrichuk took a brief statement and informed Bonnie that there were no grounds to get a peace bond under S.810 of the Criminal Code. He told her to consult a lawyer about a civil restraining order, and advised her to "stay in a public place in the future."[6]

She left in disbelief, echoing the voices of so many battered women: "Surely the police can do more?"[7] Scared for her life, Bonnie made several efforts to protect herself and her family. She got her best friend Hazel White to sleep over and installed bars on the windows. Six weeks later, on March 11, 1996, Kruska "smashed through the patio door of her rural B.C. home with the butt of his sawed off shot gun." He killed Hazel, and severely wounded her twelve-year-old daughter, Michelle. Bonnie, Michelle, and her other daughter, Kristy, escaped while Kruska set fire to the home and killed himself.

Certain the RCMP could and should have done more to protect her, Bonnie pursued the matter. She became the first ever to sue all three levels of the state: the RCMP, The Attorney General (AG) of B.C., and the Solicitor General of Canada. She launched a civil action on the grounds that *reasonable steps were not taken to ensure the "safety and security of her family."*[8] Women's groups across the country wrote letters to the named authorities demanding that they stop making Bonnie fight in court and that they assume responsibility.[9] Rape Relief called a meeting with the Director of Police Services, Kevin Begg. We asked why the AG of B.C. was in concert with the federal government, making Bonnie fight in court, as it was in their interests that their own policy on wife assault be upheld. Our concerns were forwarded to A.J. (Tony) Heemskerk, Assistant Deputy Minister of the AG, who replied that they were not a named party in the case.[10]

I faxed copies of the court transcripts that showed the AG as a named party. He later called back and told us that he had recently learned that the "Fed's" had retained a lawyer on behalf of their ministry. He said that he had lodged a complaint with the Solicitor General of Canada, for not advising him sooner, but did little more.

The case proceeded. The defence lawyer on behalf of all Canadians, George Caruthers, argued Bonnie was the "*author of her own misfortune*," stating a protection order would have done "*nothing*" to prevent the shootings.[11] Women's groups were outraged when Justice Collver announced the dismissal of the case stating although

> ...a careful investigation was warranted but not undertaken...[but] there was no clear connection between Constable Andrichuk's failure of March 11, 1996 and Kruska's fateful trip...seven weeks later...the officer's inaction did not materially increase the risk of harm to the extent that [the state] must bear responsibility for Kruska's acts.[12]

Collver's decision went on to quantify damages to be awarded to Bonnie and her children in the event that their claims were to prove successful on appeal. They came to less than $500,000.[13]

Rape Relief filed an application to intervene in the appeal so we could inform the courts of a feminist perspective before they made their decision.[14] We knew that Bonnie's experience was shared by thousands of battered women and it was important that this case be placed in that context. We asserted in our application that the individual constable's failure to follow the guidelines on wife assault guaranteed Bonnie and her family would not be safe.[15] We stated that the negligence, agreed to by Justice Collver, did not uphold the *Charter* values that Bonnie and her family had to the right to *life, liberty, and security of the person and the right to equality before the law*.[16]

When Bonnie ran into that Prince George detachment, the constable made several sexist stereotypical assumptions about all battered women, and "*left her out to die*."[17] He "deprived her of her right *to security of the person* by subjecting her to the very real risk of attack by her ex-partner."[18] Women know that the police judge battered women in this way; it's because of this that so many women do not go to the police for protection from male violence committed against us in the first place.[19] And still we fight. We fight with the belief in equality and with hope for all women who follow. I hope that Bonnie receives some compensation for so much of the life she has lost and that other women may be spared the same ordeal. The case continues today, awaiting hearing at the Supreme Court of B.C.

Notes

1. Transcript of *Bonnie Mooney v The Attorney General of Canada, The Attorney General of The Province of British Columbia, The Solicitor General of Canada, Corporal K.W. Curle, Constable E.W. Roberge, and Constable Andricuck*, T.V., T.V. 3, pp. 570-573.

2. Transcript, Vol. 2, p. 197.

3. Transcript, Vol. I, p. 131, lines 22-44, p. 134, lines 40-42, p. 135, lines 2-19.

4. A.B. V1, p. 68 "The Judge accepted the Appellant's statement to the court (A.B. V1, pp. 8-9) and remarked in sentencing Kruska to 21 days that he was "relying a great deal on what Ms. Mooney had told me."

5. A.B., Vol. V, p. 1030, para 16, (RFJ) Transcript, Vol. I, p. 153, line 22 to p. 154, line 9, and p. 156, line16, to p. 157, line 10.

6. Trial transcript, February 23, 2001, line 34.

7. Trial transcript, p. 7, line 23.

8. Trial transcript.

9. Some of these groups were: Aboriginal Women's Action Network, Phoenix Transition House, B.C. and Yukon Society of Transition Houses, Canadian Association of Sexual Assault Centres.

10. Letter addressed to Louisa Russell from A.J. (Tony) Heemskerk, Assistant Deputy Minister, Attorney General of British Columbia, April 23, 2001.

11. Kwan, K. (2001, February 20), Abused Wife Wants Cops to Pay, Vancouver: *The Province*, p. A3.

12. See Transcript, Reasons For Judgment of the Honourable Mr. Justice Collver.

13. Court of Appeal Appellants' Factum p. 8, section 21. A.B. Vol. VI, p. 1062.

14. Intervener status was granted and our intervention was heard in November 2003. The government lawyer argued that Bonnie was only *inquiring* about protection and that she was only a *potential* client of the police and had no claim to protection once they refuse her.

15. Court of Appeal Proposed intervener—Notice of Motion, January 2003, filed by Gail Dickson, Q.C.

16. Canadian Charter of Rights and Freedoms, Part 1 of the Constitution Act, 1982, being Schedule B of the Canada Act, 1982 (U.K.), c11 [hereinafter "the Charter"].

17. Transcript, p. 7, line 23.

18. *Jane Doe v. Metropolitan Toronto (Municipality) Commissioners of Police*.

19. *The Daily*, Statistics Canada, November 18, 1993: "The Violence Against Women Survey," p. 7, "violent incidents experienced by women 18 years and over by type of victimization and criminal justice processing, Canada, 1993: Total: 20,543; Total reported to Police: 2,796; not reported: 17,571; of those reported to Police (2,796) Perpetrator Arrested: 913; Not arrested/Charges not laid: 1,671."

Bonnie Mooney's Story...Continued

Suzanne Jay

"IF ONLY THEY HAD done something, two people would still be alive," Bonnie Mooney told me as we walked back to the courtroom on Thursday. The two dead were her best friend, Hazel White, and Bonnie's ex-common-law partner Roland Kruska. Kruska was trying to kill Bonnie when he broke into her house and shot Hazel and Bonnie's twelve-year-old daughter. He set the house on fire and then he killed himself.

Several weeks earlier, Bonnie escaped Kruska after he threatened to kill her and chased her through town. She asked the Prince George RCMP for protection. They refused her, and thus, they failed her. I think the RCMP's refusal to arrest allowed Kruska to escalate to murder. I was shocked when the lawyers for the RCMP and the government claimed in court that their refusal to arrest and the shootings were two unconnected events.

I'm not a lawyer, but that assertion does not make sense to me. I don't believe the police can absolutely guarantee my safety or the safety of any woman. However, I expect the police to be more effective than a woman alone in stopping a man with a gun. This belief is the main reason why I'm willing to allow the police to have guns, cars, training, and power that the ordinary citizen does not have.

Are the police claiming they were powerless to stop this dangerous man? What kind of message does that send to women? I'm a small unarmed person, should I just stand aside and let men beat up or rape whoever they choose: Should I just not bother calling the police? Are they really more helpless than I am to prevent this kind of violence?

Bonnie survived the attack in 1996. With help, she compiled evidence about the police attitude, behaviour, and policy related to her case. She found a lawyer to help her sue the RCMP and the government of Canada. In the first trial, the judge agreed with her that the RCMP had been negligent. But he failed to see that Kruska's rampage was facilitated by that negligence.

Vancouver Rape Relief and Women's Shelter supported Bonnie's appeal because we've heard similar stories from far too many women. We engaged a lawyer and got intervener status. We provided the judges with information about how those women's interests are involved in the case and how women's rights can be positively affected by good public policing.

My heart and mind raced while one of the lawyers for the government talked about other Kruska attacks on Bonnie. I remembered her telling me she reinforced her front and back doors, she used a stick in the runner of the heavy glass patio door and sometimes, when she couldn't bear the fear anymore, she would call him to make sure he wasn't actually lurking outside her house. Hazel stayed with her and the girls; it must have helped them feel better to have each other.

I have deadbolts on my doors, bars on my windows, outdoor security lights, and I live with someone. I make an effort to know my neighbours, and I draw the curtains at night. I'm not hyper-afraid, but then I'm not dealing with a man who has beaten me, has guns, and has threatened to kill me. I'm not responsible for children who are counting on me to protect them too. However, even without children, I am entitled by law to police protection. And so is any other woman.

Yet, the lawyer for the government describes Bonnie as a "potential client" for the RCMP, as though she is required to buy her policing. They claim they had no obligation to serve and protect her—as if police have that option. They claim she was not entitled to expect anything more of them after they turned her down.

We directed our lawyer to remind the judges public policing is guaranteed by the Charter of Rights and Freedoms to be available to everyone in a fair and non-discriminatory way, including women. Although I'm sure it is something that the judges know, it's a relief to hear this asserted in the courtroom by our lawyer. Beside me, Bonnie turns and whispers, "Good for her!" It was as though even she wasn't fully aware that it was her case that had been making this point.

It would be fair and just for Bonnie to win this appeal. It would confirm to those watching that police have a responsibility to protect us from violence against women—especially when women ask. I think it would be a long overdue and bittersweet victory for Bonnie. It would be a victory for every woman in Canada, including me.

Local **Documents** Reviewed

A s we began this book, we were especially interested in whether and where policies and procedures to address violence against women failed to meet our understanding of the Charter obligations to women and equality. We were tired of training personnel in the state machineries of Health, Justice, and the Solicitor General, tired of chastising individuals, and individual offices, or departments when the problems seemed to us to be much more systemic.

We examined the international law and context, the restructuring of Canada, the Charter cases, and processes. We also decided to examine, using those discoveries, the documents, and policies affecting local officials as they handled violence complaints. Gathering documents was an instructive activity in itself. We found that where once women begged for institutionalization of policy to instruct the ignorant and contain the erratic, we now found ourselves buried in paper. The system seems to have adapted to our attempts to curtail problems by keeping huge numbers of civil servants and contractors writing policy to the exclusion of much effective change.

Getting the documents is difficult. Officials guard them with suspicion that some wrongdoing will result from citizens understanding the obligations of state officials. When we asked for assistance, despite a letter of introduction from the Justice Department, we were repeatedly refused. Apparently there is some suspicion of danger at that level too. But when we actually secured what we could, we wondered why anyone would worry. There is little possibility that anyone could follow the chain of command, be reassured that they know what the legal policy or procedure is, or be assured that they could find the offending ignorance or obstruction to the enforcement of that policy. No ordinary citizen could possibly know what is going on or how to use the existing policy and procedure to her own benefit. Obfuscation is the order of the day.

CASAC LINKS was interested in their compliance with Charter obligations, as we understand them. We undertook a simple analysis: Do the documents identify and acknowledge that violence is gendered and oppressive to women in particular? Do they apply a substantive equality notion to the situations about which women call?

What we were looking for, of course, was reassurance that workers in the police department, or crown offices, or 911 call centres, as well as court workers, are instructed to treat women as humans with their own worth who always merit, by their existence alone, the equal access to and protection of the law. We hoped to find instructions to address the conditions in which women find themselves. We wanted to see that these public officials and functionaries are instructed that such treatment of all women is nothing more than the law requires.

A Document Review: 911

The mandate of the 911 operators in most places is to establish the correct response to a call: that is, to ensure it gets an appropriate response from the fire department, the police, or an ambulance. In each site we examined, different players were responsible for the running of 911—police, fire department, the province, or a corporation. There is no consistent gender analysis, and no training on violence against women, and/or to assessing women's safety. There is no notable difference in the training or procedures, regardless of who is in charge. The Canadian public gets much of its expectations these days from American television. They think 911 operators have a lot of control and access to emergency staff. Commonly, the 911 operator is instead working in a call centre atmosphere and being supervised by police. There are standards such as goals for the length of time it would take to handle each call such as, "average 40 seconds, goal 35," which apply for all calls, with no indication of when extra time and attention should be given.

Currently, there is a fiction consistent with television that operating the 911 system is overseeing police response in that it will record all the incoming calls and record the assignment of the call. This is not true. And the chances of using what systems exist to hold police accountable is laughable. Even with concerted efforts we had a very hard time securing the basic policy and procedures, much less directions to make any record of any call. The 911 personnel and systems often understand themselves to be contracted and managed by the police, and in small places, even feel personal loyalty to "our members" meaning the police.

The procedures recommended to the operators indicate no relation to the criminal code. This undermines the potential assessment of which law, and also which policy the police should be following. Wife assault and battering, up to attempted murder, is referred to as "domestic" in every case. It seems to us that if there is no relating to the criminal code, and no relating to gender, there will be no relating to the Charter either. There is no revealed reference to criminal code and no revealed priority placed in relation to the particular offence or crime. We saw no other method of identifying the particular danger to women.

We certainly imagined that there would have been some safety assessments, including asking if the attacker is still present, asking whether he had access to weapons, whether he is an ex-husband or boyfriend and so on. We know women sometimes say these things voluntarily, but we were looking for acknowledgment that the likely danger for women is different from an ex-husband with a gun than even from a balcony rapist working a neighbourhood for unlocked or easy to pick doors. We found no such incorporation of the common knowledge of the dangerous situations for women. Some policies refer to "domestics" as "dangerous for the responding member" meaning the officers coming to investigate, but there is no equivalent caution about the increased danger to the battered woman to whom they are responding.

There is a Canadian Supreme Court Case, *R. v. Godoy SCC 1999* about police responding to abandoned 911 calls. It is referenced in the E Division RCMP policy. It contains understandings, which could and should be generalized to all calls responding to violence against women. In the specific *Godoy* case, the woman called 911, but the call was not completed. In Ontario, these calls are given "priority two" and the police are also to get back up to respond. Four officers arrived at the door. The attacker answered, refused to let them in. The police went in and found the woman with a swelling on her head. She informed them her husband had hit her. The police arrested him and charged him with assault and resisting arrest.

The trial judge dismissed the case, because firstly, the woman denied in court that he hit her, and secondly, the police entered the premises against the wishes of the accused. The Crown appealed, and the Ontario Court of Appeal ordered a new trial. The Supreme Court did also. The Supreme Court decision lays out police responsibilities, and specifically names expectations of police response to "spousal abuse," in relation to the Charter. They say the police have more obligations to see to the dignity, integrity, and autonomy of the 911 callers than they do to the attacker's dignity (of not having the police in his home). They discuss:

> Further, the courts, legislators, police, and social service workers have all engaged in a serious and important campaign to educate themselves and the public on the nature and prevalence of domestic violence. One of the hallmarks of this crime is its private nature. Familial abuse occurs within the supposed sanctity of the home. While there is no question that one's privacy at home is a value to be preserved and promoted, privacy cannot trump the safety of all members of the household. If our society is to provide an effective means of dealing with domestic violence, it must have a form of crisis response. The 911 systems provide such a response. Given the wealth of experience the police have in such matters, it is unthinkable that they would take the word of the person who answers the door without further investigation. Without making any comment on the specific facts of this case, it takes only a modicum of common sense to realize that if a person is unable to speak to a 911 dispatcher when making a call, he or she may likewise be unable to answer the door when help arrives. Should the police then take the word of the person who does answer the door, who might well be an abuser and who, if so, would no doubt pronounce that all is well inside? I think not.[1]

Thus in my view, the importance of the police duty to protect life warrants and justifies a forced entry into a dwelling in order to ascertain the health and safety of a 911 caller. The public interest in maintaining an effective emergency response system is obvious and significant enough to merit some intrusion on a resident's privacy interest. However, I emphasize that the intrusion must be limited to the protection of life and safety. The police have authority to investigate the 911 calls, and, in particular, to locate the caller and determine his or her reasons for making the call and provide such assistance as may be required. The police authority for being on private property in response to a 911 call ends there. They do not have further permission to search premises or otherwise intrude on a resident's privacy or property. In *Dedman, supra*, at p. 35, Le Dain, J. stated that the interference with liberty must be necessary for carrying out the police duty and it must be...[2]

The charge against Godoy for the attack on his wife was dismissed—the Crown appealed on the resisting arrest and assault of an officer charge only. This is the charge the Supreme Court ultimately sent back to be re-tried. The Crown clearly put the injury to the officer, the resisting arrest, ahead of the assault on the wife, and did not enter any arguments into the appeal about why the charge for the assault on the wife should not proceed without her. They have a police witness to the injury and what she said on the scene, probably her original statement. There was no consideration by the Crown of her Charter Rights.

Overall, the case presents us with some hope. The Supreme Court has mandated the police to enter premises on reasonable grounds in order to assess the safety and liberty of 911 callers. But once again, we are in the position of hoping that power is used to protect women. The decision provides women with some expectation that their Charter Rights will be seen if the batterer disconnects her phone call. Surely they could be seen in other circumstances before she is at risk of death. The willingness to pursue men who challenge the police or the court directly is not new. But it is difficult for women to direct their anger at the authorities. And it is humiliating to women to experience that the system responds much more aggressively when abusive men hit a police officer or defy a court order than when they hit women and children. Sometimes it is deadly.

With the Supreme Court clearly stating that the emergency response systems are in place to secure the 911 callers, and this is since 1999, there seem some grounds for transforming the 911 policy training and procedures Canada-wide towards a policy, which better directs the dispatchers to this priority.

A Document Review: Police

What we get at this level is contradictions. There are violence policies in every outreach of Canada, though less about handling sexual assault than policies about handling battering. There are gender specific references but not consistently. There are still many hidden gender references (persistently degendering) as though either police forces don't know it is men who batter and rape and women who are on the receiving end or they don't know it is legal to say so. Surely they can no longer be worried that too many men will be arrested or that the lone woman attacker will be ignored. There are many women who have negative judgments about the police handling of their cases, but even more often women are scared, frustrated, incensed, defeated.

Women across Canada tell us that they want certain police responses. We have passed that on to policy writers and police educators. We were looking for a reflection of that learning in the documents directing police at the beginning of this next century. We expected to see directions that we have long sought:

- To inform women of what to expect at each stage of the process;
- To make women officers available whenever possible;
- To give information to women in a timely manner with respectful delivery;
- To refrain from sexist comments;
- To refer without disrespect to women's equality-seeking advocates and services;
- To advise women of the difference between a police-based victim assistance worker and an independent advocate;
- To protect and observe women's privacy;
- To tell the legal truth, not their personal opinion of the merits of a law;
- To have a kind and helpful manner;
- To give immediate and enduring protection of the community through the state from the attacker and from reprisals;
- To collect and take women's evidence and include all the possible evidence in photos, statements, forensics, witness statements into a formal active police file;
- To record the case properly and to recommend to crown promptly;
- To act themselves, based on that evidence;
- To act based on women's rights so that women are safer and men are held accountable for their violence and for their defiance of the law's acceptance of women's equality and the law's controls on violence.

This is the kind of policy in which women could see their right to equality with the attacker, the members of her community, and the policeman taking her statement. On the whole, this is what police policy promises:

- To take her statement;
- To investigate fully: gather evidence, secure the scene, interview potential witnesses;
- To refer to victim's services (usually police-based) and sometimes community agencies (occasionally identifiably feminist);

- Sometimes they are told to take violence against women calls as seriously as any other crime;

- Sometimes they are told to fill out a VICLAS booklet on all Sexual Assault Reports, whether charges are laid or not;

- Sometimes they are to have a supervising officer sign off on the report to crown counsel when recommending or not recommending charges;

- Sometimes they are to liaise with the community groups that work with battered women to provide information and assistance (not to get information or assistance);

- To consider their own safety when responding to "domestic violence" calls;

- To not ask victims if they want charges laid;

- Sometimes to secure medical attention in the immediate emergency after the attack.

We saw neither mention of women's Charter rights nor any attempt to state those rights or to enumerate the usual manner in which police have failed to uphold those rights. No understanding of women's rights was embodied in the policy.

Police providing information, in and of itself, does not secure women's Charter rights. But it is a vital part of women being able to protect their own rights of safety and security. To know what the police will and will not do is terribly important. Giving women copies of their protection orders as per policy, and arresting on the breaches of those orders, as per policy, gets us closer to this aim.[3] The police continue to refuse this basic request to tell us what is going on. As suggested under the Crown section, the police behaviour about handling information and response to women's requests and frequently advocates' demands seems to be about maintaining the mystery of the investigation. At this initial stage, police often "explain" that the needs of a conviction require that they refuse to inform women of the details of the process.

In response to the police refusal to co-operate with women victims of crime, governments created victim's services across North America. The clamour of women was behind the installation of volunteer services at police and crown level. Of course, so was the plan to eliminate the free standing advocacy centres that women had created for us. The job of the victim assistance offices too often seems to be to placate women by doing the things the police refused to do. She may not get a woman officer, but she will get a woman who will treat her kindly. She may not get a copy of her statement, but she has someone to call and complain to when she is dissatisfied. The victim's services worker duly writes these things into the file, which become part of the investigative file, and the investigating officer is saved from the urgency and insistence of the woman. He does not have to examine his methods to ensure he is following policy. He is left to "do his job," which apparently does not include respect for, or cooperation with, or accountability to the woman attacked, in any policy across the country.

Of course the victim's services worker cannot provide safety/protection from the attackers—it is the job of police to see to the life, liberty, and security of the person in violence against women. They are meant to be fully investigating for evidence, not for protection worthiness, arresting him in a timely manner, recommending arrest clauses on bail orders, arresting on breaches of bail. The victim's services worker provides the pamphlet describing the criminal law at issue, or Protection Order Registry (B.C.), or the Conditions of Bail. No one in the system is accountable for achieving what the woman can and should expect of the police or the crown.

The victim services worker does not secure the crime scene, collect forensic evidence, take the pictures of the scene, or her body. Too often neither do the police. But for the sake of policy considerations alone, it is important to know that the victim services worker cannot interview witnesses, recommend charges. The police must do that. That is why it is the police to whom women want to talk, to aid in getting that evidence found and recorded, to insist that these things be done in their cases. Victim's Services provides a buffer for police, a "friendly face" to the justice system, and are offered as a panacea to the numbers of dissatisfied and angry women.

If the women persist in trying to get access to the police, the victim assistance workers protect the police. Women are told not to "tell the police how to do their jobs." Or they are instructed that they should "trust" the officer in charge because the victim assistance worker "knows" him. The most blatant cases we have seen include the role played by the victim assistance workers in the Vernon case and in the ongoing case of dead women at the Pickton farm.

In both cases the victim services workers manage the families and communities with "support" while inappropriately shielding police from angry citizens and distressed victim/witnesses. In a meeting with the RCMP victim worker, in front of RCMP officers, we were told that the woman in Vernon made herself vulnerable (to being killed) by being "boldly in her carport." In Coquitlam, at the pig farm, a feminist aboriginal women's group, AWAN, was blocked out of the family contact centre by the police-based victim service worker, Freda Ens, and her boss in the Attorney General Ministry, Susanne Dahlin, according to the AWAN organizer, Fay Blaney.[4] Families, including the Crey family, have complained that they have been denied support services by the same victim services. They were denied access to meetings of the joint families of the dead because they spoke to the press with their concerns about the police investigation.[5] The Crey family and AWAN have provided leadership in the public demand for inquiries into the police activity and inactivity. Feminist anti-violence groups like Vancouver Rape Relief and Women's Shelter have been denied access to information and opportunities to offer assistance on the pretence that race sensitive services were being offered by the state, which required the absence of feminists. The fact that members of the families were already consulting and working with women's groups was over-ridden. Clearly, support through Victim Services is used as a disguise to block community and women's organizing for better policing. How is this consistent with an understanding of violence against women, including the murder of these women, as a matter of women's equality?

While some of the policies do address particular realities of violence against women, none speak to responding to violence against women as a matter of individual women's Charter/equality rights, or as a matter of the hateful crime, and the terrorizing of women as a community or population.

Many women are aware that various police entities across Canada have loudly stated opposition to the Charter. Individual officers blame not being able to "do anything" on the Charter (because of securing the attacker's Charter rights). Which may help to explain the failure of even the best policies in that while many of these policies seem to promote a high level of police thought and action in each investigation, it is clear from what women tell us that there is systemic and systematic interference with the application of those policies.

There are two quite good policies: the B.C. Attorney General Policy and the RCMP E Division Policy. They expect investigation and procedures to ensure the criminal code is followed. Both provide very detailed step-by-step guidelines for the police, from the minute they respond through the entire investigation process. If every officer followed these guidelines, step by step, there would be more potential for cases to proceed to court and conviction. It would require thoughtful, detailed police work, very carefully done, with attention to detail of all the people involved, and in particular, attention to the woman attacked.

These two documents do provide a standard for investigation of any criminal case in their region, but as they apply the Canada-wide criminal code, they are the standard we want to be able to expect nationwide. CASAC does, however, protest the gender-neutral language that remains in even these policies. The refusal to name the victim as woman will almost always allow for every level of the police to ignore the Charter Rights of the "victims" they are serving and protecting. The degendering of policy regarding violence against women allows for the discretion of the individual officers to take precedence over the policy, over the criminal code, over the Charter.[6] The Ghakal family in Vernon and others across the country paid highly for that failure even though the B.C. AG policy was in place. Bonnie Mooney explains the earlier point that policy is too commonly contradicted in daily practice.

The discretion of the individual RCMP officers is supposed to be limited (in battering cases) with the supervisor's signing off on the check sheets. Embedded in that document is a line of "mandatory checks"—did the investigation include looking for previous complaints?—but then goes on to find out if the success or failure of those past charges are the result of the woman's (here 'victim's') changing of evidence, reluctance, lack of co-operation. These screening options based on ideas about her pervade all of the documents at police and crown level. It is as though they are invited to look for an excuse for the lack of previous convictions and to use that previous failure to excuse a current one and to place the blame for both at the feet of the abused women.

At the crime scene women tell us that the police act out that same inclination. They always seem to be able to generalize in the field any of the sexist errors remaining in the policies. They say, "What do you want me to do?" "Do you want to press charges?" They imagine excuses to refuse to establish the men as the "primary aggressor." They offer her excuses for him that shakes her resolve like blaming alcohol consumption. They tell her the police restraining order won't stop him without offering to stop him another way. They misrepresent the law by telling her she has to wait until he "does something" as though beating, threatening, confining, harassing were not grounds enough for charges. They refuse to arrest him on the current crime or refuse the work of evidence gathering.[7]

All these reveal to her the police reluctance to enforce and consequently construct her hesitancy and reluctance. Some police act like they are doing women a favour, giving women a choice, by asking if women want charges laid. They know women are conflicted for all the sensible reasons women are conflicted about the arrest of men, but police use that momentary reluctance against her instead of adding in the necessary problem solving or referring callers to women who will.

Instead of responding with effective action to women's fear that this man will escalate this time, they respond by using her fear to exempt themselves from applying the policy. Sometimes they act as though they believe they have been trained and mandated as social workers, mediating and pretending to negotiate rather than imposing the rule of law. Often that takes the attention away from securing safety and evidence.

So what if she does let him back in tomorrow? It's not a legal requirement that she promise anything. How are the police instructed to proceed only on those cases that they deem personally acceptable, and which they personally believe ought to be winnable? While the policy is weak it does not account for the repeated wrong-headed understandings expressed by police across the country. They fail to hear that, in law, once police are called in to these events, this is about her and crime and freedom and human dignity, not about the personal frustration of the police or the management of the police time and/or the police budget or even the police version of equality.

The officer on the scene uses his discretion too often in favour of "keeping the peace," meaning the immediate quiet. He should be securing her a chance for freedom from violence and the community's interests in criminalizing violence. So far the policies have not convinced the police on the beat or their immediate bosses of this simple fact. They remain convinced that they are entitled to judge whether she caused it, or whether she shouldn't have been there, or whether she will just take him back tomorrow, or how they should "both" back off and sleep it off. There is no caution in the texts that we could see to the individual police officer to curtail their own resentment and avoid, for instance, becoming punitive and diminishing of women.

It is a common experience for women to be chastised by police during an investigation for exercising our freedom to go where we would like or to do or wear what we would like. It is also common for women to be punished by being humiliated in front of her children for insisting on aid from the police. Sometimes the policy directs them to call in social workers as though the children are at risk when she has been hit. But how and why this is done makes all the difference. Too often police behave as though the woman has caused the violence and pulling in a social worker is the consequence. Children who witness violence are being damaged, of course, but by the hitter, their father, not by their mother. And if seeing one's mother beaten does the damage, surely the best response of the state would be to make sure the children immediately see their mother being respected by the community authorities. Why isn't that policy?

None of the documents regarding battering of wives refer to rape in marriage. It seems there should be a standard question about this. Feminists ask, "Does he force you to have sex?" "Does he rape you?" or "did he rape you before or after the assault." During any safety assessment, police should be asking if he threatens or blackmails her into having sex before or after he is violent. Of course such questions are only safe after they have removed him from the scene, while they are taking her formal statement. This will provide them with another level of understanding of what she is facing, add to potential charges, give an indication of potential medical care she may need, the stipulations required on any no-contact order/bail provision.

A Document Review: Crown

Women express in recent years almost as much anger at the behaviour and manner of the Crown personnel as they express about the police. But we find that anger much less informed and so much more directed at personality, courtesy, and manner. We know that in spite of crown and court-based victim services, women have very little or no comprehension of what is happening to them in court, and in preparing for court, and they are often ignorant of who is responsible for it. Not telling women what we need to know forces women to comment on personalities and exercises of personal/professional/political discretion instead of legal processes.

Often the protest at the end of a trial more properly belonged at the beginning. We know that prosecutors are overworked and that the jobs are under-paid and in many places prosecutorial work is now a dead end job left to women. The few women who get as far as court have rightful expectations of the system of justice and should not be so often disappointed. Most of the women working with us and calling us are unaware of the Canadian particulars of the interaction between the political directives from the provincial and federal Attorney's General and the protection of independence of the courts. Much more education is needed here. That information should also be available to women and their advocates seeking justice on their particular matter. It is in the interests of the justice system to reveal the political.

Women and the general public, we suggest, are unaware of what to expect and what work to demand and how to complain effectively about prosecutors. It is not in the interests of a good system to keep women ignorant of these legal processes and methods of accountability. In fact, we think there needs to be a more serious examination of how to introduce equality seeking into the consideration of which cases to prosecute and how, from the perspective of honouring the legislative intent of the Charter and the case law interpretations that have accumulated. There is a pressure from the bottom that can assist in the accountability of the system in moving toward a better and better delivery.

Too often both American television and the police with whom she has worked give women the impression that the prosecutor and judge are exercising only personal opinions against her even when they are doing a good job. The political directives from elected officials are invisible to them as are the rules of court and evidence. They are quick to see the nature of law and legal processes as malleable to political and personal interpretations of legal officials, but they are too often deceived about exactly from who and how the pressures are coming.

More materials need to be developed like *Tell it to the Judge*[8] designed by a family law lawyer in B.C. to help women cope with the courtroom dilemmas of how to speak. This is the kind of material that cannot be developed within the system but must come from trusted advocates in the community. Funding such projects or circulating them once they emerge could help many women to direct their anger usefully in their own case and collectively. We include this example because there are few such documents to instruct women how to cope with the crown.

If sometimes we, as women, are ignorant of what should happen according to existing rules, CASAC is aware that the system itself has almost no information about what actually does happen. Few lower level court processes are recorded or digitalized. Few administrators at the provincial or federal level are aware of the normal handling of violence against women. The process of recording only the exceptional cases works against proper understanding, supervision, and policymaking. But it is with this level of the prosecutorial process, crown obligations, and lower court judgment that we are most familiar. Consequently, when speaking to each other, advocates, and federal officials are describing two realities.

Women know to demand to be seen before trial but rarely are. Usually they are held off by the crown-based victim assistance worker who shows them around the court house or court room, but has no equality driven understanding of why the woman has complained, and what consequently she may need to know to participate fully in her own case. Women are taught to be in awe instead of comprehending the system. And they are virtually never taught how to get the best from the system unless by an advocate. Jane Doe's story, as told in her book and somewhat less vividly in her movie, tells about this promotion to isolation, inappropriate individuation, and patronization.[9]

Advocates are rarely treated with respect by the crown, as though to declare oneself as interested in one's own advance as a historically disadvantaged group impairs the case. Must the crown insist on disentangling each incident from the social understanding before it can be tried fairly? We don't think so.

Often women are advised to drop their connection with advocates so as not to offend the judge. Victim assistance workers who claim a direct link to the wishes of prosecutors tell them this. Even when system personnel tolerate advocates, they do not regard advocates as a useful part of the legal struggle or as important discussants in the construction of the legal case. But this divide and conquer tactic often convinces the women complaining that they must be dishonest about this support because the crown prefers their isolation. It communicates instantly that the crown sees no relationship between this woman and disadvantage. Often it seems to us the legal professionals try to exclude advocates and the community groups they represent in order to avoid the work of informing and accounting to the community. Sometimes the motivation seems as banal as to avoid any critical over sight of their work styles or legal methods.

The individual women are handled with a combination of charm, rudeness, maintenance of their ignorance, and then a reminder that they are ignorant when they express a concern or opinion about their case. It works in the short term but usually backfires sooner or later with anger and non-cooperation from the women.

Many women, both within CASAC and within the group that calls us for help, are very opinionated and have definite judgements about not only how they should be treated, but also about what should have happened at every court step. Their lack of information, however, may undermine their judgements.

Few women succeed in entering the courtroom to complain or witness against violence compared to the numbers that complain to us and even compared to the numbers that complain to the police. That drop-off drastically affects the accumulation of expertise. Even the advocates are much less informed of the rules of court, the methods of insuring fairness, the possible actions, and the democratic considerations at stake. Not only do we need much more research at this level but also advocates need access to learning and teaching opportunities.

The speed with which courtrooms are emptying of violence cases, however, and alternate processes are being privatized may make such interventions a waste of time. There is no role tolerated yet and no role expected for equality advocates in the new privatized mediation, restorative justice, and counselling-based approaches to justice. We think that will exacerbate every current problem for women but hide those problems at the same time until women reorganize to collectively protest or until the system of justice is in such disrepute that women abandon it altogether.

Quebec, New Brunswick, Nova Scotia, Newfoundland/Labrador, and British Columbia all have Crown policies/directives from Attorney General/Solicitor General etc., which we were able to get and analyse. All but the Quebec government deal almost exclusively with violence against women in relationships, or battering. Quebec alone has a complete policy regarding sexual assault, including a training manual for crown on the social/political context of rape.[10]

We are left wondering why the two sites of violence against women have been separated from each other as the first step in attending to violence. It seems a backward initial step. Surely a policy affecting the relationship between women's equality and violence should have come first to be followed by the specific needs of each crime site and relationship that supports abuse.

There are three documents that speak about women's equality as a consideration which are worth thinking about:

New Brunswick Public Prosecution Manual—Chapter X—Family Violence[11]

590-1-2 Since many complex social factors arise in a decision to prosecute or to continue a prosecution where the accused and the victim live or lives together in an intimate relationship:

(b) Violence against women is depriving many women of their ability to achieve equality;

(e) The elimination of violence against women requires a strong response by officials responsible for enforcement of the law.

Crown Counsel Policy Manual Core Policy, Ministry of the Attorney General of B.C.—Charge Approval Guidelines[12]

2. Public interest test: Public interest factors in favour of Prosecution;

(j) The offence was motivated by the victim's race, national, or ethnic origin, colour, religious beliefs, sex, age, mental or physical disability, political views, or sexual orientation.

A handbook for Police and Crown Prosecutors: Criminal Harassment[13]

4.4.2 Evidence at Bail application hearing: Consider invoking Section 7 (life liberty and security of the person) and Section 15 (equality before the law and equal protection and benefit of the law) of the Charter of Rights and Freedoms in balancing the victim's right to safety with the accused's right to freedom.

These documents are no doubt well intentioned, but are weak, and thin in any understanding of the case law and the general promise of the Charter, it seems to us. They certainly cannot be seen to be a forceful application of law to the urgent situation of violence against women. Together they make it clear that much work needs to be done to promote attention to improving the normal crown counsel response to sexist violence.

They also indicate the weakness of the political directive coming from each Attorney General or Solicitor General by each provincial government. It can hardly be seen to be giving the matter political importance.

The above are all in policy or directives to Crown about battering, not sexual assault, and do not seem to apply where the charge or plea bargain hides the violent or sexist nature of the criminal incidents, or the normal occasion of the charge not matching the event in seriousness, or comprehension of the events are part of a system of repression. So many of the situations in which an equality analysis would be useful simply slide through the screen, nearly all are cases of plea-bargaining and pre-judgement diversion, for instance. This would also be true in most cases of charge consolidation as well.

The Quebec manual mentioned above quotes Justice L'Heureux-Dubé extensively, including her analysis from *Seaboyer* on rape mythology. It should also be noted that while the Quebec documents go to great lengths to describe the condition of women and violence against women, the Quebec researchers found no actual policy that would change any of that condition. Again we deal with government policy that acknowledges injustice without redistributing the power that would end the injustice.

The Quebec policy seems to be heavily based in the case law: *Seaboyer, O'Connor and Mills*: all describing the Rape Shield law in its various forms. There is specific direction about the victim's records as a result. In the documents, the equality interests are to be considered and factored in only at Charge Approval and at Bail Hearing.

There is no indication that this line of thinking should be applied to each step of the prosecution. There are some other notions included that we do value. "Since woman assault is a crime and will be treated as any other serious criminal matter, the onus is on the police and not the victim to initiate the criminal process."[14] This would be a somewhat useful application of law, but it is also true that woman assault is not just another criminal offence. It is a human rights offence, a challenge to Charter promised equality, a matter of systemic injustice, and requires a specific approach, and seriousness quite different from the crime of robbing a bank for instance.

Police are to consult Crown as soon as possible about the possible prosecution of the charge, and "reconciling is not, in itself, a sufficient basis upon which to stop a prosecution."[15]

> The Crown should be particularly vigilant when the offence involves spousal assaults and when there have been any previous breaches of Court Orders by the accused...[16]

But vigilant of what, remains the question. If he has already breached, surely the route is already determined. Constantly building in the possibility of non-accountability for men is the problem.

Many of the documents remain degendered: "spousal," "domestic," "victim," and as such, reflect no will to particularly ensure these crimes are prosecuted or prosecuted with equality in mind. While degendering implies neutrality or universality, in fact, it is the application of formal equality at best and damages women's access to substantive equality. The Crown and crown-advising personnel, of course, know this in law and ignore it when they could correct it for the sake of women. Sometimes equality is mentioned in a way that reduces it to safety alone. And too often there is no indication that the political response or the Charter response to violence against women should be generalized to other crimes or the general treatment of women and women's cases of violence.

In B.C., while the AG's VAWIR policy is gender specific at every line, and often speaks to the known and documented conditions of women's lives, at no place does it speak to the AG's intention to promote the prosecution of violence against women especially, and to be guided by its role in securing women's equality.

The B.C. policy on wife assault is the best policy in our opinion and has the potential to influence the case law in violence against women. As noted by the researcher though, too often, cases were reduced (even before pleading) to section 810 Peace Bonds. Is that because the Crowns do not apply Section 15 to the Public Interest consideration?

In any case, the technique of peace bonds has been much debated as a way to move the struggle away from the individual woman by making it a matter of his cooperation or compliance with an order of the state. But too often now the peace bond or restraining order route seems to be understood within the system as ways of reclassifying or gender-ghettoizing the event of violence against women into a space in which it can be seen to be a private matter and not a real crime. The technique of directing the struggle as being between the man and the state doesn't currently work.

The B.C. AG participated in consultations about a sexual assault policy but did not develop one. The political will did not seem to exist to advance the cause of all violence against women. VAWIR policy does not deal with the rape of wives at all, and this is echoed across the country.

Also built into the "good policies" are more and other sidetracking devices that can undermine Charter provisions.

Charge Approval 4.3: diversion or alternative measures it says *may be* inappropriate.[17] This in spite of enormous concern expressed by women serving violated women in every province. The critique has been carried out at the national level in the Justice consultations, and we were promised by Allan Rock that a strong message discouraging such diversion would be put forward by the federal government to the federal-provincial meetings of Attorney's General at least as far back as the year conditional sentences were legitimized. Of course the message has been undermined by the breakdown in federal-provincial relations, which leaves the administration of the new sentences and legal aid problems hanging at the same time. Another shell game?

"4.5.3 additional Conditions: in cases involving former intimates, consider whether the exercise of the accused's rights to child access *may interfere* with a no-contact order with the victim."[18] Are we to infer that his right to access the child whose mother he beats could ever supersede her right to escape him with her children?

In these provinces, referring to "woman abuse" and "violence against women is a crime" in a sloganistic way was perhaps prepared for newspaper copy rather than advances in the use of law.[19] The same policies can avoid advising with specific directions as to which criminal code charges to consider and how vigorously, in which circumstances, which would be the keys to moving the rhetoric into action for women, etc.

Crown attorneys will prosecute a spousal/partner assault charge (there is no such charge of course so what does this mean?) whenever they are satisfied that sufficient evidence exists regardless of the victims/complainants wishes unless public interest considerations dictate otherwise.[20]

Wouldn't Section 7 and Section 15 be in the public interest? And wouldn't the better advice be to pursue a charge consistent with the complainant's wishes? This way of phrasing and conceiving of her hesitancy sets up the system against her. Why not recognize the burden that has been placed on her unfairly to resist him alone and relieve it. Most complainants and witnesses in trials against powerful violent offenders have to be encouraged with safety and enlightened approaches. So do women witnessing against the men who have over-powered them.

Many of the convictions are plea bargains and diversions. Many pleas bargained were for battering. It is still very unclear how many of the plea-bargained incidents of violence against women were committed by men known to the women. This area requires much more research. We suspect that familiarity with her helps attackers use the Crown in and out of courts to avoid consequences and together the Crown defence bar and the attacker avoid the work of equality considerations.

A Document Review: Court

We saw a judge in Vancouver (whose name we lost along the way) speak wisely to a young woman in court. She asserted that the man who beat her and was being held in jail pre-trial could come home to live with her now. They were reconciled. The judge explained that he would not be releasing the man from jail until he had a separate address because the charge was serious and they each had separate interests in the months of proceedings, that those separate interests had to be protected. The assault charge had to be handled. He did not lecture her about her choices or her past choices. He simply took the power in his hands to protect her interests and kept the man in jail until he made other plans and protected her with the legal processes. She was satisfied that she was handled as an adult with full responsibility for having called the police and complained of violence and who may well reconcile with this man in the end. We wished that many prosecutors in and out of the courtroom had been circulated that particular judicial speech for use.

Trying to understand how women's cases are lost in the courts is a life's work of course. And we are grateful to the women lawyers and academics that give their lives to understanding and resisting this force against women. In this WORK, we limited ourselves to much smaller goals. We wanted to get more familiar ourselves with the court room since rarely do our cases move past police complaint, recommendations to crown, and the Crown's authority to deal and divert and past the political road blocks being imposed through directives. It is rare indeed for women to have their day in court. When they get there and face shockingly ignorant and damaging judicial behaviour, they are devastated.[21]

CASAC centres have, in recent years, intervened in high profile cases to offer assistance to women already isolated from advocates and facing alone the commercial media and the alienation of court processes and the hostile political climate.

We have done so irregularly as court observers, as accompaniers who offer emotional support, as political campaigners, and as legal "friend of the court" interveners. This is in many ways an area of work forced on us.

We observe that at the local level, for one reason or another, some women seem determined to challenge male attackers in the courts. They seem to us to be trying to use the courts against fathers, institutionally appointed or surrogate fathers, men with community prestige, and professionals using their positions in the community in particular.

They know the odds of a conviction are not good. They know that they will be pilloried in the press and that the process itself is arduous. But they are rarely prepared for the hostility they face. Many centres now approach women complainants to offer assistance at all levels. Sometimes the initial court battle is only the beginning of the process. This forced us to learn more about the system as it exists and as it is changing and to develop techniques with which to be politically useful. No centre is paid for such work nor for the media and public education work that must follow, but for the movement to ignore the need for it would be foolhardy.

The women's movement internationally is becoming more and more integrated with anti-racism, anti-globalization, and insistent on economic equality. Simultaneously, we experience the abandonment of many liberal feminist leaders, especially those working within the justice system and the professions. Many were only attached in their actions to formal equality achievements. We know that Canadian working-class women are having to acquire the expertise to play more of a role in leading our own legal strategies, both defensive and aggressive, because we want those efforts to contain and be consistent with a world-wide integrated feminist analysis. Of course, in so doing we construct the new alliances that assist women in their individual cases.

The understanding of links between trafficking, immigration, and labour policies controlling domestic workers, and the rape cases they bring is an example. The crown is unlikely to make those connections without our presence. The prosecution of a man abusing his mail order bride is another. The prosecution of a psychiatrist, or police officer, or father requires similar contextualization unlikely to happen in the telling of an individual woman and the hearing of an over-worked crown official. But without that context, the case will not protect the Charter rights of the women involved and certainly will not aid the women who never get to this level of the engagement with system.

Women complain to us about the plea bargaining process, the length of time to get through each step, the manner (behaviour and speech) of the judge, the diminishing of the status of their women lawyers, the not so subtle diminishing through racializing of their lawyers, the continued allowance of the defence's ill-treatment of themselves, being treated by court officers like a mindless agency-less "victim," the disinterest of the key players in the well-being of the women and children involved, the public, uncontested, cavalier (often off the cuff) admonishment for her life decisions.

All of these things are matters of law, not just attitude.[22] They do not show up as problems corrected or behaviour curtailed in any of the documents collected by researchers. The people who impose and/or witness and tolerate these indignities make the decisions and conduct the case legally. Women and their advocates are aware of the breaches of equality and are clearly cognisant of these as statements of the alignment and allegiance of the justice system. Women often complain that even in winning a conviction they suffered more indignity than they counteracted. This is the current state of the system's disrepute.

Our document searching focused mostly on criminal court where we expect to find violence against women but of course it dealt with family courts as well because that is the site of most violence decisions.

Nova Scotia Family Court Act, Section 5 has clear statements of "equality principles." Direction is given to the judges to "strive to be aware of gender, race" etc., to "disassociate themselves and disapprove of irrelevant comments demonstrating discrimination," and "should not be influenced by attitudes based on stereotypes," even going so far as to recommend demonstrating "sensitivity and correcting such attitudes" as they appear in the courtroom. And while the policy does not direct judges to be particularly aware of women's participation in the courts, gender and sexism is primary.

Rewarding and directing such behaviour in provincial and federal courts, particularly those lower courts dealing with criminal cases, would go a long way towards changing both women's perception of the courts and how we are treated while engaged there.

The *Saskatchewan Victim's of Domestic Violence Act* would be an example of exactly the opposite—no specific direct references to violence against women at all, no analysis of the violence in relation to gender, race, or class. There is definitely no way to infer a concern for Charter rights. This act is relating to criminal law, not family law.

We clearly made a mistake in research design by not asking more questions that would link the policy to the charge-tracking sheet.

A Document Review: Sentencing

This area of the justice system remains the most mysterious to the women interviewed, the women using the rape crisis centres and transition houses, and to the advocates themselves. Documents affecting sentencing exist across the country, but few of the researchers were able to get them, in fact, many were denied access to them outright. Most women did not understand the connection between the federal guidelines for sentencing, and the provincial administration of justice policies, and the political pressure for punitive responses to other crimes, and how they work together.

Victim impact statements, as a pre-sentence document, are in use nation-wide. We encounter it more often because these forms and outlines for these documents are often handed to women in their initial crown appointment. They are told to fill them out and hand them in before trial starts. Women are given the impression that they are affecting the case. Of course, they are ignored until the sentencing (after both trials and judgement) and are not a legal statement, but defence lawyers who have access to them pre-trial have the right to cross-examine women on their contents. Often they pathologize her version of events, including her opinion. It sometimes seems to us that women are invited to declare themselves destroyed mentally, socially, and even medically as proof that rape or beatings are hurtful subjugations. A backward legal assertion and dangerous to the case. We have never seen encouragement to express her opinion about how the violence constituted or demonstrated indignity, or even interference with security or privacy, or other expressions of equality understood before the Supreme Court. Certainly she is never asked if his behaviour undermines her equality with him and other men, her ability to live life fully as described in the Charter. She is only asked to describe her interior, her feelings, and her body, and to medicalize those descriptions.

Women are left with the impression too that there will be a direct connection between the harm they assert and the sentence, which is misinformation, of course. When we tried in the project to examine the impact of specific references to violence against women, etc; the impact of the use of gender-specific terminology; and the impact of references to women's inequality, we found ourselves at a loss. The instances of references to women and violence against women are so seldom as to be negligible. And the morphing of criminal and civil processes into medical and "community" ones somehow just disappears from the documents.

The absence of women from hate crime legislation is annoying to many. But inclusion would be of very little benefit since recognizing violence as hate crime in this way would only affect sentencing. The merit we can see in such a proposal is the public discussion that would ensue. Many women are unaware of this omission on the part of Parliament, and the matter has been raised again in response to Svend Robinson's leadership regarding the inclusion of hate crimes against gay people.

When they are mentioned, it is only as a degendered victim or spouse whose feelings must be considered in sentencing. Once or twice, considerations of her safety are built into policy—victim notification of release dates, etc. These are ostensibly so that she can use that information to protect herself: a useful but woefully inadequate response to women's danger. Protecting her or us collectively is not the point in any sentencing considerations that we can see. The references seem to leave the researchers with more questions, and they are unable to find the answers either from a person or another document. Overall, the documents gathered do not measure up to even the most basic demands for law reform.

We did not have a corresponding policy question for sentencing: were there sentencing guidelines? Where they followed? But more importantly, we didn't follow the diversions to various sites. This again is research needed from the grass roots that should be pursued. Our observations are that most cases of violence against women are not criminalized in the first place. of those that are, they are dispensed with as:

- Common assault in response to rape and wife assault resulting in diversion to medicalized responses imposed without legal consideration for equality effect, (certainly without considerations of women's dignity, or equality, and also without mind being paid to men's and boys' rights as accused persons and prisoners);
- Peace bonds with or without bail conditions but no equality and safety considerations;
- Diversions without charges to an education model called "John schools";
- Incarceration of young women in social service centres or juvenile detention;
- Civil Restraining Orders unsupported by enforcement;
- Break and enter charges completely hiding the character of the crime;
- Incarceration for drugs, theft, and other crimes, rather than for the sexual violence;
- Murder plea-bargained to manslaughter.

CASAC has not endorsed a call for longer sentences or greater incarceration, but we have insisted that pre-court diversions must end.[23] We need public, legal, and recorded processes to increase accountability within the courts. Progressive approaches to sentencing are fine with us but the current pretence is not.

Most women never see their cases get this far but when they do, there remains both a lack of information and a lack of understanding. Women using rape crisis centres and transition houses usually report being dissatisfied. Even having come this far, they are offered no hope from the justice system that they will be safer and freer as human beings. And in that moment of disappointment and distress, they are approached by the commercial media and other political forces inviting them to make statements that would satisfy vengeance, rather than equality. We all live with the consequences.

Notes

1. *R v Godoy.* (1999). Supreme Court of Canada pp.21-22.

2. *Ibid.*

3. Others think this too. See: Rigakos, G. (1994). *The Politics of Protection: Battered Women, Protective Court Orders and the Police in Delta.* Burnaby: Simon Fraser University.

4. Told to CASAC in front of a class of students in Aboriginal Studies at Langara College. Tape available at CASAC office.

5. Culbert, L. (2003, September 24). Families say they're left out after talking to media. *The Vancouver Sun,* p. B3.

6. Judge Josiah Woods's inquiry of the massacre at Vernon. Wood, J. (1998).

7. Gorin, T. (personal communication, May 14, 2003).

8. Ruth Taylor a treasured local family law lawyer finally produced her own public education tools for women facing the courts this was one of the most useful handouts we had seen. Taylor, R. *Oh Yeah Tell it to the Judge: Every Women's Primer on Testifying in Court.* Notes available at Vancouver Transition Houses, including Vancouver Rape Relief Shelter.

9. Doe, J. (2003).

10. Gouvernment du Québec (1995). Guide des Practiques Policieres. Agression Sexuelle. Author. Gouvernement du Québec (1995). Agression a Caractere Sexuel. Directive. Enquete Criminelle. Surete du Québec. Author.

11. New Brunswick Public Prosecution Manual (1996). *New Brunswick Public Prosecution Manual,* Chapter X, "Family Violence" (p. 590-1-2). Fredericton: Author.

12. Crown Counsel Policy Manual Core Policy (1999, October 1). Ministry of the Attorney General of British Columbia. Subject: Charge Approval Guidelines.

13. Prepared by the Federal/Provincial/Territorial Working Group on Criminal Harassment for the Department of Justice Canada.

14. New Brunswick Public Prosecution Manual (1996). *New Brunswick Public Prosecution Manual,* Chapter X, "Family Violence" Fredericton: Author.

15. Newfoundland Attorney General and Solicitor General (1996). *Crown Policy Manual: Directive of the Attorney General and the Solicitor General Regarding Spousal/Partner Assault.* Author.

16. *Ibid.*

17. New Brunswick Public Prosecution Manual (1996). *New Brunswick Public Prosecution.*

18. *Ibid.*

19. Newfoundland Attorney General and the Solicitor General (1996). B.C. Ministry of Attorney. (1996). *B.C. Attorney General Violence Against Women in Relationships Policy.* Victoria: Author B.C. Ministry of Attorney General (1999). *B.C. Attorney General Violence Against Women in Relationships Policy.* Victoria: Author.

20. Newfoundland Attorney General and the Solicitor General (1996).

21. The *Ewanchuk* decision and debacle in Alberta is an example of the trial judge; *McLung's* sexism undermining both the case law and required sanction of the judge at the SCC level in order to see to the woman's right to a fair examination of the evidence before the court.

22. Wilson, B. (1993).

23. Lakeman, L. (1993).

May/Iles and Hadley
Wife Murders
and the Use of Coroner's Courts

The willingness of some men to end two lives rather than lose a woman has created its own category of crime."[1] She was referring to the deaths of at least Arlene May and Gillian Hadley. Thanks to the outrage of the community and the advocacy and organizing of the Ontario Association of Interval and Transition Houses (OAITH) with assistance from METRAC, both cases remained front and centre of the media and government agendas for months. Within two years of each other, both focused coroners' inquests on wife assault and both coroners' juries made wide-ranging recommendations for equality-based systemic changes.

OAITH, among others, used these inquests as legal venues in which to intervene on behalf of the women dead and those still under threat in their marriages. Both women had struggled to leave abusive men and had tried to use the state for protection. Both men had a history of violence and were under court orders to stay away from the women. Both men could have been detained and were not. They are typical, not atypical.

In the 1998 inquest into the death of Arlene May, the jury made some 213 recommendations. Randy Iles had been free on bail while facing charges of stalking, assaulting, and attempted murder.

By 2000, Ralph Hadley had been examined by police in the previous six months for incidents involving threats and actual violence against Gillian, his ex-wife. Each time he was released.[2]

We fear Risk Assessment is the newest boon-doggle for government funds. Already there are lobbying efforts to use the public discontent with the justice system in these cases to train, test, monitor, and evaluate risk assessment tools. While we have no objection to such tools, they will not compel officers to do the right things, nor will they deal with the time limit attitudes and promotion/peer review issues that seem to most directly affect these decisions. What assessment tool could possibly be necessary to improve on the understanding that each official would have made in dealing with Iles and Hadley? Officials including court personnel, prosecutors, police, all knew these men were dangerous to their ex-wives. No check-off list is needed. They had repeatedly threatened and abused. Law and policy was available. Criminal justice resources were available. The media coverage of the May/Iles inquest should have been adequate reminder to those dealing with Hadley.

According to Statistics Canada about one in five women who leave a violent partner will continue to suffer abuse—often on a more severe scale—after the separation. The killing of a spouse accounts for at least one of every five homicides across Canada. Femicide!

Adequate police enforcement will deter men from breaking court orders.[3]

But we must decide, too, if the process of examining deaths in public inquests and inquiries will make a difference. CASAC argued for inquiries and the public funds for the participation of equality-seeking groups.[4] In these cases, the process did respond to public pressure and did focus some government attention on the problems. Some new transition house beds have been funded, and some policy changes have been made. It was massively time-consuming, expensive, and, so far, only minimally productive. The Ontario government has already adjusted away from the most important recommendations. For instance, although deaths from wife assault will be examined, the results will be revealed only to the chief coroner's office. The public response will be controlled through secrecy. There is no obligation to reveal to the public the results of those examinations.

The 24-million-dollar introduction of a new divorce court system is promoted as a response to the murders and inquiries, but is, of course, something that was planned much earlier as a response to the costs of the administration of justice. That planning has not been adjusted to better insure equality interests.

Notes

1. Huang, R., and Appelby T. (2000, June 21). Baby Saved as Husband Shoots Wife. *The Globe and Mail*, p. A3.

2. Luciw, R. (2000, June 23). Risk Assessment Could have Saved Slain woman: Advocacy groups. *The Globe and Mail*.

3. Eyherabide, E., and Shess, P. (2000, July 2). Spousal Abuse: How to Stop the Killers. Law-enforcement Officers Must Treat all Acts of Domestic Violence as a Crime, Say the San Diego District Attorneys Pioneering Spouse Protection. *The Globe and Mail*, p. A11.

4. Lakeman, L. (1993).

Another Hundred Women
Tell Their Stories

In the interviews we were interested in what a new group of women might tell us of their experience trying to use the "justice system." We were also curious about what they understand about their entitlement to dignity, equality, fairness, and justice from the system. We also attempted to hear what understanding of the law, equality, and violence the rape crisis workers and the women themselves hold.

CASAC LINKS interviewed 108 women during the course of the WORK. These women were callers to their centres, callers and users of other centres within the region of the participating LINKS centre, or women who answered a public invitation for participation in the research. Over the course of the research and analysis of the data collected, 92 interview subjects were accepted and their interviews analyzed.[1] We want, too, to thank those women who offered their stories even after they knew that they would not meet the research criteria.[2]

The following interview analysis quotes those 92 women and sometimes the advocate researchers. The findings were consistent with the experience of the other women from their centres, and the stories told to them by thousands of women who call the rape crisis lines and transition houses every year. We understand these interviewed women to be a small sample of the women who use both the Canadian state and CASAC in their response to the sexist violence done to them by men.

Official documents were collected. These included policy and procedure manuals for five levels of the "system": the 911 level, the police level, crown involvement, the courts, and for sentencing.[3] However, overarching all these documents are the *Charter of Rights and Freedoms* and Canada's international agreements as articulated in the *Convention on the Elimination of all forms of Discrimination Against Women* (CEDAW). We were interested to see how the state avoids convicting. We speculated that both sexist images of the women complainants interfered, as did a failure on the part of state functionaries to apply the equality provisions of the law.

We agreed with both the Canadian government in legislating the Canadian Charter of Rights and Freedoms and endorsing CEDAW as to the relationship between equality and violence. Since those documents are both accepted and promoted by the government of Canada, we grouped women's experiences, as described in our interviews, to see if and how their experiences revealed the law being delivered to or accessed by the women involved.

Most women who are victims of male violence, in whatever form, do not involve the state. They do not call the police to report the crime and do not voluntarily involve the system in any way. Only twenty to thirty percent of the women who call our centres also call the state. This figure has remained the same since the first surveys in the 1970s.

CASAC women continue to debate whether and when it is wise for women to use the state and when it is dangerous. We debate when policy changes serve other state agendas more efficiently than they serve women's equality interests. "Mandatory" arrest policies, for instance, are still controversial. But it has been the policy of all CASAC centres to support the will of the women calling regarding their personal situation and their personal decisions about how best to cope.

Consequently, all centres have always assisted women who call the police, complain to crown counsel, and complain to the state about the violence they have endured or survived. CASAC has never wavered from the belief that women have a right to use the rule of law and the involvement and protection and relief of the state to assist them in resisting their oppression, including the particular acts of violence we call violence against women.

For the purposes of this WORK, CASAC decided to interview only women who had called on the "justice" system as a response to a criminal attack by a man. Rape crisis workers were trying to learn more about what, whom, and how forces were thwarting the efforts of those women who did want to use the system of "cops, crown, and courts."

Although it was not part of the initial research design, workers, we learned later, set out to find women with cases that had an evidentiary potential to last in the system. In hindsight, workers accounted for this by saying they thought perhaps only their centre had so few women who wanted to report and that they worried they would not have enough cases unless they pursued willing women, beyond their own callers, as research subjects in the first research year. We did not anticipate this in the design but see the logic of the researchers now.

Because of this choice, we have stories that continue through each stage of examination. Instead of the array of "worst cases" in which women's complaints are dismissed early or even an array of "normal cases" in which most women's stories come to naught, we have interviewed a group which stayed in the system and proceeded in many instances to conviction. That this is not typical of what is experienced in our centres was confirmed in the minutes of our last meeting between CASAC Regional Representatives and researchers.

Even this group with an unusually high conviction rate expresses meaningful discouragement. Their distress and thoughtful dissatisfaction are evident in the stories they reveal and the judgments of the workers to whom they are speaking. It is consistent with our overall experience of thirty years that even these "successful" cases fail to meet the standard set in law.

Hundreds of women responded to our call to participate. The discourse, the back and forth education about violence against women, about our equality and expectations of liberty, the daily teaching and learning about the law and the criminal justice system: all of these played a part in grounding the research, and in developing the analysis of the research data. Keeping all of that in mind, the workers at the rape crisis centres who participated as researchers and forged links between centres in a pan-Canadian conversation, their co-workers (paid and volunteer) at the rape crisis centres, transition houses and women's centres, the women who complain about violence to us, have all cooperated to produce a collective wisdom in this report.

In this section we have limited ourselves to the answers given to the research questions as they emerged in the dialogue between researchers and those interviewed. In the qualitative research used here, we were interested in how similar and unique these next hundred women's voices would be. Although there is no quantitative design to the research, we have included numbers at times to give a sense of whether we are speaking of single or multiple experiences or perhaps even normalized experiences of the system.

What 100 Women Say About Emergency Response

In most of the country, women have access to some form of emergency state response to an attack. This is not true on reserves and not true in many areas of the north and rural Canada. But our study was based in urban centres. Usually, the woman interviewed has 911 emergency services available: where an operator takes a call, and makes a determination as to the nature of the emergency, and sends out the ambulance or police. For some women, a centralized 911 is not available and the local police, municipal, or RCMP act as the first emergency contact.

There is no nationally consistent 911 service, nor is 911 consistently part of, or overseen by, the police or any other emergency services of a region. Over the course of this work, many 911 services have changed, have been amalgamated, or are in the process of being so. In British Columbia, for example, 911 services are now privatized under a corporation that coordinates responses for the whole of the province. In Nova Scotia, 911 services for the whole of the province are answered out of Halifax.

We were interested in the nature of the assessment methods, the tracking of calls, and whether calls are assessed and routed in a way that maximises women's safety and equality. In some regions, as in Newfoundland, there was no access to 911 available to the women during the time in question. The women in these regions call upon the Royal Newfoundland Constabulary. In Nova Scotia, where 911 services are centralized in Halifax, women in the outlying areas, like Antigonish, rely upon the RCMP and make complaints to them directly.

- Far fewer women called 911 than we expected;
- Women called 911 themselves and fifteen women dealt with 911 because someone else called for them;
- A total of 37 women dealt with 911;
- In 49 cases she called the police directly;
- In 23 cases someone else called for her;
- A total of 73 women contacted the police instead of 911.

For some of the women who did not call 911 where it was available, they did not because they believed their attack did not warrant an emergency response. They themselves did not deserve such a response, or they judged that the danger of future violence increased because of the use of 911.

It was no surprise to us that women don't like to bother caregivers and hesitate to regard their own needs as emergency. But we were surprised that 911 operators are clearly not trained to handle the reality of assisting women.

> At the time, I didn't think of this as a crime really. And he always sweet talked me, or convinced me it was my fault, what had happened. I felt sorry for him too.

> No. I didn't think to call them because I was so ashamed at what happened and blamed myself for drinking and going with strangers in the first place.

She did not call 911 because she "didn't want to cause a scene. It was me."

> Question: What do you mean?

> Answer: I'm not important. I feared for my life if I tried to call 911.

Sometimes women cannot sensibly trust that calling for help will be safe. And this study does not provide reassurance that calling 911 will get women quick, equality-based intervention, and safety. Regularly, the imminent danger to her is neglected in the 911 processes: In only ten cases did the emergency response actively assess her safety.

Her ex-husband beat her. She tells the operator the attack is over because he has left but he has a gun. In the past and in his threats to her he expresses suicide. The police judge him more a risk to himself, rather than to her as well as himself, in spite of her judgment and knowledge of the opposite risk. Well, that risk is public knowledge.

> I told them I had been assaulted by the neighbour. They told me I was not the only one assaulted that day. They asked where he was, where the assault had taken place. They said the police officers will give me a call and then hung up.
> I called back, and that's when they said there were other people requiring po-

lice assistance, and I should be patient and wait. They hung up again. I called back and insisted. They were rude and hung up on me. She said if you get off the phone and stay off the phone then the police can call you.

Half an hour later the police came into the driveway, they hadn't called, they just showed up. There were two officers.

It was September, Labour Day long weekend. The Indy [a high profile annual car race] was on. I called 911 because he had called me at work. I said that a man with bail orders had violated the order. They asked if I was safe or in immediate danger. I said I needed to report this and get something done. Because of Indy, the operator told me it would take up to fourteen hours to get a police response. I said I'd go to my friend's house and call back the next day. In the end, I waited until the next day, and I called again, explained the details to that operator, and asked could they send someone out now. I asked how long it would take. They said they didn't know.

Sometimes he could be a danger to others and quick action could be preventative as in this stranger assault:

I called the police; it had to be around 10:30 p.m. I was very distraught; I had to take a breather. I sat down for a little bit and then I called. I told them, "I've just been mugged," and she said, "Hold on I'll transfer you to dispatch." Dispatch answered and I said, "I've just been mugged, I've just been attacked, please send someone right away." She said, "Yes ma'am, no problem." Then, I went downstairs. It's a secure building with a glass door, and I sat there and it must have been at least 45 minutes and still no one had shown up. So, finally I went back upstairs, it took me a bit of time, and I called back and asked where the officer was. They just complained that they were having a busy night, saying, "Sorry ma'am we're very busy tonight." "We'll try and send someone as soon as we can." I went back downstairs, and I waited and waited again, and finally an officer showed up.[4]

Sometimes there was benefit to the woman other than getting a police response, in that she got some emotional reassurance from a call handler:

Female operator answered and she was fabulous. Things had calmed down but the operator suggested she would call me back and she did, and then she (911 operator) called the RCMP for me.

In only five cases did 911 operators keep her on the line until police arrived. Contrary to popular mythology and what women see on TV all the time, the 911 operators did not usually keep women on the line, instead took the information and said the police would come or the police would call. Women responded that they were surprised about this, especially in cases where they judged that the situation was volatile and their fear was elevated. The interference with his isolation of her was part of what the women were seeking.

They do not ask if the attacker is her husband or ex-husband. It is a vital link to any assessment of the imminent danger. The danger of ex-wife murder and assault by ex-spouses is common knowledge now. It is shocking to realize the implications of maintaining a wilful ignorance. All women should be assured quick intervention and proper policing. In our judgement, the risk to life and security goes up tremendously if the man threatening, harassing, or even lurking has been an ex-husband within the last two years.

In one case where the caller, who is racialized, is known to the police (because of past calls of wife battering), the 911 operator did ask about weapons and elevated the priority of the call as a result. The police arrived en force in this case and arrested the man. The inappropriate, racialized and infrequent nature of this leaves women wary and not trusting of the police: "They take their sweet time. If he came down to kill me, then what, I would have been dead."

> I called and explained that my husband had dropped off the kids and assaulted me. The female operator asked "Is he there now?" I said, "No, he has left." The operator then said that the RCMP would get in touch with me soon. She didn't ask anything else.

In this case the RCMP did not respond to the call and the woman called again and the police still did not attend to the call.

Women Did Not Get the Emergency Medical Treatment Required: In Only Five Cases Did 911 Ask if Medical Care Was Required

This woman called following an assault by her husband. The police did not ask about injuries despite the fact that it is later revealed at hospital (she went on her own the next day) that she suffered a broken tailbone and broken nose. She had a dependent baby at home and in the emergency she did not want to leave without the baby. The police did not secure her safety or that of the baby.

> They just told me about shelters. I told them what was going on, but I didn't have any visible signs at that time, I guess. [Interviewer: Did the police take a statement?] I'd written one before, the time when I called them at 9 p.m., but not this time that I can remember. [Interviewer: Did they take pictures?] No. [Interviewer: Did they talk to your neighbours?] No.

Women were not advised as to how to secure themselves in the situation (i.e., going to a shelter, securing her locks, having someone come over).

> An RCMP officer called one hour later and asked if my husband was still there. And he asked what happened. He then said that he was getting off shift

and couldn't come that night. He said, "I will come talk to you when I get back on shift" (in three days). This RCMP officer never called her back.

They didn't give me numbers for victim's services or a transition house—they didn't give me anything.

They sometimes make the situation worse by asking, inferring, or suggesting that she was exaggerating the danger by inferring she was in the wrong.

No, nothing was said to make it easy for me, there was no concern, no caring attitude, I was treated as if I was a nuisance, I was made to feel as if I was add-ing to their workload, like I was making it up.

No, they don't make anything easy. They ask questions in different ways. "Are you sure? Are you sure?"

In the case of this woman calling about her husband's attack the response is: "Is it an emergency? Is he there now?"

While it was rare, a woman did tell us of a full and helpful response from 911: 911 as-sessed the level of danger and got the police there in force. The caller had indicated weap-ons, past assault, children in the home, suicide threats.

They wanted to know what was happening, if he had weapons, where my child was, what was my name and information. They kept me on the phone. They wanted to know if he was on drugs or drinking, and his name and his birth date. I told them all that information.

Women call for help in situations where they understand themselves to be overpowered and at risk, and are clearly calling for state intervention to save their lives and liberty, even if they have low expectations of delivery of that aid. Women expect to be treated with respect, to be taken seriously, and to have the police attend, immediately.

Women did not get immediate, dignified, or secure treatment of her person, or of women in general, as promised by the Charter of Rights and Freedoms. We can even say that sometimes 911 staff and the police collude with patriarchal power against her or against women in general. Women are made to feel sometimes that they are either a nui-sance and/or that their situation does not warrant emergency response. Often they are encouraged to feel grateful that someone believed them at all. They rarely experienced that we have given all as a community using state resources determined to assist her.

100 Women Assess Initial Police Response

CASAC has documented for ourselves that 70 percent of the women who report to rape crisis centres refuse to officially report the crimes against them to the Canadian state. That percentage has remained fairly constant for thirty years. Anti-rape workers dis-cussed it in our first national exchanges in the 1970s, and we discussed it in the May 2003 meetings between the CASAC regional committee members overseeing this report.

CASAC has speculated and surmised at various points that women have many reasons for not reporting, but in this study, we looked to see if one factor is their understanding of the inadequacy of the protections of rights including women's rights in the criminal justice system. The women in this study decided to report and were consistent in their efforts to engage a response that worked for them.

Did the police come? In 60 cases the police responded. In 15 more cases she went to the police station herself to file a complaint as an immediate response to the attack. In the other cases, the attacks were historical and an emergency response was not required. In the following case of an ex-husband attacking when at her place to pick up the children for visitation, the police did not respond:

> An RCMP officer called one hour after (the call to 911) and asked if my husband was still there. And he asked what happened. He then said that he was getting off shift and couldn't come that night. He said "I will come talk to you when I get back on shift (in three days)." (This RCMP officer never called her back.) Ten days later, I called the RCMP and said that no one had gotten back to me. He came within an hour, took my statement. He wrote as I spoke, then I signed it.

> The following day, I took myself to the hospital with a friend (at the suggestion of her lawyer) and had my injuries documented by the hospital (bruises, head swollen).

On the whole, women say that the police response was timely, except for some notable exceptions, as in the case mentioned previously where the 911 operator stated the police wouldn't be attending for at least fourteen hours because of the Indy race; also the case above where the police did not attend at all, and the following:

> The police said that they would be there within a half hour but did not show up until two hours later. "She had to make a second call to see what was taking so long. She was afraid the attacker (her boyfriend) would come back," noted the LINKS worker.

The definition of timely manner was not responsive or inclusive of her safety, prevention of crime, and respectful of her. The following positive example of police response is rare. In this situation the woman has called about her current husband's attack and the police respond within fifteen minutes. She called directly to the police, not through 911. The police in this case arrange for her immediate safety and prevent imminent harm by taking her to a transition house and arresting him.

> They were very nice, supportive. I wrote down what happened, he read it back and I signed it. He told me they were going to press charges. I didn't want this. I told them this. They gave me 45 minutes to pack and meet them back at the station. They offered to come with me to get my stuff. I started crying because I was sad and felt stupid for not knowing the law. I had to go to a transition house.

There are a few cases where the response from the police demonstrated a serious attention to the threat and danger she is experiencing. Two notable examples involve a stranger rape where the police attend promptly and take the woman to the hospital for forensic exam. The other is the case of a racialized couple when the man, who is known to the police, attacks his wife and she calls the police. The man is known to have weapons, and there are children involved.

> The police came, brought dogs, when they came in they took all the things they needed for the court—coffee cups, bedding, my housecoat. They took me to the hospital in the ambulance, the ambulance attendants were fine.

> They came within ten or fifteen minutes. Police cruisers and a van came. Maybe eight officers came. He's well known, that's why. When the police came, I walked out to the alley to meet them. They wanted to know if he had outstanding warrants that I was aware of. They ran his name before they went in. They asked if he was alone with my baby, if there were any other exits, and what he was like temper-wise. I told them what was going on. They asked if he had weapons, and I said, "Not that I know of, just kitchen knives." I told them what I knew. They wanted to see picture id from me.

Women told shocking stories of police responding to their situation with what they interpreted as disdain, disbelief, rudeness and, in at least one case, blatant racism. This does not seem to us to secure her dignity as a person or her general liberty. Nor have these women been treated in a manner that suggests respect for women in general. Women are reluctant to call in the state for fear of rejection and disbelief, and the response from the police in many cases underlines the reason for their mistrust.

> I remember going up to the police station, going up to the desk, to the female, *not* the male officer, thinking she would be more compassionate. But she was loud, and asked questions of me at the desk, in the lobby: "What kind of Assault?" "Was it Rape?" "How did I know him?" "Where and how did it happen?" "Did he ejaculate?" "Did he complete?" "All in public!"

> I went to the police and the police say, "Why did you wait?" So I said, "I was scared, and the policeman was one of his friends." So, he knew I was French, and he was French, so he made the interview in English, and he was completely French too. I was really upset with the police. I said, "You're one of (husband's) friends," and he said, "No, I just know him like that." And he tell me that he is going to arrest him, and he's going to be in jail for the week, and he called back that night, and he said, "Well he's not in jail," I say "why," and he say, "because he's working."

A young woman tells:

"My mom said to call the police right away," and I did. They (police) wanted me to go there, to the station at 11:00 p.m. I had no way of getting there, "Can you have an officer come and get me? I don't have a vehicle, there are no buses after 11:00 p.m., and I'm certainly not walking there." They said, "No, we're not a taxi service." I said, "Fine, well I'm coming in the morning then." He says, "Well this must not really be important to you then." I'm like, "No, I just don't have a way of getting there. Do you want me to get killed or raped on the way there? It's called common sense here pal. I'm not like you, I don't carry a gun with me everywhere I go." So, I went in the morning.

We called them and they came over. They sent two investigating officers, one man and one woman. The man was obviously the main investigator. He was tape recording and he wanted all the details—he was very rude. It's like he would get mad at me because I was crying and stuff. He would stop the tape and yell at me. He'd ask me the same question over and over. He'd say, "I'm not here for a joke, if you're just making this up." He was there because it was his job, not because he wanted to help someone.

The police came and they were really ignorant. After I told them what happened they asked me, "What did you do to get him so angry?" After that I wouldn't answer any of their questions. I couldn't believe they were blaming me when I didn't do anything wrong.

He is Eskimo, he was wearing shorts, and they said "okay, chief, get your coat." So there were racist remarks. I was going to say something, but I thought it wasn't up to me anymore. They said, "I'm tired of you Indians beating each other up." The police never looked for weapons, but maybe because I told them there weren't any.

When women call the police and request intervention in an instance of male violence, they expect that the police will protect them, arrest him, confirm with evidence that a crime has been committed, and that someone other that her believes an injustice has been done and will be righted. Often police did not attend to safety and her personal security.

The woman's ex-husband had called her and told her he was coming over with a gun and she should call 911. When she reports to the community police and asks that they come around to her house they respond with "why should we go to your house." The woman's reaction is: "I guess I live in a dream world."

Her husband beats her and terrorizes her. Nine hours later she escapes while he is passed out. She goes to the police. They agree to arrest but have trouble finding him. When the husband calls to say he is coming over she calls the police to let them know. She asks that they not announce their arrival because she is fearful he will become violent again if he knows she has called them. They endanger her by agreeing to the plan of having him in the home alone with her and ring the bell when they arrive instead of coming straight in.

She is physically assaulted by boyfriend/common-law and runs out of the house. She called 911 and told them that a man has beaten her. Police take her back to her place where she expects he still is but he is gone. Police say call if he comes back knowing that he lives there and surely will return. She is hesitant to leave perhaps because this is subsidized housing she cannot afford to leave to him.

Her husband was choking her in front of her infant daughter on Christmas Eve. Her family arrives and his brother arrives for a celebration of Christmas and they all hear her. Her aunt goes downstairs to her grandma to call the police. They wait an hour for the police who stay two hours. The police separate them: him with baby and police in one room and her with family and another officer and her husband's brother who is a lawyer in another room. After questioning the police ask her if she would like to leave and she says "not without my baby." Police say there is no threat in spite of the visible marks on her neck and face and the witness statements. The same officer says to her mother that he didn't feel this was a dangerous situation and that in spite of her mother's concern it would be safer for "all of us to leave." She pointed out that if there was a suspicion of abuse they had an obligation to press charges. They continue to respond as if she were asking a question about the appropriateness of a charge rather than that she was asking for implementation of the law and policy. No pictures are taken and no charge is recommended.

Ex common-law is harassing her. She and her sister return to the flat to find that he has broken in. He was gone. She and her sister call 911. Police responded quickly in seven minutes. Attacker comes back as police arrive. He has a friend with him. They separate them to get statements. Then bring him into her flat saying, "They are trying to resolve it in a way that will work and quickly for both parties." They do not arrest him. She had already inquired weeks earlier about some way to restrain him and had been told she did not have grounds or a means. Her perception was that she was being stalked and this event of "break and enter" was a dangerous escalation. They suggest a way for him to get his stuff at a neutral site and warn him verbally to stay away from her. He calls her again and she calls police: "in the computer it is a resolved case"…on yet another occasion he is warned again. There are at least four reported events. Her sister observes several of these. He is eventually charged with criminal harassment but not until she and her sister think there have been many dangerous moments that could have been prevented. She suspects that he is charged because he has been picked up on a charge of sexual assault of another woman. After that they pay more attention to her statements about him.

CASAC can only imagine they now perceive him as dangerous when they did not before, maybe because this latest attack is not on "his woman."

This woman is, in her own words "mentally challenged." She calls police with the benefit of a feminist advocate because she says men are coming into her apartment without her permission and assaulting her at night. The advocate asked the local police to check on her that night, but the police respond: "we don't do that, why would we do that?" After more advocacy an officer does come to her house that night. The police did not take a statement or help her secure her house or advise any course of action. No investigation proceeds as to the crime or her security.

Woman was raped and reported to the police after a few days. Police take her statement and do video statement with a detective. They keep her pants from the night, which we can assume is a search for DNA, and put out a warrant for a male witness (hostile). They told her they couldn't find him. She phones often for news and tells the police that she has learned that her attacker is in jail now on some other charge. "The file is in the drawer inactive and we will pull it out when he rapes another woman." There was no charge laid. She was a young woman partying and they don't believe her or don't believe she will be believed in court. So we wait for the next rape that will surely come.

Woman reports to police after lengthy history of wife assault including beatings and attempted rape and humiliation in front of her twelve year old son. She escaped to transition house with her son and reported to police two weeks later while still at the shelter. They took her statement but told her they did not plan to arrest because they had warned him to stay away and he was now at his job. They did charge him later with assault. But she, the other women at the shelter, and her son all had to live with the lack of arrest.

He is her neighbour. She is a woman of colour. She sees his attack as criminal harassment, which she had already reported to police, and that their inaction now allows the resulting escalation including sexual assault with bruises. In that case too they do not lay charges but lecture both about "respecting neighbour boundaries." Later when she has film documentation of her injuries and the medical report, they charge him with theft and assault ignoring the sexual nature of the assault; he grabbed and twisted her nipples.

At the time they treated both as offending parties, and, therefore, communicated to him that he had crossed a social, not legal boundary. She irritated police by insisting on her rights. She received the lecture too but had not crossed any legal boundaries.

Women colloquially ask for restraining orders or peace bonds because they have learned about them from TV or friends, but it is a common language way of saying someone more than her needs to be involved in stopping him. Commonly women have little or no experience and knowledge of the law when first contacting the police and the state for intervention.

We are not lawyers, nor should we be expected to be. Often police perpetuate the illusion that women can decide whether a charge is to be brought, rather than reinforcing that the crime is one against the state and the law of the community. The police are in a position to explain all the options to her and to take the full power of the state to ensure her safety and security. In many cases this is not what happens. In the case of the woman from above whose ex has broken into her apartment:

> So I went to the police to get a peace bond and they said "we don't do that here" and they told me to go to the Public Prosecution Service. They asked "was he threatening you?" The reason I hadn't gone to the police was because I was afraid the police weren't going to take me seriously. The RCMP officer asked me: "Are you legally separated? How do I know that you are not harassing him? How do I know that he's not entitled to be there and you are harassing him? Just call your lawyer." My lawyer said, "There are good cops and bad ones...you got a bad one." "I had the right to live in my house."

She is distracted by the police from getting police protection for which she has already called, explaining the difference between civil and criminal peace bonds and restraining orders, instead of charging him appropriately or restraining him appropriately.

> She tells the police three months after a rape about a whole history of abuse from an ex-lover who used to live close by. They had dated when they were neighbours. The rape she is reporting happened after the break-up and after his moving. She tells a story of rape and abuse involving other men as well and of his threatening to come back. When she moves and is ready to tell on him she says she wants a "restraining order." The police respond that they would only be able to do that if they gave him her address.

As though there was nothing they could do on the basis of the past criminal activity or the current criminal threat.

It is often true that attackers get the woman's address through the process of seeking a civil order through the courts. This can be prevented and sometimes is.

> She has left her husband because of his abuse and finds out that he has been bothering the children at school. She seeks a "restraining order" and police

come to her house for a full statement. "The officer said that there is so much that it would take all day to write it out, so one officer says just tell of the one assault with a weapon to myself, and each of my four children and I could lay other charges later as there is no statute of limitations on assault." A fuller picture might have better informed crown, and she could have been better informed as to what an order could do and not do and what charges might proceed and might be provable.

The older male officer dominated the interview stating, the "facts," discouragingly, that they could arrest my husband if I wanted to charge him with assault, BUT he would be released in a few hours, and that nothing would be in place to stop him from coming home and being even angrier and hurting me even more. Did I want that? The female officer was repeatedly but quietly saying on the side: "You know you could charge him, you can go ahead if you want and we will keep the file open." I got the feeling that she would have laid charges if the other officer weren't there. I felt like the charges were useless to pursue because the male officer basically told me that it would actually make things worse. I was naive because I had no idea about the law. Basically this was another man telling me I was overreacting, and that was just what my husband was telling me. I really felt pretty powerless in this.

A knock came at the door and he identified himself as police. I was on the phone with the women's shelter. He asked me questions like, "Is there a problem here, and what do you want?" I told him I wanted my dog and my car. I had my ownership in my hand. He said, "I already told your husband he could go back to the Sault. I told him he could take the car." He already talked to my husband before knocking on the door! My husband says the same thing all the time, "she's bonkers, she needs help, and she's sick and so on." "My destiny was already decided outside that door." "I didn't make it clear that I wanted him to be charged with assault."

She believes it is up to her to educate the police about the possible charges that can be laid, this despite physical evidence of an attack and possible witnesses to question. They do not take a statement from her and do not proceed with an investigation or charges of assault.

A woman reports past rape by uncle. When giving her statement to the police:

He told me some of the things I was telling him weren't as serious and he didn't write them down. He was professional about it. He tried to use words that were softer, not harsh. He tried to be objective. He asked me to start from the beginning—what incident I first remembered. And, he let me go from there. And, he would ask were there any other incidents I remembered. I was aggravated that I couldn't tell him everything because he would say it wasn't as big and we didn't need it. This led to me having to give another statement later on. He could have done a better job. He did a good job, but it could have been better.

We wanted to know how do police deal with the question of formal vs. substantive equality and compounded inequalities when responding to male violence against women? Such a definition of equality should be embodied in the application of the law, in the use of resources and the attitudes modelled from the first and most common moment of contact with the system: initial response of the police to a crime.

It's not really a question of being treated as equal, formally or otherwise. It's whether or not she's going to be treated as a human being. So many of the women I spoke with, especially native women, were treated like they did something wrong to begin with and were bothering the police by calling them. And I hate it when I work with a woman and have to tell her that no matter what I think, and no matter how much I believe her and don't blame her, the police will likely make her feel like there was something she could have done to prevent the attack from happening. Especially if she's young and has been drinking. Women are all sluts to them then.[5]

Women want to feel validated when they call the police. They want to speak to a woman cop because they think she is more likely to understand where she's coming from. In some cases it's really helped to have a woman there. I think we should have that as policy everywhere.[6]

She is a woman of colour. Her boyfriend physically attacks her; there are bruises on her face. She calls 911 and the police arrive approximately 45 minutes later. They take her statement, give her their card, and tell her to call them next time he comes around. When asked to comment about the police she responds, "They took so long to show up. They were treating it like, oh whatever, this happens to all the Native women…" The police did not investigate, they did not take pictures of her injuries, and the case did not go further. He was never charged.

Young woman is attacked, attempted rape, by casual acquaintance at a hotel. There is alcohol involved, drugs, and possible situation of prostitution. It (the statement to the police) took about two hours, word for word, detail for detail. Then he sat there and goes, "O.K. let me just take five minutes here and throw out some comments to you. How much had you had to drink?" I said, "five or six drinks," whereas I'm used to consuming 10-12-15 drinks. "Well, rye is a pretty heavy drink for a woman your size, you know you're only supposed to have two or three or so (police)." Like I mean come on. How many twenty year olds do you know drink one an hour? He asked me, how much have you had to drink, who were you with, did you provoke them in any way, were you talking dirty to them, did you have intentions of having sexual intercourse with them in their hotel room, did you give them the impression that you were? How do you really know if you don't remember all the details? How do you know that that actually really happened? I said, "well why would I have bruises on my neck and hands for one, if I was just going to the bar socializing with my friends? Nobody goes up grabbing people by the neck and hands...you know, and I was crying through all of this. It took me two hours. He said, "here's a pen we'll let you re-read it, and anything that is not in there you just go ahead and write it yourself and put your initials. He signed the bottom, I signed the bottom, and I said, " can we take pictures now?" "No, that's not necessary, we'll do it some other time, besides, we have your statement (police)." And that was it.

Nothing further comes of her involvement with the police. No charges are laid in connection to her attack. However, bruises on her neck and wrists would indicate consent was not present.

A stranger at a dance put on by a predominantly black social club physically assaults a white woman. She leaves with male friend who is black, and they call 911. "Police attend and are racist and dismissive of the danger to her."[7] They were rude, disrespectful, and unwilling to go after the assailant. They were insulting me and laughing at me. They were actually abusive but seemed to be enjoying tormenting me. They took my friend and I into the police car and asked what happened. They asked things like, "Is he your pimp?" and "Are you one of his girls?" I told them I wasn't a hooker and they kept laughing at me and saying there was no way they were going after this guy. I was really angry. They asked my friend if he was a pimp. He said no. He was so embarrassed. They asked him if he saw what happened and he told them this guy walked over to her, out of the blue, and hit her in the face with his cast. He didn't know the guy before either. I asked them to come back to the social hall with me and I would point this guy out...the guy that did it. They said, "No. We're not getting involved in this kind of thing.

The woman is francophone. Her common-law husband of three years continues battering and attempted rape and murder threats, "my lawyer told me to contact police" the officer to whom she reported is francophone and recognized her as francophone but insisted that they speak in English. "So, he knew I was French, and he was French, so he made the interview in English, and he was completely French too."

Aboriginal woman, possibly drinking, who they suggest has to leave her house after a domestic dispute. She doesn't want to leave her house, saying she pays the bills; it's her house, so why should she leave? During that settlement, "One cop grabbed me, pushed me up against the wall, and handcuffed me. He swore at me several times and said he wouldn't put up with a stupid bitch like me."

Ex-boyfriend who stalks and has assaulted her, and the cop says: "you get yourself into these things, you got to get to know someone first. Why don't you hire a PI?" Blames the woman for faulty judgment instead of the attacker.

The woman is explaining why she was reluctant to call the police when her husband beat her up. She had had bad responses in the past. "The response time of the police was always despicable. And their actions once they got there. They always under-reacted. Like it was 'just another day in the North end'."

When responding to a case of wife battering involving a native man and woman, where there was drinking involved, the police arrest her instead of him because she is seen as being non-responsive and uncooperative with them. They do not arrest him, rather they tell him to go outside and cool down, and do not consider the woman's situation of past abuse or financial dependence on him. They do not recommend a transition house, do not secure her safety, or promote her equality.

I didn't tell them what happened. I just sat with my head down. My friend told them. [My ex] showed them his papers with my address on it. They said, just go out for the night and calm down. I didn't want to make it worse with [my ex]. He was right there. They charged me with that charge you get when you're hurt and don't want to go to the hospital.

Native woman is physically assaulted by her common law. "The police came and they were really ignorant. After I told them what happened they asked me, "What did you do to get him so angry?" After that I wouldn't answer any of their questions. I couldn't believe they were blaming me when I didn't do anything wrong." The police end up taking a statement from her friend who has also been assaulted but do not pursue the matter of the crime against her. Their dismissal of her prevented her access to the law.

After accessing the police file through freedom of information, one woman learns that the police do not proceed with investigation of the crime because they say she is out for revenge. In her statement she had in fact answered to the question: "what do you want to happen": "I want him to pay for what he did to me, to know he has committed crimes against me." In this case the police have deliberately taken her statements, which to a woman is read as a plea for someone to intervene and confirm that he has broken the law, which he had, and not impugn her motives. She is not treated equally under the law and is denied access to the law by virtue of being a native woman who presumably did not know her place.

- In 36 of the 92 cases the attacker is "picked up" for questioning;
- In only thirteen cases is the attacker arrested immediately;
- Thirteen women do not make it past the initial police response;
- The majority (nine) of the women of colour were dropped at the police stage of the system.

The police did not take further action. As documented in the police section of the research report there are lots of incidents of overt and subtle racism by the police and this explains to us why they do not proceed. The underlying assumption seems to be that the woman of colour and her man, who is a man of colour (except in the case of neighbour sexually assaulting her: she is woman of colour and he is white. They both get peace bond) deserve their lot and are wasting the time of the cops and the rest of the system.

There has to be a case built to convict. There has to be a proper police record of the call, an adequate investigation, a recommendation brought to the crown, an application made to the court. Secondly, it is more than useful if there is an open and respectful relationship between the woman complaining and those working in the justice system beginning with the emergency response and the initial investigators.

Emergency services do not respond to the particulars of violence against women. Sometimes the medical emergency is sacrificed for the case and sometimes the case for the emergency. There is a lack of training for emergency staff. Staff are pressured with too little time to ascertain the danger. They have too little information and a lack of appropriate classification of calls to assess the situation. There is a lack of priority given to violence against women calls.

When we started the LINKS project, we assumed that women usually call 911 in an emergency. We imagined that, by now, the various systems in place to deal with these emergencies would have protocols to prioritize these calls and send out appropriate police response. We weren't prepared for how few women actually call 911. In some cases, because it isn't available (as was the case in Newfoundland), and in some cases because the system is new and women are used to dealing with the old system of local police detachments (RCMP and local) as is the case in Antigonish.

In many cases, women did not use 911 because they thought their situation either was not, in their eyes, or would not be seen by others as an immediate emergency, although the danger was very high or a violation had already been carried out. But they did expect that the government, including these emergency services should respond to violence against women for themselves as well as for other women.

Of the 67 attacks reported that were in the present or immediate past, only 37 women used or had someone else call 911 (22 women called them on their own). For a lot of women, the reason they gave for not calling 911 is that they don't think their situation is an emergency, in the sense of immediate life and death; they don't think they warrant that kind of attention or, as in one case, "you can't call 911, you just get beat worse next time." Often the 911 responses were inappropriate or inadequate in that women needed faster, more inclusive responses made on the basis of information about danger and risk. Such assessments are unlikely in a situation where the operators are not trained or allowed the time to make such decisions.

Usually 911 centres don't seem to be the place where the cases get dropped. There are some cases where the 911 operator did not fully do the job: as with the case in which the 911 operator told the woman she would have to wait fourteen hours to see police at her door because of the Indy race; the one in Fredericton who told her that the RCMP would call her back, and they never did and did not show up. In both these cases, the women were persistent and finally got attention for the attack. But it didn't make the complainant go away or the case get lost at this point. Emergency response, in the broader sense of police and RCMP, Sureté de Québec, responding to the first call or seeing the woman in person, is not so positive. In some instances, the police desk clerk is rude and gives no weight to the dignity of the woman reporting the crime (there are several cases where the woman is put in a public situation to answer the questions) but these aren't the situations where the cases are lost either. The women persevere through the experience and do get to see a uniform officer. They build that perseverance on the political understanding that violence against women is a matter for government intervention.

Notes

1. See Designing the Research: Stepping Into The River section of the report for criteria and process.

2. It is interesting to note that some women participated in the interviews knowing that they did not fit the criteria for inclusion. They were eager to tell their story, and the fact that the results would not be published did not stop them from telling their stories to the interviewers. Of the sixteen interviews not selected for further analysis, most were rejected because the time of her involvement with the state fell outside our criteria, and some because she did not chose to use the state at all.

3. See appendix for list of documents collected and Designing the Research section for methodology.

4. Researcher's note: Initially, according to the police, the first call was not recorded, and the second call was recorded at 12:00 a.m. The first call was finally tracked down at a later date.

5. *Ibid.*

6. *Ibid.*

7. *Ibid.*

911 Death By Indifference in Winnipeg

Nicole Robillard

CORINNE MCKEOWEN and DOREEN LECLAIR are dead: stabbed to death while the 911 operator listened to their fifth disregarded call for assistance. William John Dunlop murdered them in February 2000 in their Winnipeg home.[1] He was a vicious ex-partner of one of the women, and he was more credible to the police than were the women themselves, and more credible than the two decades of information available to police and their staff as to the pressures on women in the moment of reaching for assistance in an emergency.

Shamefully, the tapes revealing the failure of the 911, and police response were not released until friends and relatives forced that release through the courts. Initially the courts provided access to the transcripts after an application by media businesses. "We want the people to know exactly what the hell goes on with 911 operators," said Hank Meadows, brother-in-law of Corrine and Doreen. He lives just a couple of houses down the road from the murder scene. He said people could read the transcripts over and over and not get the true sense of what happened without hearing the tapes.[2] We think the transcript alone contains plenty of information.

- *9:00 p.m.:* Ms. McKeowen called 911 claiming her friend had been shot and no one cared. Police responded. When they found "no one hurt" they accepted the false name offered by Dunlop, therefore, also missed that he was under a restraining order to stay away from the women, and that he was just out of prison and had a serious history of violence. They say they were convinced by Ms. McKeowen's insistence that there was no problem. We have no statement from her of course.

- *11:52 p.m.:* Ms. McKeowen called again, "I am having trouble with a guy that got out of the pen, and I have a restraining order against him." "Uh, well right now this man is not at home, and uh I'm visiting my sister's place. (He had taken money and gone for beer). Now this man is threatening me, he already stabbed me." Since he was not in the place the operator reasoned it was not an emergency and told the women to call the non- emergency police line.

- *12:15 a.m.:* Ms. Leclair did as she and her sister were told and called police directly. "They are not fighting yet, but he has stabbed my sister." "He what?" the operator replied. Ms. LeClair repeated, "He has stabbed my sister." "Ok, well one of them has to leave so you choose which one," the operator said, as the initial part of her lecture of Ms. Leclair who then handed the phone to her sister. Also part of that lecture was a patronizing accusation of drinking too much, and a quiz as to why the women had admitted Dunlop in the first place, and a personal legal opinion of the situation. "OK, so, Ok right now you guys are both in breach of this order (the Restraining Order on Dunlop). You are not supposed to be around each other," says the operator. She promised to send a police car, but then, "So he is not even there?" says the operator about Dunlop being out for the beer.

She retracted that promise of help and told them to lock the door while Dunlop was out getting beer. "Ma'am he is not gone, he just phoned, and he's on his way back." Operator says, "You know what, you guys are lying to me." The operator mocked them for wanting the police to remove someone already gone, then advised them to lock the door and refuse to share in the beer he was buying with money he stole from them.

- *2:46 a.m.:* The women called 911 again to complain again. "Oh please help me, they're fighting," Ms. Leclair said. Dunlop was in the house. She had been patched through directly to police, and the operator engaged the women for some time and promised to send a car. It never came.

- *4:45 a.m.:* A woman can be heard moaning and dogs barking wildly. The line goes dead.

- *5:15 a.m.:* (thereabouts) The operator calls back to the house and gets Dunlop reassuring her that "everything is fine." That he is Hank Wacko.[3] After failing to get a woman back on the line the operator dispatches a car. The police find the women dead.

In the police investigation that followed, five workers are held responsible for the decisions. This is not one error of judgment but a systemic problem. Jack Ewatski, the police chief, said two dispatchers, a civilian, a duty inspector, and another unnamed fifth person who quit were responsible.[4] Racism is denied. Sexism is not even considered. Class bias is obvious.

January 19, 2001, New Domestic Abuse training begins in the Winnipeg Police Service. October 29, 2002, Judge Judith Webster releases her report into the inquiry and recommends a complete review of police communications in Winnipeg and the hiring of more staff.

Notes

1. 911 Calls Unheeded; John Dunlop Murdered Two Sisters: Pleads Guilty (2001, March 13). *Canadian Press* wire story.

2. Lunney, D. (2001, May 3). 911 Tapes Released (Sisters Died) Tapes release lauded. 911 tragedy broadcast publicly. *Winnipeg Sun.*

3. Hank Wacko is a stage name in professional wrestling.

4. Perreaux, L. (2001, May 3). "You are lying to me": 911 Operator. *National Post*, p. A3.

Preparing **the Case**: The Detective's Job Determining **the Crime**

Normally, policy indicates that the initial police interview is to be followed by an interview with detectives once a report has been filed. Usually, if the police come a second time, they take a statement: 73 women made an initial statement, 38 have a second interview, and 56 make another statement with detectives.

For the purposes of this research, we interviewed women with cases that would most likely stay in the system. Our criteria was clear—that, in our opinion, a violent crime had been committed against a woman by a man, that this woman wanted to engage the system and had done so after January 1, 1997. In many cases, the women had engaged the help of a women's centre, rape crisis centre, or transition house prior to involving the police. But in some cases, she has proceeded on her own or with family support. It is our assessment that these women are unusually persistent in their use of the system. They are confident that they have a right to state intervention, and these interviewed women were unwavering in their steady and persistent expectation of state action.

> In our centre we are lucky if the woman gets past the investigation and the crown recommends a charge, let alone conviction of a crime. In all my years of working with women on the crisis line, I have seen three men get convicted and given some kind of sentence for beating her up.[1]

One worker says of one of the women she interviewed:

> "I was so impressed by her tenacity and by her determination. She had to hound the cops into doing their job. I don't know if it was me whether I would have gone to so much trouble. And this is talking from the point of view of someone who calls the police on behalf of other women all the time.[2]

> I know some women have chosen to do this on their own and I think they're very courageous. It's a difficult thing to do without back up. We have to fight all the time to get women to be taken seriously by the cops in this town. In the end, she got a better response because we were advocating for her, but it's never an easy fight. You'd think the cops would just automatically proceed when they know how hard it is for her to come forward.[3]

Her husband assaults this military wife after they move off the base. She calls 911 and the RCMP call her back and ask her does she need them? Her husband is standing next to her at this point so she says "no." Later she sees the police drive by and she runs out to the street to flag them down. She receives police response in this case because of her persistence and determination.

Do They Take Pictures and Collect Evidence of the Crime?

Women know that bruises, cuts, and other visible signs of damage matter as evidence in a police investigation, and they aggressively point them out to police. To the women, it is proof enough that a crime was committed and it is ample proof, in their minds, to have him arrested and charged. Yet physical evidence of the crime is rarely collected and the police consistently do not take photos of the injuries for their investigation. Police took photos of a woman's injuries in only six cases.

> Woman is raped by an acquaintance. She is persistent about police involvement. "They took no photos of me. They voluntarily called me once, returned one phone call in beginning, then took two and a half weeks to get them to return my calls, and then going through the SGT, it took at least eight to ten calls. They did not interview my friend, who was the first person I told, they did not go to the place where the attack happened to collect evidence."

> Woman had visible signs of bruising on her neck as a result of the physical attack by her husband. No photographs were taken, no evidence was collected, and even though they were there for approximately two hours, only a one-paragraph report was made at the police station.

> So, when I got there, they brought me into a room and said, "Okay well— cause I had bruises all on my neck from when he held me down, and I had them on my wrist as well. Well, they didn't take pictures; they said they would do it next time. I said, 'My bruises will be gone away then, you know. I mean, they're already purple and blue right now, tomorrow they will be green, and they will go away the next day. Like come on, they wouldn't take pictures; they said we'd do it another time. They're going to be gone.' It doesn't matter, we have your statement" (police).

> Woman has been confined by common-law partner for eight hours and manages to escape and contacts the police. Did they look for other evidence? Take pictures? "No, just my word. Other than the policewoman looking for marks the day I reported the assault."

> Woman is the victim of a stranger rape in her apartment. She is confused by the police's lack of concern for physical evidence. "I would have checked if there was hair on me or traces of semen or body hair. That's what I found strange. No one checked my body or my clothes, they didn't keep anything."

The police did take a sketch of the assailant two months later, but failed to collect forensic evidence that could have identified a dangerous attacker.

We are so unaccustomed to the police taking photos and treating women's injuries in a serious manner that in seven interviews we did not ask and, therefore, could not ascertain whether the police took photos.[4] When the police did record or photograph the injury, in one case they told the woman the injury was "too small to photograph," implying, in her opinion that it was too small to matter.

In the instance where a complete police investigation took place and where a complete body of work is presented to the crown, the man is convicted of the charge of sexual assault with a weapon against his common-law wife:

She has been confined to her apartment by her common-law husband for two and a half days, physically assaulted, and raped. "After the forensic medical exam, the investigators were waiting for me and asked if I could make a statement. I agreed in order to get it over with as soon as possible. We went to the investigation centre of the sexual assault division. I told my story" (verbal statement). A photo technician took photos of everything that might show up my injuries. The investigators came back and asked me to write my statement. This was twelve hours after I first arrived at the police station, but I wanted to continue. They asked if I had a place to go. I was given referrals to resources for battered women. I chose to phone a girlfriend whose address was unknown to him. The investigators drove me there. They told me they'd be back the next day to pick me up to search the apartment and make the arrest. "You must come with us to identify the right person. You will be safe."

The next day the investigators came to pick her up and explained they had search and arrest warrants. They assured her the attacker wouldn't see her. "When we left the police station, I was with the investigator in the car and I was chatting with him." All of a sudden, the respondent saw the attacker across the street, who came to get the car. The investigator and the technical team arrested him on the spot. I went with them to the apartment. I had the keys. The place was completely clean. I was furious. He had left a note saying he was sorry, to forgive him, and come back. I thought to myself he must be an idiot if he thought I'd go back. He didn't realize, as if what had happened was unimportant. The note would be a first piece of evidence because the police officers said he knew he had done something." To look for evidence, the police officers asked her to tell them how the place looked before it was cleaned up.

The mop was in the bathtub, proof that the place had been cleaned, and also the respondent never left the mop in the bathtub. Clothes had been washed and hung up to dry (he had thrown wine at her) and traces of wine were found on the walls. The bedspread had wine stains on it, etc. Under the bed they found the board the respondent was attacked with.

In one case, they took as evidence the pants the woman had been wearing, and told her when she was concerned that she didn't know the man's name that they have ways of finding people. Yet, she had to call the police to inform them that she knew where he was and still no response from them: "They kept the pants I had worn too. Later, when I found out where he was, I told Det. (blank) he's in jail in Surrey, please go look in computer, and I'd do a line-up. He said he couldn't do that." There is only one case of wife assault where the police took pictures of the scene of the attack.

In the following case the police not only neglect to conduct an investigation of the premises, they pretend that their hands are tied and that the assault is really better handled in civil court.

He was out in the bushes when they came. He just came out of the bushes right to them. They arrested him then. The whole conversation happened out in the yard outside. He was in the back of the police car, threatening me, giving me the finger the whole time. They gave me a card for victim's services and explained the differences between a Restraining Order, and Section 810 Peace Bond. They were probably there for fifteen minutes or so. We telephoned the police to tell them about the knife. They stopped the car, got the knife. They left me with my parents. They did not offer a transition house or anything like that. My mother actually worked at Women's Place at the time. My parents got there right after the police. The nice cop, he said he was frustrated with the system, said there was nothing he could do, he really wanted me to go to family court about custody of my son.

Often the lack of concern for evidence and conducting a proper investigation results in nothing being done at all.

There was no investigation, except for our names. They did not ask about the clothes all over the yard. C at the time was supposed to refrain from drugs and alcohol. He was on probation. And that night, he was drunk. So the cops did not check him out. The police did not take a statement. There was no further follow-up by the police.

I don't think they conducted it in a proper manner. I'm the one that had to get the documentation of the bruises. I had to call the RCMP twice. The first one never got back to me. A week and a half later one came after I called again. I don't think they ever spoke to my husband about it.

There were many examples of women being needlessly humiliated or suffering personal indignities.

They told her that they were going to do a video statement. She had to sit in front of male officers and lift her blouse and skirt to show them her bruises and the fingerprints on her and boot marks from the perpetrator. This was very embarrassing and difficult to do. She was not told that they were going to do this, and she would have asked for females to be there, not males. She felt she was re-traumatized. The woman from victim services was harsh and made her feel worse and shamed. Everything was so rushed, very cold, and uninformative. Things were not explained to her.[5]

She felt embarrassed as she was still in a Johnny shirt at the hospital when all six police officers showed up. Afterwards, it took about six to seven hours to get the investigation officer to show up. They questioned her in her Johnny shirt in a cold room. She told them she was not comfortable being there with them. They showed no understanding or concern for her. They told her she had to stay and finish a statement. One officer asked her why she would not look at them, and she told them she was uncomfortable with them as they were men and she was just raped by a man.[6]

I'm very disappointed. I'm disgusted with the way they talk—professionally. It's all the same—monotone. They just come out with whatever questions are on their mind. They blamed me...Just say no, no is no, and you're not to blame, is repeated over and over in the policing course. It should be drilled in their head by now. You don't say that. They'd rather be doing something more exciting, and they don't want to have to fill out the paper work.

There's no way I would ever treat anybody else the way I was treated.

He (the investigating officer) was kind of mean. He scared me when I called him once to tell him that I ran into him [the rapist]. I called the police who said, "you called me to tell me that?" I felt I was losing his precious time.

They made her sit down and answer questions in front of a man who was there for other reasons. She was very uncomfortable with being observed. They did not tell her not to shower, or tell her to go to the hospital for a rape kit, or anything. They were very insensitive and did not seem to believe her. She felt very exposed.[7]

In 35 cases they did interview witnesses, but did not in 26 cases. There is missing information on this point in thirteen stories/interviews. The police say in quite a few cases they did interview other people in connection to the case. But this level of investigation is often conducted in a way as if to confirm that she is not a liar, rather than uncover evidence that supports a charge against the attacker.

A stranger who confines her to her apartment for several hours before he escapes rapes her. "The next day I went into the station. Const. E. took my statement.

Told them what happened. He did ask me if I had any reason to make it up. I was very upset and said no, no of course not. He tape-recorded our conversation. By the end of the interview, he said he believed me. When I was doing the statement, the taxi driver who had driven him that night had come into the station and given a statement and seemed to know where he was. At first, they didn't believe him, but then they found the guy—I wouldn't be safe now if he (taxi driver) hadn't come forward. Police took no pictures nor took me to the hospital but Const (blank) did take note of visible bruises. I was at the station for a couple of hours. They took a statement from my mother, too."

She was raped. The police have forensic evidence taken from hospital, identify injuries, but do not take photos. They interviewed her friend. Cab driver that drove her home the night of the rape was interviewed. Doctor at hospital and crisis worker were interviewed. "The officer (blank), called her to let her know that she was still working on the case, and that the police had interviewed the accused, and his sister, her former partner."

In some instances, the police do appear to interview witnesses for the purpose of getting more and better evidence for conviction.

The woman is attacked by her husband and has bruising around her neck. She contacts the RCMP who attend, and she makes a statement. The woman reports that the RCMP talked to her neighbour who verified the presence of the red marks on the woman's neck from the attack. This neighbour agreed to testify in court. Although useful as a witness to the injuries, the same could have been achieved by photos of the injuries that the police did not take.

Two men, a business acquaintance, and his friend, who is a police officer, rape the woman. The attack began with drugs in her wine at dinner and later at the man's apartment. For evidence, the officers wanted to get the cassette from the security camera in the lobby of the building in which the woman was assaulted. The building's janitor refused to give it to them at first because he didn't know if his employer would agree. The officers told him that he would be charged with being an accomplice to the crime unless he gave them the cassette. The cassette was handed over and it proves that the woman was with the two men on the night of the assault. There were roughly 80 witnesses in the restaurant. Some of the witnesses were questioned, and they confirmed what the woman said.

Often the woman has provided the witnesses and sent them to police or directed police aggressively to them herself. We could not find an example of police thinking of and finding someone who would or could or might have given evidence that could be useful, for instance, neighbours, or professionals, or friends, and relations. It is speculation, of course, but this did indicate in some way an attitude toward the seriousness of investigation and the application of investigative techniques.

> The next day, Thursday (after calling police) she went to the station with her mother and gave an oral statement. The officer wrote it down. A social worker was also in the room, but her mother wasn't allowed in (she would be a witness). Then she was asked questions about her statement and was asked to name other victims or witnesses. She named her two friends who had also been assaulted as victims, who then became part of the whole court process. She also named five witnesses, who were never contacted.[8] "They took my statement, my mom's statement, I brought witnesses to them, my running partner's statement." He pled guilty.

> The woman has laid a complaint of wife assault. She gives them ten or twelve witnesses: her doctor, coworkers, friends, and parents. The police do interview all of them and eventually charges are laid against the husband.

Sometimes the police use her evidence as a way of prosecuting him on a lesser or less revealing charge, as in the following example.

> She is sexually assaulted by two male co-workers and goes to the police. They take her statement, and polygraph the two men. The results of the polygraph suggest the men did not lie. The police say to her that they will not proceed with the possible charge of sexual assault but could still get them on a public mischief charge.[9]

We wondered was the investigation conducted in a way that added to the understanding of the law? Women often find the process of engaging the state as a response to the violence done to us completely overwhelming. We lack knowledge about the system, about the law, about what we can and should expect from the police, and the investigation. The whole of the system is generally out of our experience. We expect that the process will be explained to us and that the professionals, in this case the police, will aid us in getting a conviction.

Police and other professionals substitute words like "charging him," "peace bonds," "restraining orders" for what women actually seek when going to the police: safety and security for ourselves and those around us and acknowledgement that a crime has been committed. In public legal education materials, women are taught to trust the police to keep us safe, and yet we are swamped with examples of what happens to women when they report against a man, especially reporting rape and sexual assault. The contradictions confuse women and make us distrustful in the face of state power. In most cases, police did not take the opportunity to educate about the law, the system, or about a woman's rights generally as a person.

> They were very nice, very warm, apologizing for keeping us waiting. They separated my friend and me; they needed to talk to me alone. They did not take a statement, only talked about very general information, explained the Rape

Kit, how long it would take, and explained the court system, explained with me being out of province, they wouldn't be sure of the timeline of everything. They were encouraging of me because it is something they specialize in, and it is their job. They drove me and my friend to the hospital, walked me into emergency to get checked in, waited for the nurse, bought us coffees, and waited in interview room with us. They wanted to ask my permission for the female cop to sit in and watch—she was new. The nurse did the forensic kit, and gave the kit to cops at that point. The unit is all at the hospital. I went in after the medical to give my statement. It wasn't as bad as I thought it would be, especially with the female officer (everything from the beginning of that night to the coming to them), they discussed when they would do things. For instance, they were supposed to call witnesses. At no point did they call witnesses though, my friend called them.

He did end up giving a statement. They said as we were leaving, "If you are in touch with so and so (another witness) tell him to give us a call." There was one phone call where I phoned to find out if they had talked to him (the attacker). I kind of got a verbal tongue lashing, you know, "we're busy, don't tell us how to do our job!" It was three weeks before they contacted him, and then they asked him to come in voluntarily. They did arrest him that day. They released him on his own recognizance. He did not appear before a judge as far as I know. They actually called me for once and told me they had arrested him and the court date. This was a phone message. I called back and they explained the court process. My biggest concern was would I have to come back to testify? They kept saying they didn't know. I think I may have omitted (to tell them) something because of their behaviour at first.

The front desk clerk's initial behaviour did not promote this woman's full access to the law when she made her ill at ease and unsure if she remembered to tell them everything. The woman is very grateful when the police tell her something about the system and believes she is being informed. However, they obviously do not explain that the attacker had to have been before a judge to be released, that there would be no preliminary trial without his appearance in court, and that it is within the right of the accused to come into the police station on his own steam. Despite the police's appearance as good guys and on her side, they still do not do all their job, do not interview witnesses, do not keep her informed or behave in a way that suggests she has a right to be informed about her case.

This woman was raped by her ex-lover and says the following about the interview with the detectives: "I didn't tell the police everything while I was being videotaped. I didn't know how much I was supposed to say, and he never asked me to give more detail."

> The woman's common law husband beats her and she calls the police. They tell her she must leave the house, but she refuses at first. "This is my house...I pay the bills so why do I have to leave?" They said, "He needs to sleep...he has to go to work in the morning." I told them I didn't think that was right because I was the one who was assaulted. I showed them my bruise on my back and they said, "How do we know it wasn't there before?" They told me my boyfriend said he didn't do anything to me. Then they told me again I had to leave. I was afraid to argue, so I said I'd have to call my sister to tell her what happened and ask if I could stay over at her place.

The police in the above case could have taken the opportunity to tell her that if her name is on the lease she does not have to leave, or could have told her about her right to public housing units, or her right to her things, or her right to information.

In some cases the police not only neglect to inform women about our rights, about the law, and what we can expect of the system, but in some cases deliberately misinform.

> The constable came to my work, he was young, but nice...but it was embarrassing. He said, "I'm here to get you to sign this thing, for charges. The Crown wants you to...but you don't have to. It's going to make things worse" ...so I asked him "if it was your sister, what would you tell her to do?" He said to "get a peace bond." The crown does lay a charge against the ex-boyfriend (section 17, assault level 1). The woman in this case did not believe the police constable and inquired directly to the crown.

In the following example, the woman, who is pregnant and beaten by her husband, is confused and misinformed by the police.

> As for the no-contact order, I wasn't informed of the options I had, or given any choices. The officer said if I didn't want him to come after me, I'd have to write a statement that I was afraid and afraid for my life. And I knew he'd be angry since he'd just been charged, and that he lived in the apartment too. The officer explained what a no-contact order was, but not how long it would last or much else. I didn't know about peace bonds. So that's what I did. I was afraid and in fear.

Or in the case of the disabled woman who was beaten by her husband:

> I called that officer back to say I was on the night shift and they could contact me in the day. Then I called the Domestic Conflict Unit, and they said the officer has to investigate and make a charge before they can contact me. [Worker: Did they do anything about your safety?] No. They mentioned a peace bond. I asked how much it would cost and they said $800. But I can't afford that. I'm on Income for the Severely Handicapped and Canada Pension.

A woman, when she wants the police to charge her husband for a rape that occurred some time ago: "I wanted to charge him with the rape, but they said it was too long ago."

The implication for the woman is that there is a statute of limitations and that it had passed already. Another implication, of course, is that she should have gotten over that a long time ago, and why would she want them to bother with that now. In some cases still the police deny her the right to the rule of law. In response to going to the police to report a rape, the woman is told that most sex offenders don't get charged and maybe she should reconsider laying a complaint.[10] Sometimes police destroy evidence:

> Woman is escaping an abusive husband who is also involved in drug trafficking. She is fearful that he will find her in her new location. The police officer offers to write to her social worker to promote the granting of a cheque to pay for a ticket out of province. This could be an escape route for her. The police officer abandons the case though and it does not proceed. The woman got herself safely out of province with the help of a women's group.

> Young woman is sexually assaulted at a party. There are witnesses to the events surrounding the crime. The assault was videotaped and the police have the tape. Policeman says he has viewed the tape and it looks to him as if she were "enjoying herself." He tells her it won't do her any good in court and that she "doesn't have much to go on." Feeling pressured by the police she withdraws her complaint and the police do not proceed. It is her opinion they destroyed the video once she decided not to proceed with the complaint.

> After his (perpetrator) appearance in court for his plea, I was questioned by the crown who said that a second statement should be taken because not enough details were given and more offences could be given than was in the first statement. I was then interviewed by (a second RCMP officer). He videotaped and tape-recorded this second statement. "The audio tape didn't work." When asked if anything had been done that made it harder for her to give the information to the police the woman answers: "Going back to do a second statement because it wasn't done right the first time."

In another case a woman is raped and feels frustrated by the lack of police response. The case did not proceed beyond initial investigation contact with the investigating officers.

> She does not believe they even looked for him. She gave a clear description of him and the car. They seemed disinterested. The police phoned her a year later to see if she had ever seen him again and to tell her it would be on the books for ten years. The police did not explain any procedures to her or any information about pursuing the rapist.[11]

We found no examples of the police explaining that she was entitled to more than she asked for. Sometimes they do inform about the process and policy and sometimes law, but in most of the cases she informs herself.

I called the police each time I found out where he was. They kept missing him.
He was finally picked up later that weekend, had a bail hearing, was released,
and he skipped to Calgary. Six months later, I found out he was in Calgary jail,
I called the Crown, who got him brought to Prince George. I handed in my
written statements; I'd called them and let them know what was going on,
not the other way.[12]

As for making sure she has all the information needed about the law and going through the system...well, if the cops are so poorly educated, and they are
the first persons to take on the case, no wonder so little is done. But I don't really think it's a question of lack of education. I think it's a question of not
wanting to take the cases of violence against women seriously as crimes.[13]

After calling the police and learning that the police officer that took her statement about a
rape did not file a report, the woman contacted a rape crisis centre. Together with the
rape crisis workers, she returned to the police and made another statement that was then
filed. With the rape crisis counsellors, she went to the hospital for an examination. She
filed a complaint against the initial police officer.

I got a call Thursday from the detective that interviewed me, and he said they
picked up the kid on breach of probation. Also, the cyclist went in to the police
station to make a statement. This was all done while the so-called investigating officer was still on holidays. About four hours later I get a phone call from
someone who said his name very fast, I didn't catch it. He said, "Did you hear
we caught the kid?" I said "yes," he said, "Well since this has happened, and
charges have been laid, do you want to withdraw the complaint against Constable (blank)?" I told him that had there been no report, nothing, the kid
would not have been caught, and he may never have confessed to the crime.
Just because the kid has been caught does not change the fact that the officer
did not do his job. He said thank you ma'am and hung up.

They didn't take a statement from me, he just asked me some questions while
at the hotel, and there was no contact after that. I went to the Freedom of Information to get a copy of the police report. There was no follow-up, and it
said that the police didn't feel the need to press charges. I had waited at the
women's shelter to see what the process would be, but I was never contacted.

The woman said she put a lot of effort into remembering. She sought information, asked the girlfriend who was with her at the bar for details. "Rohypnol is
taboo." "I called [the detective sergeant] often, every two weeks. I got fed up."
"I saw on TV that there has never been enough evidence to file a complaint
[Rohypnol] in Canada" and only eleven complaints have been filed to date.
She wanted people to know this happens. She had contacts in different places
and used them to denounce assaults using Rohypnol. She was invited to take

part in a TV program where she denounced the fact that in so few cases the complaints made were accepted and processed. "I told everything." The squad corporal "didn't like that." The detective sergeant, the investigator, however, "was extremely friendly after that, I was respected."

Was the Investigation Conducted in a Way that Promoted Her Security?

When my friend was in the shelter and I was still out with him, the police told him she was in a safe house because she was afraid for herself and her family. This gave her away. There is only one safe house in Halifax, so he knew where she was. And the reason she left could only have been because I had told her what he had said. "I felt like the police were virtually trying to kill me. And I felt like I had no recourse. I couldn't go to his supervisor to complain. I was afraid the old boys' network would kick in, and he'd get mad at me, and call.

The woman being interviewed is in front of her attacker. The policeman says, "you two pulled two officers in off the street for something you probably could have solved yourselves by sitting and talking yourselves." She decides not to say anything because she is afraid of his violence. When asked by the researcher if there was anything she could not say to the police she answers: "You mean like he'd kill me if I said anything? As far as history's concerned, yes." "I called that police officer later and asked if I could pursue charges. She said, I have to warn you, he could too. I knew that, legally, I know that. He's telling people that I pushed him first. He's been with the Hell's Angels, am I going to hit him? No. He's got mercenary training; he could break arms."

In only four cases do the police let the woman know about women's shelters. We don't find examples of them actually securing her person with the resources of the state or even of the criminal justice system such as with the use of proactive arrest, bail supervision, enforcing restraining orders proactively, or of scaring him off with the power of the state.

The research documents many instances of overt anti-women bias: Police in their conduct directly with the woman, in their questioning of the attacker, in their confidence that the man is telling the truth even when physical evidence proves the opposite, show a clear disregard for women's equality.

One worker at a transition house states: "It's not just a case of women being suspect when telling their stories. We expect that the police would have some measure of scepticism to ensure neutrality and the bringing forward of unbiased facts. But the truth is that women are treated with much less respect and are right away disbelieved. It puts us at a clear disadvantage."

The overall impression of another worker is that "some cops definitely have better customer service skills (speaking of sensitivity training and the like), but no great commitment to women's equality."

In the case of the woman attacked by a wealthy business associate and his police officer friend, "The investigator also came to her work place at one point. He asked her if she would withdraw her complaint if she was offered money."

Young woman who worked as a waitress in a strip club was raped by two casual acquaintances. The police ask if she "talked dirty" to them, had intention of having sexual intercourse with them. When the police ask or imply in their questioning that she must account for why didn't she leave, or call, or do something to prevent the attack, they are implying that she already has equality and the safety and agency it affords, and there is, therefore, no need for the very state intervention that she is asking for. In all the instances of trying to get the woman to proceed with a civil restraining order rather than proceeding with criminal charges of assault, and whenever they misrepresent the law as being unattainable for her, they infer women are not as deserving of protection under criminal law.

The police often demonstrated no concern for her liberty. In many cases they tell the woman to "keep your door locked and don't let anyone in," or "you should leave now and give him some time to calm down." They insist that as women we should relinquish our liberties and freedom in order to achieve security, as if both cannot be achieved at the same time by proactive arrests and thorough and conclusive investigative practices. In the case of the disabled woman who asked that the police secure her premises because she cannot prevent men from entering and sexually assaulting her, the police refuse to investigate. Her liberty was severely limited by their refusal to act.

> It took a long time for them (the police) to respond. Investigation did not begin until a month later. They took a statement from her. He was apprehended and charged with two counts of uttering death threats. He went to jail for two nights, and was released with orders to stay away from her. His lawyer phoned the female police officer and harassed her (the officer). The investigating senior officer was the husband's family friend and began pressuring the investigating female officer; character assassination against the complainant. Female officer said, "It was not worth her time," so she stopped her investigation.[14]

Sometimes police statements were profoundly disrespectful. To a woman whose husband chokes her, "He doesn't think it is a dangerous situation, and it doesn't need police involvement." She was left to wonder what would warrant police involvement. "Go somewhere safe" was often a substitute for arresting him rather than a complementary action.

Women were often overtly blamed for being with violent men. Instead of seeing her immediate safety and security as a moment with which to build the case against him, they more often use it as an excuse for not proceeding at all. The lack of freedom it implies, however, and the restriction of movement it imposes, is seen by the attending police as an acceptable loss.

We know that 49 men were arrested, thirteen were immediately arrested. The majority of these are not wife assault. Twelve men were not arrested. In two cases we do not have the answer to the question. Police recommend 57 times that charges be brought against the man. Twenty-eight women's cases do not make it past the point of police investigation. Police prevent convictions in cases of stranger attacks by not collecting evidence:

> A stranger posing as a repairman attacks this woman in her apartment. The police appear to be kind at first, take her to the hospital to deal with her broken nose, call her sister. But they don't collect evidence at the apartment; do not ask for the medical forensic kit at the hospital. They do not proceed with presenting the case to crown. They said there weren't any fingerprints. And yet the respondent said the attacker had rummaged throughout the apartment.[15] "No one checked my body or my clothes, they didn't keep anything."

In the following case, a man attacks the woman when her car breaks down on the road, and she accepts his offer of using his cell phone.

> She doesn't even feel that they bothered looking. She could have I.D.'d the rapist if they showed her any pictures. They didn't ask her anything like that. They insinuated that her husband did it.

> This woman's drink was spiked at a bar. She doesn't know the man who offered to take her home. He raped her and left her home after giving her a card with his name on it. The police had his name. At the hospital they did not collect evidence. The police did not proceed with the case because of "lack of evidence." The forensic evidence kit wasn't used on me. "It was my word against his."

Of the casual acquaintance rapes for which the police did not recommend charges to the crown, it is usually the case that the police do not believe the woman. In many of the cases, drugs and alcohol are involved in some way in the attack.

> The woman knows the attacker and has been in a social situation with him. He takes advantage of her vulnerable state to commit the rape. The police proceed in this case with the assumption that she is lying. "He (police) wouldn't keep in contact with me, so I called him every week. Week before Christmas he met me for coffee at Starbuck's. Told me to move on with my life, go to school, etc. Then he said the file is inactive and it's 'in the drawer'. He said they'd pull the file out when he rapes another woman." In this case, the woman is attacked by a casual acquaintance. There are drugs involved and physical evidence is collected by the police. She can identify the attacker.

> "I'm not here for a joke, if you're just making this up." This is the response of the police officer to the young woman who was raped by a casual acquaintance at her friend's house. There were drugs involved, she had taken some cocaine. "Obviously the cop in Winnipeg not only made it more difficult but impossible." (Casual acquaintance rape, police do not believe her and do not proceed.)

As far as I know, they stopped it because (one of the assailants) passed the polygraph, (the other's) was inconclusive and not enough to prosecute him according to (the investigating officer).[16] This is the case of the woman who is sexually assaulted by two male co-workers. The police based their case on the polygraph test and do not believe her account of the events.

[LINKS Interviewer: Did he take a statement?] "Yes, from both of us." [Interviewer: Have you had contact with the police since then?] "They said the Domestic Conflict Unit would contact me in a couple of days, and it's been over two and half weeks and I haven't heard anything. I called that officer back to say I was on the night shift, and they could contact me in the day. Then I called the Domestic Conflict Unit and they said the officer has to investigate and make a charge before they can contact me." The woman never heard back again from the police and so assumes the case was dropped.

"At the time, he was supposed to refrain from drugs and alcohol. He was on probation. And that night, he was drunk. So the cops did not check him out." The police did not take a statement. There was no further follow-up by the police.

It wasn't what I expected. I thought they would arrest him. They wouldn't even look at my injuries. They wouldn't even come over and look at my wrist, which you could see, was scraped from where I fell. The guy said, "You guys called two officers in off the street for something that you could probably solve yourselves by sitting and talking like adults."

With stranger assaults the police manage to have the case go away by lack of investigation and evidence gathering. In all cases something more could have been done. One worker summed up the attitude problem:

I'd love to attend a cop training session where they're given 'sensitivity training' about violence against women. Clearly what they don't get is an education in the Charter to teach them even the basic principles of formal equality: where everyone who calls the police have the right to have their case heard and followed through with. Never mind any ideas of substantive equality where they could be taught that the social inequality of women's condition means that we have more obstacles to overcome in firstly, calling the police to respond to the crime and secondly, following through with a complaint. I think they're given a lot of psycho-babble about women needing to be taken care of and that's it. As soon as a woman puts up a fight with the cops (either wanting them to do their job, or questioning them as to why they have to take him away in handcuffs, or worrying about what's going to happen to the guy) they (the police) are hostile and behave as if we have wasted their time.[17]

Consistently, the primary reason that cases are lost occurs at the level of the first police response (uniform attending to the call). There are 28 cases that do not make it to the crown's desk and are considered unfounded at this point. Looking over all the cases, it's clear that the police have stock responses to violence against women: Women are often treated as damaged or psychologically fragile beings who are patronized with "everything is all right" and they will "do their best to get the man." But, those comforting statements are not matched with investigation.

The initial police response was often contemptuous of her sense of danger and dismissive of her request for assistance. Civil restraining orders do not constitute a conviction. Nor are they often a crime prevention device. They could be, but the administration of justice would have to change to oversee them properly. *This is one way that the system prevents conviction; by taking the case out of the criminal realm and letting women think that they have been heard. It doesn't criminalize the behaviour of the man,* and it doesn't put the resources of the criminal justice system to work on the problem of wife assault, or the social problem of violence against women, or the compounding impacts of inequality and violence.

Too often, women are treated as liars who want to get back at a man. Sometimes we are seen as sexually out of control females who feel guilty the next day ("are you sure you didn't entice him?"). Failing that, women are mocked for choosing the wrong man or choosing the wrong behaviour ("you guys called two officers in off the street for something that you could probably solve yourselves by sitting and talking like adults").

From our interviews, it appears that most of the cases that don't go forward to the crown have not had enough basic investigation from the initial and detective police. The motivation to do a good job is weak. The revealed sexist attitudes cover up the lack of pressure from their superiors to achieve a successful investigation. Sometimes those attitudes subvert their orders and are the reason for the lack of investigation. Both attitudinal responses must go and could be handled with a policy of promotions, quotas, and so on. Failing that, they are likely to engender more and more civil suits against the police.

Evidence gathering like pictures of the place of attack (taken in only five cases), pictures of the injuries (taken in only six cases), interviewing possible witnesses (completed in only 33 cases), is pushed aside and justified by the officer's initial sense/judgement/bias of whether the woman is telling the truth and whether the case is worth their while investigating. Police often act as though they have been given the personal discretion rather than legal professional discretion as to whether or not to investigate.

There are several cases of sexual assault where the woman has not had a forensic exam, and the police say the reason for not pursuing the rest of the investigation is a *lack of evidence.* There are also cases where the woman has given a description of the man, or even has his name, and knows where he is, and the police do not proceed. In some cases of violence against women where there is evidence of abuse, the police arrest him, and charges are brought against him eventually. But in many of these cases:

> They leave the case without work, and so it remains as 'he says, she says', tell
> her they are powerless and wish they could do more, and it would be great if
> you went to get a restraining order.[18]

One researcher says: "I don't know what the documents will show about proactive charging and whether all the regions have policies of arrest, no matter what. However, if I hear the phrase 'do you want to charge him?' one more time, I'm going to scream."

American television, jargon, and mythology about the system leads a lot of women, anti-violence workers included, into believing that individuals in Canada have the power to decide whether a complaint will proceed to an eventual charge.

> But when cops say it to women, they know or sure as hell should know, that as the police responding to the call, they decide if there is enough to go on to warrant an application for a charge against the man. What the police are in fact asking her is 'do you want to make a complaint?'...Well, why else would she have put herself in the position of calling them in the first place?[19]

This question is almost always asked of women reporting wife assault and, in some cases, child incest, but it happens too in cases of casual acquaintance rape. There are the situations where the woman is up against not only her husband and father (or uncle or grandfather) but also her socially constructed notions of her position as woman in this society. The police response does not deal with her inequality as a woman or the inequality of all women; police do not do all that they can to promote her safety and security.

It's at the police level that there is the most personal interaction between the victim and the criminal justice system. *Many women don't talk to the crown until shortly, even moments, before the case is taken to preliminary hearing or trial.*[20]

Notes

1. CASAC LINKS worker.
2. *Ibid.*
3. *Ibid.*
4. *Ibid.*
5. *Ibid.*
6. *Ibid.*
7. *Ibid.*
8. *Ibid.*
9. *Ibid.*
10. *Ibid.*
11. *Ibid.*
12. *Ibid.*
13. *Ibid.*
14. *Ibid.*
15. *Ibid.*
16. *Ibid.*
17. *Ibid.*
18. *Ibid.*
19. *Ibid.*
20. *Ibid.*

David Hilton Jr, Convicted March 2001, Sentence 7 Years

Tamara Gorin

IN 1999, TWO TEENAGE SISTERS went to police to reveal three years of sexual assault by boxer David Hilton. Hilton had been lovers with the girls' mother, and was violent to her also. Between 1995 and 1998, Hilton sexually assaulted the girls separately and together, often when other adults were in the room sleeping. The girls described many more than the nine counts for which he was eventually charged and convicted: sexual assault, two counts sexual interference with a minor, and two counts of invitation to sexual touching. They described forced kissing, forced oral-penis penetration, and eventually rape. They were twelve years old when he started and fifteen by the time he stopped.

The Crown had statements from their mother describing the battering he did to her in this time also: no charges were laid against him for these attacks, which included burning her with cigarettes and an iron, threatening her with a gun to her head, and forcing her to have sex with another man while he watched. When the Crown attempted to have this violence entered into evidence in the trial, arguing this violence against their mother potentially indicated how Hilton used that violence as a way to control the girls, the judge disallowed it, saying the testimony did not indicate Hilton exercised control over the girls as a result of the violence he did to their mother.

From the date the charges were announced, both the Montreal and the pan-Canadian press were awash with speculation about yet another athlete charged with violence against women. The courtroom was packed daily with men and women fans of Hilton, many looking for autographs and for a chance to see their working-class champ firsthand. Claims that Montreal had celebrated Hilton as their own, as the boxing family "the Fighting Hiltons" had been part of the city's boxing folklore for two generations, drowned out any claims otherwise—the small yet vocal boxing community seemed to dominate the discourse. Questions of consent and alleged blackmail dominated, along with speculation about the future of Hilton's title. The hard-luck, rags to riches life of an athlete was at stake, and the details of his crimes—sexual assault and rape of two girl-children—barely in their teens, took a back seat to what might happen to the fallen star.

Hilton claimed he did not remember much because he was drinking so heavily. Yet, it was during this time that he was training and travelling towards his goal: winning the World Boxing Council's super-middle-weight championship. He did this in December 2000, just months before the trial began. While awaiting trial, he was remanded to treatment for alcoholism. He says nothing sexual ever happened with the girls, and brought forward witness after witness who said they often spent time with Hilton when the girls were present and saw no sign of anything sexual or "funny" going on.

Both girls testified, as did their mother. The defence's position was that their mother was out to make money off Hilton—which does not make sense, considering he was apparently cash-poor at the time the charges were brought forward, he had not yet won his championship title. She would have been with him on the road during the time they were together, and knew firsthand there was not much money floating around. It is worth noting that there is no civil suit filed against Hilton by any member of the girls' family. The only hint at money comes after the charges are laid, when a publisher approached the mother to write a book.

What led to this conviction? Apparently, the police did their jobs here—interviewing the girls and their mother, providing enough investigation and background information so the recommended charges could come to trial and the Crown could start building a case. The Crown, Helene Di Salvo, did her job as well—she presented a range of evidence at trial, and the girls and their mother seemed well prepared to testify. Lastly, the judge, Rolande Matte, seems to have decided the credibility issues presented at trial about both the girls and Hilton came down to the details of attack and how each of the witnesses presented themselves. Defence lawyer Paul Skolnik called several witnesses who said they didn't see anything, and he even tried to make the girls' mother looked like she was out for money, but he did not succeed in calling into question the essential evidence at trial. Di Salvo presented a case which provided the evidence and supported the girls' credibility, and so Matte was able to convict.

The charges for the violence against both girls were brought together (instead of charging him with the assaults on one sister and using the other's evidence as similar fact), and this seems to have improved the chances of conviction here. He was charged with nine offences, which increased the likelihood that the judge could find him guilty of any or all the charges. As well, Hilton started attacking the girls when they were twelve; the majority of the charges here were related to the sexual assault of minors, who cannot legally consent. It is noteworthy in this context that the potential assault charges for the violence Hilton did to their adult mother were not pursued. The battering boyfriend seems a useful evidentiary sideline to what the police and Crown were after: a child molester. One hopes Hilton would have been charged and convicted if the girls had been fourteen to sixteen when he attacked them or if their mother had reported the violence he did to her at any point separately from the attacks on her daughters. But the law changes and so does the state's response to adult men's violation of teenage girls' and adult women's bodies.

News Sources:

CBC News-Indepth background, Martin O'Malley, CBC News Online. Retrieved online March 11, 2002 from CBC website: <http://www.cbc.ca/news/indepth/background/hilton_dave.html>.

Malenfant, L. (2001). Hilton's Grounds for Appeal: The Report Magazine. Retrieved online March 11, 2002 from the Newsmagazine website: <www.fathersforlife.org/php/hilton1.htm>.

Hamilton, G. (2001, February 8). Hilton's mother "heartbroken" by sex charges, *National Post*, p. A9.
Montreal Watches as Fighting Hiltons dealt latest blows (2001, March 18), *The Province*, p. A36.

Will We Have **Our Day in Court?**

The government is aware that those women's stories that are told to public officials can be so distorted or minimised by the process of becoming official data, as to hide great swirls of women's reality.[1] "Many had told it all, for instance, but it did not register."[2] The violence disappears, the equality issues disappear, and women's resistance disappears. We know because women tell us in their own words, in their own time, when we participate in an encouraging equality-seeking environment.[3] In these one hundred stories, all involved physical violence already committed. Nothing less than an assault charge would therefore be appropriate. And many involved breaches of trust, confinement, threats of more harm, death threats, and weapons.

It is clear from the responses to the questions relating to the crown's preparation of the case for trial, that "this part of the process is very confusing to women."[4] Criminal court cases and convictions are out of the normal experience of both the workers in the centres and the women interviewed. Neither knows enough. Women are at times unsure of the difference between pre-trial and trial, between arrest and charge, between the crown's responsibility to present the case to the courts on behalf of the state and the role victims play as witness for the state. Popular culture, television, and movies are as close to the real thing as many women will ever get, and their understanding of the system is reflective of this. And nowhere can we find in the information provided to us that the professionals in the system took any pains to educate and correct most misconceptions.

So, as we move up through the system, women (individually and collectively) have less and less experience and knowledge about the system and how it can and does contend with claims of violence. "We are so unaccustomed to having our cases go further than the police."[5] We have very little personal built up collective knowledge of the system.

"Women talk about the crown as "their" lawyer, see the case of so and so vs. the state (province or country) as her vs. him."[6] There is very little on the spot informing and educating of women. But this lingo and colloquial speech often used by victim witnesses complaining of violence also reveals that she assumes that she and the government are on the same side and that, by virtue of this, the prosecutor is her lawyer. They will perhaps not have the same interests in total but since she is the one violated and the state has declared an interest in interfering with that violence, she naturally presumes shared interests. She is often profoundly surprised and disappointed to be treated as a body of evidence or as a pawn in a power game between other people that has very little to do with her experience or violence against women.

Once the bargaining begins, charges do not necessarily go away, but the system's response to violence against women is no longer at issue. The violence and equality imperatives disappear. "The crown pleads charges down in a way that takes women and women's equality out of the picture":[7]

- Three counts of sexual assault committed against a daughter gets plead down to death threats: he gets probation and anger management;

- Incest gets reduced to sexual interference;

- Nine charges of incest-related offences reduced to three counts of sexual interference and corruption of morals;

- Wife assault results in a bond to keep the peace for one year.

Our information about what happens in court is sketchy. Between the crown office and the courtroom, the women and their advocates are reduced to passivity. "She has no legal counsel or legitimate voice in the court unless she has hired counsel of her own."[8] Crown counsel tries to avoid the defence attacks on the crown key witness by keeping women ignorant and out of contact, preferably isolated from advocates. We know from our interviews that women were ill prepared and ill informed. After the events, many cannot say clearly what happened to them or their case.

Only twenty-seven women are kept informed about the case by the crown;
Fifty-five women tell us that charges are laid;
Ten charges are dropped shortly into the process.

We know that often the police do not adequately attend to the victim nor do they investigate in a way that makes apprehension and conviction more likely. But what happens once the case is laid on the desk of the crown attorneys? What are the charges brought against men when women complain of breaches of human rights that they call criminal assault? How relevant is her story and her experience of the events to the case brought to the courts?

In this case of stranger rape, where he has broken into her apartment, confined her and used a weapon (screw driver), the police recommend sexual assault with a weapon and robbery. The crown proceeds with both of those charges. But how relevant is her situation to the proceedings? He had a previous conviction for Break and Enter and she believes they wanted him for those. "They were quite determined after my rape." Looking back, we think they want him for serial rape, but no one says so. At court she realizes he has previous convictions for sexual assault and we wonder if the police and crown already knew him as a serial attacker. So he is known to the system, is picked up because he had "broken his probation and was in a half way house when he raped me." The man re-offended since his release from the three and a half years sentence on the conviction of her rape.[9]

How do we explain the divide between her reality and the charges that are eventually brought against the man? *Why is the man not charged with the most serious crime he committed?* And why is he not charged with a crime that matches her description of the offence she is reporting? What are women meant to take from this? It does erode the usefulness of criminalizing sexist violence.

It was wife assault. The police recommend a charge of assault and the crown agrees. Yet she has given evidence of confinement and his threatening her life. He had pinned her down while yelling at her that he would "get rid of her" rather than let her leave him. The man pleads guilty of assault and is given a conditional sentence and no contact order.

He sexually assaults her and has been harassing her. She is a woman of colour and there is a sexualized nature to the harassment. He calls her "filthy stinking bitch." "Fat ass." Calls her a "thing" and "filthy bitch" to the police. He exposes her breast by pulling her clothes over her head and rubs the nipple roughly with his forearm. Her screaming and her son coming to her aid interrupt the incident. His under-age son gives her son pornography of Asian women that has been given to him by his father. She is a South Asian woman. The police recommend two charges against the man, one of assault, and one of theft. Crown proposes a Section 810 Peace Bond against both of them. In the end, the court has no information about the sexist, racist nature of the case. Of how significant it was that she was from a recent wave of immigration seen to be "moving in" to her community. This was an attack by a white male and his son.

Two men, who are known to the police, rape the woman. The crown has lots of evidence: her clothes, semen, DNA, pictures of the bruises. She had called the police immediately; the friend who found her had been interviewed. But the crown decided not to proceed with a charge against the men.

> I called the Crown Attorney's office in Saskatchewan to ask about my case. They
> said the police there had interviewed my friend and a couple of her friends that
> were there that night, and they identified the guys who the police already knew
> from other incidents. They said they wanted to proceed because they felt they
> had plenty of evidence, but the cop in Winnipeg told them it wasn't worth it be-
> cause I asked for it.

The police believe it is her fault and that she was behaving in an unacceptable manner for women. She had been drinking with these men and knew them. Obviously, they believed this "type of woman" would have consented to the events: brutal sex in a field with two men, which left her bruised after being dragged there by them. The crown could have at least argued that she was too drunk to have given meaningful consent.

Where did notions of freedom and equality go? Where did notions of violence against women as a social reality go? There are no discussions or recommendations of a demeaning and hateful crime, and never can we find in the crown's preparation of the case, the question of social impact when considering the charge. Rather than challenge the police's victim blaming in the case above, *the crown continues to disregard her right to equality and to the rule of law.*

A political directive to crowns to go ahead with trials only in cases where there is a high likelihood of conviction (now coded as a competing social interest) causes great harm. *Costs now always trump the social impact of a quick and fair judgement on violence against women.* The political directives argue against "undue" court costs, against burdening the system with difficult cases. But these cases will remain expensive and difficult and too often without conviction unless there is a concerted effort to try a critical mass of them. We would rather value the social impact of being seen to be quick and fair in the service of equality and women's Charter rights.[10]

The impact of the directives to crowns is to erase violence against women as a crime against the community (in the name of the state). The police begin the problem by constructing cases of missing evidence and missing confident, willing complainants. Crown attorneys decide not to proceed based on that missing evidence or hesitant witness and the political directives from the Attorney General. Sometimes they decide to proceed on a charge that does not reveal or respond to violence against women. That does not criminalize the sexist violence.

> It is a case of wife assault: the police have recommended a charge of assault to the crown. She is not really interested in pursuing the assault but wants him charged on the past sexual assault of her. She refuses to cooperate with the crown. When the crown loses this particular witness he decides not to proceed at all, this despite his insistence that it "has nothing to do with you, it's not your business. You don't even have to come to court."

> Another case of wife assault: the police say there is not enough evidence to lay assault charges against him, (this after not taking her statement nor forensics and photos). They inquire instead whether she would like them to charge him based on what he did to trash her house.

Sometimes violence against women disappears from the criminal justice system because of pre-conviction diversion offered for reasons of cost cutting or time saving. The same process of erasure happens with plea-bargaining to a voluntary conviction on lesser charges. In the following example, pre-conviction diversion combines with plea-bargaining.

Woman discovers after separation from ex-common law that he has made sexual advances to her daughter. She confronts him with the incest in a letter she writes after the daughter reveals the incident. He comes over and threatens her with a gun. She decides to proceed by going to the police since obviously she cannot handle this alone any more. Police recommend three charges: exploiting a minor, invitation to sexual touching, uttering death threats. He is released on bail. He comes over again with a gun, and she decides to convince her daughter to recant since obviously they are in danger and he will not be held. The threat happens after the charges are laid. The mother and daughter get scared, and they decide the daughter should recant. Crown contacts her to ask what happened. They clearly know that the mother has interfered: to save her daughter. The crown proceeds anyway but only with an order to pre-conviction anger management diversion and the criminal conviction goes away. How would anger management handle the incest problem? If the crown was going to divert why not something that captured the nature of the crime? Police and crown could have protected her before they lost the case and should have suspected the danger to mother and daughter and the reasons for recanting.

Woman reveals past incest: the police recommend four charges of incest, four charges of sexual interference, and four counts of sexual touching. The man pleads guilty to reduced charges: the incest charge is gone.

Incest. Police recommend crown uses 9 charges: sexual assault x3, sexual touching x2, inciting a minor to sexual contact, corruption of morals, physical assault x2. The man pleads guilty to the lesser 2 charges of sexual assault and corruption of morals with 2 years less a day with 15 years probation.

In nineteen cases we know men got a no-contact order with bail conditions after being arrested and charged. In twenty-eight cases, there is insufficient information to know. The question of race seems clear; only two of the cases of the twelve women of colour got conviction for wife assault and the other cases were abandoned.

Wife assault: the police attend and take her to a transition house. She is reluctant and doesn't know where the transition house is, feels like she has no control over the proceedings. The police recommend charge to the crown, but the crown does not recommend that he remain in custody.

Physical assault by ex-boyfriend who refuses to accept that she has ended the relationship. He commits several acts of harassment before he gets a no contact order, which he repeatedly breaches. He is charged with criminal harassment. The crown recommends that he should stay in jail for her safety, but this only after many instances of her safety being jeopardized by this man. In the end, the time served pre-trial is used to reduce his sentence. That is used to justify that his sentence is probation. She is then back in the situation of relying on him not breaching his conditions of release.

Wife assault: "At the bail hearing the judge asked me to leave because he was going to release him. This was for my safety apparently. I put up a fuss and asked why didn't he hold him in jail then if I was in so much danger that I required a head start?"

Eighteen women told us that they were referred to crown-based victims services. There were no women referred to independent advocates. In the instances where women had independent advocates, they enlisted their assistance on their own, prior to or during involvement with the criminal justice system.

Twenty-seven women told us they were kept informed by the crown through its own office or through victim services of the crown. But, the involvement with victim services and answering yes to the question of whether the crown kept them informed in the case still results in powerless lack of information and crippling ignorance of the criminal justice system and the law.

In the following example it is clear that even the advocate is unsure of the distinction between the crown attorney and his role as attorney for the state vs. her own lawyer. The statements also imply she has responsibility and power in determining the validity of a plea agreement and the sentence proposed. Too often empathy with her is expressed in this confusing way.

This woman cooperated with the criminal justice system in response to the attack on her. Her case merited not only a first call to the police, but sustained through the process to conviction, and no one has bothered to educate her.

The woman was consulted two days (not working days) before the trial. Her lawyer had received a proposal from the defence counsel. The defence proposed that the accused plead guilty and spend nine months in jail [actually in a halfway house]. The Crown attorney told her that if she accepted the plea bargain she wouldn't have to go to trial. The woman said she didn't know what to do at that point; she didn't know whether she should agree to the plea bargain. She talked about it with a friend. The rape crisis worker who had been accompanying her wasn't at the office. The woman decided to continue and not accept the offer. The day of the trial "everything went very fast." The case was announced. The two lawyers made their presentations. After arriving at court, her lawyer told her "we won't be able to get more than twelve months" [sentence]. The woman answered, "I'll take the twelve months." The woman did not have to appear before the judge. The woman thinks that her victim's statement made a difference in the sentencing, but she's not certain of it. Obviously, the sentencing had little or nothing to do with anything she said or did. And in fact her wish to have a trial was to serve some now unknown reason that has been solved by the crown with a deal regarding sentencing. She was dragged along, disrespectfully.[11]

Wife assault: the man is convicted of assault and is sentenced, but the woman has no idea what is going on: "I don't know how the court works," no, they didn't tell her that she could make a victim impact statement.

Many women report that they spent as much as two hours getting a tour of the facilities from the court-based victim service worker. They were introduced to the court building and were told how the day in court would go. But most women got no access to the crown counsel ahead of the days in court, and little to no discussion with crown officials, or the crown herself as to specifics of her case.

The woman reports that the court worker sat with her and was emotionally supportive but did not explain the court process according to her or to the rape crisis worker.

The crown meets with her in a rush in the hall "He met with us in the hall and said he wanted to meet with us individually. He quickly explained about the preliminary trial, and that the prelim was to prove the charges that we were there to make, to make sure they had enough information. He's a very busy man."

The crown attorney had no knowledge of their (woman and man's) relationship and about the case. Only interviewed for ten minutes just before trial. She wasn't allowed to speak. Crown did not even address her but addressed victim services worker with her.[12]

Woman struggles to get an appointment with the crown and gets a rushed ten minutes standing in a hall way.

Woman calls the crown attorney three times and she doesn't call her back before court. "I heard nothing from the Crown. They probably knew my name, saw it, and thought I would call if I had any questions. I don't know why. I made a pretty good forgotten victim."

Sometimes the woman reports that she met with the crown but it is evident in her statement that she met the victim assistance workers from the crown office and is unaware of the authority difference. She met the crown only later.

J'ai été chanceuse, parce qu'il ma contacté une semaine et quelque jours en avant. Il y avait dit que, 'bin oui, on vas le faire vite. On vas envoyer la police, la police va communiquer avec (fils), et puis on vas avoir les papiers'. Ils ont communiquer à l'avance, pas mal à l'avance. D'habitude il dit qu'il communique jusque deux ou trois jours avant, d'abord je suis chanceuse. Quand j'étais arrivé, j'ai vu le procureur de la couronne. (Translation: "I was lucky, because he contacted me a week and a couple of days ahead of time. He said: "Yes, we'll make it happen quickly. We'll send the police, the police will communicate with (son), and then we'll get the papers." They contacted me ahead of time, quite a bit ahead of time. He said that usually they would contact me just a couple or three days ahead of time, so I was lucky. When I arrived I met with the crown attorney.")

They do not ensure that the prosecution's witness, the woman making the complaint, is sufficiently prepared and participating with full knowledge of the law.

We know that 35 cases went to trial and that 29 women testified in court. Twenty-seven women were cross-examined; in 13 cases there were other witnesses called; and 13 cases saw the trial held over or delayed.

The crowns (overworked I'm sure, all of them) follow directives to a fault about not pursuing unless the case is winnable. They could also look at the woman involved and consider taking the case as a chance to advance women's equality interests. Sometimes it takes a number of such cases to begin to make this sort of case winnable.

At this point in the system, eight more cases are dropped: four for lack of evidence according to the crown, one by pre-trial diversion (wife assault, restraining order) and three to alternative dispute resolution. In one incest case he pleads guilty and gets house arrest in a "halfway house"; one wife assaulter pleads guilty and "gets weekends and a fine"; one is still on bail and she thinks they are recommending probation and counselling.

Except for the cases where the crown dismissed for lack of evidence and where they got her to get a restraining order instead, the abusing husbands do plead guilty and are sentenced. Dropping and consolidating charges though is where the violence against women starts to disappear. After initial crown involvement, 38 cases do not proceed further through the system.

In the end, this "best case" scenario of women who are interviewed because they have gone through the system or have decided to go through the system, leads to 34 convictions. Of those convictions, according to what the women know, eighteen were guilty pleas. So, in fact, we know of sixteen convictions that came out of the whole court process (that is, heard by a judge or jury and a verdict rendered at the end of the trial). There were eight "not guilty" decisions. So even in our "best case" scenario, only half of those heard (that we know about) get a conviction.

The women report being dissatisfied with the sentences imposed after the attacker is convicted. They see no connection to the seriousness of the crime or threat to their safety and security, or to his potential rehabilitation. Usually the judge does not impose jail time because the crown does not ask for it. One woman doubts what the judge says when he claims the 90-day sentence he imposes "is the law."

Women know that judges are bound by the criminal code and legislation in impos-ing sentences. And we know that they are also bound by law in rendering decisions. The judge's decisions and the commentary is what women are seeking. Here is the opportu-nity for the judge to make comment about violence against women, to pepper the deci-sion with concerns and arguments about equality, looking, as he/she must, at the Supreme Court as the guide in that decision-making.

In some of the cases, the opportunity is lost before it gets to court because the crown has decided to proceed on a lesser charge, one that may not involve violence against women. But the judge is sitting in the court and hears all the testimony and knows that the issues at hand are about male violence against women and that there are equality issues. He could comment.

Sentencing principles must be applied. Yet, if the sentences imposed don't reflect society's condemnation of the behaviour, how are the rest of men supposed to know that violence against women is a crime? There has to be someone who says, in imposing the sentence, or in the sentence itself, that the crime was committed, it was committed against the laws of the state and the state values it's citizens, all, and will uphold the law.

What is the Relationship Between Her Success in Court and Our Advocacy?

Looking into the relationship between the presence of an independent advocate (not a court or police-based victim services worker) and the experience of women bringing com-plaints of male violence against women, reinforced what we already know: women are better off with independent advocates on their side through the criminal justice system.

Of the 92 women interviewed, nine women had us (feminist frontline workers) with them from the start. Of those nine women, two cases are pending and have not gone through the system yet.

- In eight of the nine cases, the police took a statement from her;
- In eight of the nine cases, they immediately arrested him;
- In eight of the nine cases, they took a description of him (one Missing Information);
- He pleads not guilty in eight of the nine cases;
- Two were found not guilty and two are still pending;
- Out of the five convicted, except for one Missing Information, all have conditions of re-lease and a no contact order attached;
- Charges were laid in all the cases;
- In none of the cases did they try to divert the case;

• The one negative is that police are even less likely to keep women informed directly. Only two were kept informed by the police.

Women Speak About the Usefulness of Having an Advocate With Her

> The best thing possible about my experience with the crown was having my advocate from the rape crisis centre there with me. I don't know what I would have done without her.

In the case of a woman who did not have her rape crisis worker with her when she met with the crown:

> Ce qui m'aurait aidé c'est d'avoir une intervenante avec moi. Pas de rencontre avec le procureur. (Translation: "What would have helped me was having my advocate with me. Not meeting with the crown.")

> I didn't even think about it as a crime until I went to the shelter. The workers there showed me how I am worth more than that and he doesn't have the right to kick me around. I went to the cops after that, but it took some time for me to get there.

Workers noted too that things happen, the police and crown move once, there is an advocate in the room. Women who tried previously to get information about their case, or tried to get the crown to proceed, were successful once the advocate was there. In any event, the stories from the 92 women show that having an advocate with them gets better police response, better crown attention, and, therefore, more likelihood of conviction.

When compared to women's experience with the crown-based victim services workers, who behave more as court tour guides, it is still more obvious why it is useful for women to have advocates. In one case the victim services worker writes a letter to victim's compensation for her (the police have refused to proceed) and says: "This is an open and closed case, call me if you need anything else, she's been through enough."

Even when a woman is pleased with the victim services worker, she can see that there is more that could be done:

> Victim services (court based) were great. Very understanding and supportive. Nice and courteous but could offer a more varied service—not just in court. Women need to be trained and prepared for what will happen in court. Support is important but preparation is vital.

Though praise is not always forthcoming for victim service workers:

> In imitation of Victim Services (court-based) she said, "here's the court room—don't say anything about your case." While saying this, the woman turned her head away and put her hands out to indicate that the Victim Ser-

vices workers gave indications that not only did they avoid hearing about the case, but were not interested in engaging with the woman as a person.[13]

The following numbers, while not clearly indicative, do leave an impression. Of 34 cases of wife assault reported to the state: twelve women were native or women of colour; 22 were white women; 31 were poor or working class.

> We decided not to focus on regional differences but something stands out in Alberta with wife assault and I'm not sure how to talk about it or even how to find evidence to support the conclusions. Many of the cases we recorded were wife assaults on native women. In Alberta there is a Domestic Assault Court, yet of the thirteen cases of wife assault in Alberta, only three got to conviction. I know the numbers are too small to prove anything, but it sure looks like racism. All ten that drop out do so at the police stage. Of the three who do make it to conviction, there is one native woman and two white women.[14]

Of the twelve wife assault convictions: two were women of colour and five were poor women. All others are working class and white women (one case is pending and one we lost contact with so there is no information). The question of race seems clear, since only two of the twelve women of colour got conviction for wife assault.

Of the fifteen women who did not make it past the police stage of the system: nine women of colour and six white women, ten poor or underclass women and five working class women.

Two women did not make it past the crown level of the system; of those two, one was a woman of colour and both were poor. Two women did not make it past the preliminary court stage; both are white and working class. One case is pending.

Is it more likely that a casual acquaintance will escape conviction, as opposed to a stranger or a professional on the job? Where do those cases drop off, and is it a case of lack of evidence or lack of police follow through? Where there is no conviction, what is the stated reason?

Of 27 sexual assaults (not incest cases), nineteen were casual acquaintances, six were stranger rapes, and two were professionals on the job. Of the casual acquaintances, four resulted in convictions, three not guilty verdicts (one stay of proceedings because the man died at the time of the court process), and nine terminated before court at police level (two still pending). Of the not guilty verdict, all were because of lack of collected evidence. Of the casual acquaintance cases, it is usually the case that the police don't believe the woman and allow that to infect their investigation responsibilities.

Of the stranger rapes: three convictions and three terminated before court. All three terminated at police level. Of the professionals attacking while on the job, one case was terminated before it got to court, at crown level, the other found not guilty.

Their judgments about court are often mixed up with their judgements and feelings about the outcome, of course. However, it also seems that the powerlessness they feel in court renders them complete outsiders to the process.[15] It limits their understanding to judgements about: Who was polite to them? Who did not cause them indignity? Who did not put them at higher risk? And that is expressed as: Who cared? Who tried?

In many cases we don't have enough information about sentencing. In some cases, women don't actually know what the man is finally charged with and don't know what the plea agreement is. In some cases, they just know what the sentence is. In some cases they don't even know that. One can speculate that crown prefers not to carry this diversion and plea bargaining information back to the women. The crown no longer needs the women, as witness, so there is less reason for crown to make time for the women.

Often women are discouraged and alienated by the end of this ordeal. The reputation of the justice system is built on the word passed from one to another of these experiences. So, too, the disrepute of the government builds in the eyes of women. Often by this stage of a case the women are gone from the process. They have turned their attention to their own lives and what they can control. Safety, dignity, and equality will often have to be assured by other means.

Notes

1. Not meeting the standard of proof of criminal or civil law conventions, use of terms of categorization like "family violence," for instance, which hides who is doing what to whom, or the refusal to recognise incidents of rape of wives or prostitutes as a legal matter, or the use of charges like "break and enter" in a rape case in which the police have not constructed a legal case of sexual assault, or the charging and jailing of women who defend themselves from violent men, rather than understanding women's self defence.

2. CASAC Links worker.

3. Lakeman, L. (1999). A Consideration of Feminist Process. In Meister, J., and Masuda, S. (Eds.), DAWNing: How to start and maintain a group. Vancouver: DAWN Canada, pp. 85-98.

4. CASAC Links worker.

5. *Ibid.*

6. *Ibid.*

7. *Ibid.*

8. *Ibid.*

9. *Ibid.*

10. *Ibid.*

11. *Ibid.*

12. *Ibid.*

13. *Ibid.*

14. *Ibid.*

15. *Ibid.*

Former Nova Scotia Premier, Gerald Regan
and Eighteen Sex Related Charges

Irene Smith

IN 1993, RCMP REPORTS they are investigating Gerald Regan for crimes of sexual assault (at the time it was against police policy to release the names of suspects before charges were laid). Regan was the Liberal Premier of Nova Scotia from 1970 to 1978. In 1980, he became the Federal Minister of Labour and Mines responsible for Fitness and Amateur Sports. He lost his seat in 1984.

March 1995, Regan is charged with eighteen sex-related charges involving thirteen women. Most of these women are in their early to late teens (14-24 years). The complainants included six family babysitters, a secretary, a political intern, and a young reporter.[1]

Most of these assaults occurred almost 40 years ago.

Regan hires one of the best known and most highly paid criminal defence lawyers in the country (Mr. Ed Greenspan) and drops out of sight. In March and April 1995, the RCMP lay a total of eighteen charges against Regan, including rape, indecent assault, attempted rape, unlawful confinement involving some thirteen women in the years between 1956 and 1978. In April 1996, the preliminary inquiry begins and runs for one year. His lawyer alleges mistakes by the prosecution and RCMP endanger Regan's chances for a fair trial.

January 19, 1998, Greenspan, for Regan, motions for the case to be thrown out on the basis of an assertion of misconduct of Police and Prosecutors.

April 2, 1998, Justice Michael MacDonald throws out ten of the charges involving nine women. He ruled that these are less serious incidences of sexual assault and that to proceed with them would jeopardize the integrity of the Justice system.

November 9, 1998, three years after the original charges were laid, the case goes to trial. November 24, 1998, on the fifteenth day of the trial, Regan's lawyer (Greenspan) cross-examined two of the complainants both of who are 56 years old now. They testified that they were fourteen years old when Regan raped and attempted to rape them. Greenspan's cross-examination was brutal, suggesting that the women made up the whole story. He made reference to one woman's past sexual history without objection from the crown. However the judge did object and cite Seaboyer.

Avalon Centre staff notes that his adult children, two daughters, their husbands visibly supported Regan. His son and his wife accompany him to court and often sit behind him in the courtroom. One of his daughters, Nancy Regan, is an ATV anchorperson, and his son is a lawyer in a prominent law firm. His wife, who is expected to be a witness, is not in court for much of the graphic details of the rape and attempted rape. Avalon's position in that first three years was to support the women who called them and to speak publicly through the media as to their courage. Avalon Centre women attended and monitored the case.[2]

After two months of sensational evidence and legal pyrotechnics, he was acquitted of the eight most serious charges including rape and attempted rape.

Before the trial began, Nova Scotia Supreme Court stayed nine of the charges, saying that the crown had tainted the evidence by talking to the victim's witnesses ahead of trial and by "shopping" for a judge without a shared history in his political party.

February 14, 2002, in a dramatic 5-4 split, Supreme Court rules that Regan must face charges. They said, "the police possessed serious evidence that Mr. Regan had sexually abused vulnerable young subordinates who trusted him. Victims of sexual assault must be encouraged to trust the system and bring allegations to light." Mr. Justice Louie LeBel wrote for the majority (including McLaughlin, L'Heureux-Dubé, Gonthier, Bastarache), "The evidence in this case exposes the systemic concerns that sexual assault complainants often have."[3]

The *Globe and Mail* catches the public mood and response in an editorial that applauds the ruling as a confirmation that this was "far from being a case of backlash against the powerful, as Mr. Regan argued, this case illustrates the difficulties in prosecuting charges of sexual assault" and speculates "whether the complainants will still wish to proceed after this drawn out legal battle is an open question."[4]

April 17, 2002, in Halifax, the director of the Nova Scotia Public Prosecution Service, M. Herschorn, announced it would not prosecute the former premier and federal cabinet minister citing the staleness of the cases, the high cost of a second trial, and the likelihood Regan would never see the inside of a jail cell; "It is not in the public interest to proceed."

Notes

1. Boomer, R. (2002, April 18). Nova Scotia prosecutors give up on Regan case. From Halifax, *Daily News*, carried in *The Vancouver Sun*, p. A6.
2. Smith, I. (1998, November 25). Memo to Lee Lakeman of LINKS: Profiles on Current Issues in Nova Scotia.
3. Makin, K. (2002, February 15). Top Court Revives Charges Against Regan. Ruling Exposes Sharp Division Among Justices As Majority Decides Ex-premier Should Face Sexual-Assault Allegations. *The Globe and Mail*, p. A3.
4. *Ibid.*

Just For Laughs:
From Guilty Plea to Unconditional Discharge

Diana Yaros and Danielle Tessier

GILBERT ROZON is the founder and the director of the "Just for Laughs" comedy festival in Montreal. He is 44 years old, married and the father of three young children. On February 17, 1998, Rozon encounters K.C., nineteen years old, during a fundraising evening at the Manoir Rouville where K.C. is working as a croupière. They talk about her interests and where she would like to work. Rozon offers to help her get started. In K.C.'s words:

> Before the assault he was kind. He wanted to know what I wanted to do. He gave me his telephone number. He told me that he would offer me a job. He said he had many contacts. I was happy that such a well-connected person was interested in me, a little black-jack croupière.

Social Class

It was agreed that they would continue this discussion elsewhere when the gaming tables closed. Rozon invited K.C. up to his room to discuss job opportunities. Rozon tried to obtain sexual favours from K.C. without her consent. Despite her resistance, he continued to sexually assault her. She eventually succeeded in fighting him off and ran out of the hotel room bumping into several people who later testify to her panicked state. Media attention highlighted the tenacious prejudices still surrounding sexual assault. Rozon's actions are minimized (considered a grey area of what constitutes seduction), as are the consequences for the woman. Despite the fact that the accused pled guilty to sexual assault, he received an unconditional discharge from the Québec Superior Court.

The First Judgment

On November 30, 1998, charges are laid for sexual assault, unlawful confinement, and simple assault. G. Rozon pled guilty to a reduced charge of simple sexual assault. The crown prosecutor, Mme. Josée Grandchamp, then informs the court that the only charge is a summary offence of simple sexual assault. There is no mention of the initial charges. Before going any further, here we have encountered the first problem and major obstacle to women's equality rights guaranteeing security of the person. The banalization of sexual assault by reducing the charges laid in order to obtain a guilty plea. Because of the prosecutor's choice, we remain ignorant of the full extent of the criminal actions of the accused. Most importantly, all future analyses of this case by the media, as well as the sentencing hearings, are limited by this harmful decision of the crown prosecutor. Despite widespread media attention, Judge Robert refuses to accept the defence's argument that public attention is punishment enough and refuses to accord an unconditional discharge to the accused.

On December 11, 1998, Judge Denis Robert sentenced Rozon to a fine of $1,100.00 (maximum sentence is eighteen months in jail) despite the defence's additional claim that Rozon should receive an unconditional discharge because he needed to travel for his work. "The accused must receive a sentence in accordance with his actions, not for who he is." Rozon will have a criminal record. How can one evaluate a sum of money that corresponds to the attack on the integrity and security of women?

The first judgment was based on several factors: The unpremeditated nature of the attack. The absence of a previous criminal record, and excessive intake of alcohol. Rozon's intentions are not questioned but the victim's are. Her agreeing to go to his hotel room is seen as suspect, she must have known what was going to happen. This despite the fact that article 33.1 of the Criminal Code forbids the use of voluntary intoxication as a mitigating factor in sexual assault cases. Would we use this argument if we were dealing with a drunk driving charge?

Appeal of Sentence

An appeal of the sentence is registered in Québec Superior Court on February 19, 1999. The defence reasons that public interest is not served because the sentence may harm Gilbert Rozon's ability to continue to organize the Just For Laughs festival with potential loss of jobs and revenue for the city! Does this mean that any wealthy individual who owns a large business is above the law because their criminal record may harm the business? Surely other individuals could carry out the work.

Furthermore, the defence continues, the sentence is too severe considering the minimal nature of his actions. Little or no traumatizing effect on the victim is cited, this despite the woman's claim to the contrary, as stated in media reports. Finally, the defence adds that Judge Robert made a "mistake of principle" when he considered the crime involved: sexual assault. While Judge Robert considered the actions and not the man, the Appeal Court Judge Béliveau thought it was more important to consider the career of the accused than the consequences for the woman.

The defence also argued that because Rozon was a well-known person, the excessive media attention was more punishing for him than it would be for a lesser-known individual. This sets a dangerous precedent where any high profile case can effect the defence's ability to insist that the accused has been punished enough and so merits a differential treatment in sentencing. Do we now have a two-tier justice system where the wealthy and famous are absolved from jail or criminal records while the poor are sent to prison? No one brings up the negative impact of media attention for the woman.

Justice Has No Gender?

High-profile media attention as a mitigating factor in sentencing has now set a terrible precedent. In the months following the Rozon trial, two more men, both accused of sexual assault, are granted an unconditional discharge. Luigi Leoni, a Québec restaurant owner is granted an unconditional discharge because the judge considered that the unfavourable media attention was punishment enough. The principal of Arvida High School in Québec was also granted an unconditional discharge after his conviction because the judge thought that having a criminal record would have negative consequences in his work with teenagers. Somehow the sexual assault was not considered to have a negative impact on his work, only the fact that he was found out and convicted!

The Regroupement Québecois des CALACS (a Quebec coalition of sexual assault centres) along with fourteen other women's coalitions, petitioned the Québec Justice Minister, then Linda Goupil, to appeal Rozon's sentence. The minister refuses to appeal the unconditional discharge granted to Gilbert Rozon. "I denounce violence against women...For a legal judgment involving violence against women, the Rules of Law apply because justice has no gender." Various editorials continue along these lines, most of them making a special point of the insignificant nature of the "assault," seeing it more as a seduction scene gone bad than as violence against women. Women and sexual assault centres are accused of exaggerating the seriousness of the crime. Three decades forward and four decades back, once again we are faced with the same myths: women lie and exaggerate about sexual assault. This is justice with no gender?

Rozon Epilogue

Following the criminal trial, K.C. took out a civil suit against Gilbert Rozon. An out of court settlement with a confidentiality clause prevents us from revealing the agreement. K.C. was demanding her Charter rights to live in safety without being sexually assaulted. She was putting into practice something that many feminists have insisted upon with respect to justice issues. K.C. was stating publicly that sexual assault is unacceptable in Canadian society. She gave us a context for understanding that protection is a right as granted by the Canadian Charter of Rights and Freedoms.

Canada has also signed an international agreement on the Elimination of all Forms of Discrimination Against Women. Clearly, the banalization of sexual assault through the granting of unconditional discharges to men guilty of sexual assault, as well as refusing to lay more serious charges in the interest of obtaining a guilty plea, or to save money, is discriminatory of women. It undermines the confidence of women in the criminal justice system. It perpetuates age-old myths about the severity of violence against women, implying that we are asking for it, exaggerating or vindictive. It certainly leads women to know that justice in Canada is not objective. It does, indeed, have a gender...one that is not ours.

How Does the System Prevent **Convictions** in Cases of Violence Against Women? What is the Connection to **Women's Rights** and **Violence Against Women?**

Conclusions and Recommendations of CASAC LINKS

As Dworkin said:

> A woman sits in her living room reading. A woman makes her way to bed. A woman works, eats, sleeps. She walks along the street. She does the work of the house even if she is not a housewife. Then somewhere, sometime, somehow, in the landscape of the ordinary, she is battered or assaulted or raped or molested; she is hit or punched or touched without her desire or consent. Some of the crimes are repetitive—for instance battery may not happen every day but it happens often and it creates an ongoing environment of threat and hostility. Some crimes happen once—for instance, the rapist who is a stranger rips apart a woman's life, shreds it with his bare hands, a penis, a knife, the poison of an amnesiac drug, and after that every shadow has the possibility of a rapist folded into it. Nothing about being raped by a stranger guarantees that she will not be raped again: by a stranger or acquaintance or friend or a husband or lover.[1]

A Summary

This inquiry considers how to express more fully what it means to the Canadian Association of Sexual Assault Centres (CASAC) to seek a better and feminist future for women in Canada. Our current reality of a system of violent repression of women's rights persists. We seek a future in which it will be a rare occasion when a man abuses a woman and in that future the response will be swift and just. We look to a future where women live in autonomy, peace, and freedom, without the hideous enforcer phenomenon of violence against women.

CASAC has always been concerned with the low conviction rates and high attrition rates in cases of violence against women. In the CASAC LINKS project we focused our inquiry on the questions: How does the system prevent convictions of violence against women? We asked how do the policies procedures and practices of the justice system impact on the low conviction rates of violence against women and what is the relationship of these impacts to women's inequality. We looked for and found one hundred criminally assaulted women who would tell their stories of using the Justice system in eleven locations across Canada. And we grouped their answers in relation to: emergency response, police investigation, crown attorney decisions, court proceedings, and sentencing

By law each of 92 cases women brought to the system merited conviction on at least one charge. The justice system convicted men in only 34 of women's cases.

We asked for the justice system's documents regarding policy and procedure of those justice functions at the same sites. We examined those documents for consistency with understandings of the Charter of Rights and Freedoms. That data was collected and analyzed across Canada at both the eleven sites and further collected and analyzed nationally. It was compared and added to the international positions Canada has promoted and the current national situation as seen by our member centres and as understood by the women who engaged the justice system at those sites. In combination we expected to see some of the nature of and reasons for low conviction rates and high attrition rates in these and other cases of violence against women. And we did.

We found that the Charter obligations to the women of Canada are ignored by those responsible for emergency services, police intervention, and those prosecuting cases. The promise to women in the Charter of Rights and Freedoms is broken when it comes to women who complain of violence against women.

We found that women calling the police expect that they are calling on their rights to equality and on Canada's obligation to protect those rights. We found that women around the world are complaining of the same horrors of violence against women and poverty. And most national groups of women complain of their government's response. In coalition with other Canada wide groups and in conjunction with women's groups around the world women are saying that we know we have a right to be free of violence against women, as well as poverty, and that we are developing an international agenda, mechanisms, and a movement to address those concerns. We have come together to complain of that violence and poverty through the World March of Women to national governments at International Social Forums, at the World Bank, and World Trade Organization (WTO) processes, and at the United Nations.

We read the Charter of Rights and Freedoms together with international documents outlining human rights agreements of states in the United Nations: each document being designed to inform the other. The United Nations, Convention on the Elimination of All Forms of Discrimination Against Women (CEDAW) committee, criticized Canada in January 2003. After our report to them they criticized Canada's failures to over see with economic mechanisms that all levels of government comply with international agreements that Canada signs. They criticized the failure to support substantive equality, including the provision of social welfare, funding for equality test cases, Canada's treatment of aboriginal women, women's poverty, immigration policy, the treatment of women trafficked. The United Nations made a special point of urging the Canadian government to "step up its efforts to combat violence against women and girls and increase its funding for women's crisis services and shelters in order to address the needs of women victims of violence under all governments."

We operated with some hope of improving the treatment of women and children.

In this project we were connecting the restructuring of Canada with respect to social programs, the function and effect of feminist women's anti-violence centres, the women who use them, and the Charter of Rights and Freedoms. That new Charter in the constitution promises all women in Canadian equality under the law and protection of the law. We were connecting that promise to the lived experience of women who complain to the criminal justice system after an incident of sexist violence. For five years we participated in local national and international meetings coalitions and actions. We saw that globalization is changing the Canadian state and changing violence against women. We saw the promised indivisibility of rights and, therefore, assessed the impact of other inseparable issues of women's equality. We saw among other things increased trafficking of women, the loss of welfare to women, and shifts in the criminal justice system that effectively decriminalize violence against women. We found that the changes from Canada Assistance Program (CAP) to the Canada Health and Social Transfer (CHST) and the Social Union Framework Agreement (SUFA) are changing federal provincial relations. Those changes must be adjusted to prevent further undermining of the promise of equality and freedom from violence made to Canadian women.

We hoped to encourage change along the way. We had already made public *99 Federal Steps Toward an End to Violence Against Women* as a program that could reduce violence against women. Throughout that document, and this one, as well as across the five-year span, we recommended guidelines for policy changes on issues of criminalizing violence and developing equity. We hoped we might improve the policy development of police and crowns at least in relation to wife assault, sexual assault, criminal harassment, peace bonds, and sentencing. We knew we would be of assistance to women beaten and raped including, within the family, as well as those at risk on the job, and those driven into prostitution. But at the end of this five-year project we find the situation is worse for women reporting violence for criminalization.

The project was also conceived to benefit rape crisis centres, many of which have existed for years in their communities with too little or no federal government funding, in spite of the start up funds of the 1970s, which identified these centres as vital to the advancement of the equality of women. That usefulness and the demand for the centres is evident in the numbers of women who call every year, the numbers who want to be involved with the independent women's movement, and who want and need information about the law and their rights under the Canadian Charter of Rights and Freedoms. We found that the involvement of independent feminist advocates in a legal case increases the likelihood of conviction. At the end of this five-year project women's centres against rape and wife assault have less access to federal dollars than five years ago. CASAC LINKS has regenerated a commitment from Canadian feminists to insist on the political and economic support necessary to sustain women's centres, transition houses, and rape crisis centres, as the best tools women have to decrease their isolation, and vulnerability to violence against women, and to increase the convictions that criminalize that violence.

Some Key Recommendations Arising from the Local Document Review and the Cases of Another 100 Women

There is no one document or one woman's experience that we could find that applies the law, policy, and procedure while taking into account women's disadvantaged status. CASAC reconfirms our recommendations made in *99 Federal Steps Toward an End to Violence Against Women* and reconfirms our recommendations made in the consultations with the department of justice over the last ten years. The following recommendations are made in addition and updating of those standing recommendations:

- Canada should establish publicly owned and operated 911 emergency response service in every jurisdiction.

- CASAC recommends to the departments of Justice Health and the Solicitor General and the Status of Women that those services not be submerged under police control but managed separately or jointly with other emergency response systems.

- Canada should set national guidelines for 911 response, using the *R. v. Godoy SCC 1999* case as part of the standard.

- CASAC recommends that any procedure and response policy should be consistent with the Criminal Code.

- CASAC recommends that the importance of the operator be recognized by establishing in job descriptions that operators have the time as well as criteria with which to accomplish their job of assessing and making appropriate referrals.

- CASAC recommends that all 911 calls be recorded and preserved (for at least five years) as public record of emergency response especially to violence against women.

- CASAC recommends that the Solicitor General in conjunction with the Minister of Justice should affect a national policing policy that acknowledges the gendered nature and function of violence against women and the historical disadvantages women face when accessing the justice system when reporting criminal violence against them.

- CASAC recommends that the above policy should be designed to affect all police in the country to be more consistent with the promise of Sections 7 and 15 of the Charter of Rights and Freedoms. That policy should include actions meant to address and compensate for the disadvantages of women as a group and the disadvantage of particular groups of women. That policy should be public.
- Establish national targets and methods of evaluating the implementation of policing changes toward the promise in Charter Sections 7 and 15.
- Establish as a nation-wide norm that police investigate all reported crimes of violence against women.
- Establish as a norm that appropriate initial investigation includes collection of all relevant evidence including her word in a well-taken statement, all physical evidence available, and all supporting witness statements available. Any police discretion as to the merits of cases should be applied after that initial investigation and not before.

After an appropriate investigation as above CASAC recommends that police pursue a charge toward conviction: not divert cases by redirecting women to civil court orders; and,not divert cases by pursuing criminal protection orders.

We recommend that only when a criminal charge is not fully supported by the evidence (and after a full investigation) police provide criminal protection orders, and they automatically and immediately enforce them.

The roles of the police and crown-based specialized victim's services should be understood by the women who use them to be limited to the provision of public legal information and supplementary supports to the justice system:

- Police-based victim's services should identify themselves as working for the police and that they are not independent advocates;
- Police-based victim assistance should also indicate that they are not themselves police and do not hold police investigative or evidence gathering functions or powers and that victims are free to refuse them;
- Crown-based victim's services should identify themselves as assistants to the crown prosecutor, therefore, not independent advocates;
- Crown-based victim services should also indicate that they are not crown and do not hold evidence presenting or prosecutorial powers;
- Crown-based victim services should be instructed to educate about court processes not just court buildings;
- Specialized victim's services programs may be based in community groups. They are independent, but should indicate that their mandate is limited to supplement the justice system with some services to women, and not to support women in contesting any action or inaction of policy procedure or functioning of the system.

- CASAC recommends that it is consistent with the Charter that police and crown charge approval policies incorporate that it is in the public interest, particularly women's equality interest, for charges to proceed before the courts.
- CASAC recommends that Attorneys General be encouraged to make public all charge approval guidelines, particularly ensuring availability to women complainants and their advocates.
- CASAC recommends that Attorneys General be reminded and encouraged to direct the management of court cases involving violence against women toward particular attention to the historical disadvantage of women and, therefore, the Charter involvement on recommended bail conditions, preparing women to witness in court, supporting women through trial, and making sentencing recommendations in order to protect women's equality rights.
- CASAC recommends and digitalization permits now that Canada should establish that written judgments with reasons are recorded and available at all levels of courts.

The current unequal status of women and the current level of violence in marriage should shape policy, law, and procedure in any future discussions of the divorce act and other legislative changes particularly regarding property settlements, custody, and access agreements during and after marriage. CASAC recommends rejection of any normalizing of shared parenting principles or any other application of formal equality because of the reverse impacts guaranteed to follow.

Some of the Key Recommendations Arising from the Charter Case Section of the Report

The Charter is written with the recognition that women as a group are disadvantaged; this disadvantage requires government action in achieving our civil social, political, and economic equality.

- CASAC recommends increased funding for the Court Challenges program and expansion of funding for the legal costs to assert our rights. To implement legal strategies equality-seeking women need access across Canada to provincial Test Case Litigation funds and funding for other legal moments where women's Charter Rights are at issue such as coroners inquests and public inquiries.
- CASAC women see huge expenditures of public money and time on training and education of police, prosecutors, and judges with little positive change. This model of gaining compliance is not working. CASAC recommends more strict requirements so that legal professionals meet the Charter standards and that professional's standards include incorporating an observable commitment to Canada's Charter promises of women's equality.

- CASAC recommends that the federal government fund national women's non-government groups to meet discuss, write, and otherwise give voice to and act as equality advocates. Such funding enables women's groups to contribute to the meaning given to and to monitor the implementation of rights legally encoded in the Charter.

- CASAC recommends that Industry Canada recognize CASAC LINKS as a successful pilot project, which should be enlarged and repeated among anti-rape centres. It can be understood as an example of infrastructure development in civil society that is building the capacity of women and women's groups to continue to increase participation in Canadian democracy.

- CASAC LINKS web site and resource library should be supported and maintained as an important component in public legal education regarding access to Supreme Court decisions and lay discussion about how these decisions can be used by women's equality-seeking groups to maintain and keep alive the promise of the Charter to women in Canada.

Canadian women know that the federal government is culpable and liable for the high attrition rates and low conviction rates on crimes of violence against women. Increasingly, they are holding the policies and practices and personnel of the government to the test of law and of the Constitution: the Charter. CASAC recommends that once the facts have been established that the federal government should accept liability for its mistakes rather than fight in the courts to the point of exhaustion and financial disaster those cases brought by women such as Jane Doe and Bonnie Mooney.

Some of the Key Recommendations Arising from the Section on the Restructuring of Canada

Freedom from violence is intricately connected to women's autonomy and economic security and is best assured with women's political participation.

- We recommend that the federal government recommit to redistribution of income by requiring provincial and territorial governments to provide guaranteed annual income that meets nationally set standards in order to get federal transfer money. These national standards should embody the Charter.

- We remind the federal government that any governance scheme with municipal governments is not exempt from Charter values or CEDAW obligations.

- We recommend the federal government redistribute tax income to remove pressure on municipal governments to accept and manage prostitution.

- Alternative Dispute Resolution mechanisms do not meet Charter obligations of substantive equality to women and current ADR practices actively interfere with women's equality interests in both civil and criminal legal realms.

- We recommend the federal government review the application of ADR to examine the effect of these changes in philosophy and policy on the implementation of women's Charter rights. Everywhere in the country, equality-seeking women's groups have protested pre-conviction diversion, pressured or mandatory mediation, many so called restorative justice processes, administration of justice changes that reduce access to legal counsel. Too often the application of ADR effectively reduces the opportunities for equality-seeking interveners, prevents the benefits of the involvement of equality-seeking advocates, requires the loss of the role of legal advocates, and the loss of the role of the public courtroom where justice can be seen to be done.

The United Nations CEDAW Committee called on the federal government to require compliance from all levels of government to application of the international convention.

- We recommend the federal government implement the FAFIA (Canadian Feminist Alliance for International Action) five-point plan for a national mechanism to oversee compliance with the CEDAW agreement.

- We recommend that the federal governments do as the United Nations urged and increase funding for women's rape crisis centres and transition houses in order to address the needs of women victims of violence under all governments:

The federal government's obligation to improve the status of women can be effected through directly funding these organizations or directly funding the component of their work identified as equality seeking. The federal government obligation to improve justice for women should motivate direct funding to these centres as depots of legal education and sites of community engagement with Charter rights. The federal government has a role to play in assuring the availability of women's advocacy equally in all parts of Canada. The federal government has a role to play in assuring the availability of women's support services from the provinces that cannot be abandoned with changes in federal provincial relations.

CEDAW and CASAC point to Canada's treatment of aboriginal women and Canada's failures to support women's organization addressing violence against women as two key issues that must be addressed in any compliance strategy.

Some Key Recommendations Arising from the Section on the International Discussion: Violence and Equality

Women around the world have shared our stories and a common understanding that though the details of our lives are different much of our oppression and the sexist violence we face are the same. We are building an international movement to end violence against women and women's impoverishment.

In the United Nations the Canadian government has recognized the historical disadvantage of women and agreed that all governments must account for and compensate for that disadvantage. The Canadian government is aware of the public support for and the legal need for independent advocacy work from feminist or equality-seeking women's groups. CASAC recommends that the Canadian Government meet its stated obligation to cooperate with feminist and equality-seeking women's groups to improve democratic governance.

CASAC endorses the worldwide demands of the World March of Women Against Poverty and Against Violence Against Women.

The Canadian government is complicit in the global conditions that have forced women to migrate to Canada legally and illegally: women are trafficked in the form of indentured labour, prostitution, mail ordered brides, and domestic workers. Trafficked women often find themselves targeted for criminalization.

Domestic workers only have temporary residency and are without adequate social security. They are forced to stay in the homes of their employers and are often punished when leaving abusive employers for breeching the conditions of the Live In Caregiver Program. We wish to restate our earlier recommendations to eliminate the live in requirement of the program.

Trafficked women are in the hands of their traffickers forced into indentured labour and prostitution. Canada should refuse to criminalize these women, protect their rights to establish themselves as refugees, involuntary migrant workers, and trafficked persons who are to be protected under UN and Canadian conventions. Canada should refuse to blackmail them with offers of only temporary visas based on their contribution as witnesses against their traffickers. CASAC recommends all women trafficked into Canada receive:

- Adequate settlement services;
- Legal representation including for their gendered status;
- Genuine achievable routes to landed immigrant status.

> To understand the enormity of the crimes against women, one must first accept that women are human beings and like all human beings have an intrinsic value that need not be earned. No special pleading is required to say that an assault against a woman is anti-human, that it distresses the flesh and wreaks havoc on the mind. The boundaries of a woman's body are the boundaries the perpetrator violates. Usually he believes he has a right to transgress against those boundaries. Until the Women's Movement challenged that belief, law and social policy supported it.[2]

Notes
1. Dworkin, p. 58.
2. *Ibid.*

Postscript

This book records our advocacy in significant sexist violence cases and records the research and development project of CASAC Links to make it publicly available. One hundred women raped reported to police and sought the advocacy of their ten anti-rape workers located in ten urban feminist centres. That was coordinated by and aided by their five Canadian regional representatives in CASAC. But in the end the book was authored by me, one woman speculating on the agreement of the others to a complex pan-Canadian feminist analysis. The collective process of the Links project and the two CASAC conventions since I began, confirmed my speculations of what would reflect the collective praxis. Since the circulation of my original draft report, the other women in the ten hosting centres and regional groupings approved and endorsed my analysis and advised me to return the results to the rest of the CASAC membership. So with reports of the work in my suitcase I travelled across Canada to many frontline anti-violence centres to invite criticism and support of the transformation of the LINKS project into policy for CASAC and this book for the public. I wondered by the time I arrived if the stories of women trying to use the system would have advanced to any more acceptable outcome? Would the issues identified still be those originally highlighted by the centres?

Would the centre members find my conclusions too radical to use or too removed from their everyday experience? In the book I claim I observed a sweeping lack of application of Charter encoded notions of equality in the delivery of criminal and civil law for women. It amounts, I said, to the decriminalization of violence against women and the criminalization of women's self-defense. I claimed to see an inseparable and worsening spiral of interconnections between women's poverty and violence against women. In particular I argued the loss of welfare, the use of family law (particularly financial maintenance), the pay equity evasions of government, and the obvious targeted criminalization of poor and racialized women. We worried that the government would back up from the best research it had produced: the Violence Against Women Survey.

I made accusations that the decriminalization and industrialization of the worldwide sex trade industry is amounting to the promotion of prostitution/trafficking of women and children by government power holders. I pointed to the entrenchment of, and insistence on, the patriarchal family particularly in the processes of family court, violence in the family and the divorce act considerations, the handling of the gay marriage debate. I warned of government policy attacks on the natural and accumulated authority of feminists to fight for women. In particular the ideological and financial attacks by government on the effectiveness and even existence of the NGO's not only national coalitions like NAC and CASAC but also on women's centres, rape crisis centres and feminist transition houses that are an important backbone of the independent women's movement.

Core Funding, Pay Equity, Nellie Nippard

I travelled to Newfoundland in the fall, where I met with Tracy Duffy and the St John's women at their new centre. They have a smaller, less central, office because without the financial support of our research project they have too little operating money. At their invitation a hundred of us took to the streets to Take Back the Night to a spot where I would speak. I was tempted to stay on for a week to join and encourage those women planning to protest the inaccessibility of provincial ministers responsible for the Status of Women who were meeting in a St John's hotel. They presented five key demands including one for core funding. As this book goes to print the Parliamentary Committee on the Status of Women has again recommended core funding be added to project funding available to women's groups and that the federal government increase funding to women's groups by twenty-five per cent. They also recommended greater cooperation and consultation with the equality-seeking women's groups. Even though that committee is headed by Anita Neville (the very effective chairwoman of the ruling Liberal party women's caucus) it has so far been ignored. Perhaps the new budget will bring relief.

For our equality purposes there were two other huge issues to update the equality fight in Newfoundland. The federal courts just pronounced that the provincial government could evade pay equity obligations to its employees. It owed millions to the poor public sector worker women.[1] Newfoundland authorities asserted that the province was too poor to pay. The Supreme Court required no proof, no payment plan, no consequences. That equality decision appears to also exempt the federal government (contrary to all international notions of federal obligation), from all economic responsibility for equality decisions of its components. Of course they are wrong.

And for us the other sadly important issue: Nellie Nippard, battered woman and fierce advocate for the right to the protection of criminal law for battered women, died without having experienced a day of peace from the fear that her husband would kill her.[2]

Women Only Space, A Provincial Restorative Justice Moratorium, The Pictou Statement On Women's Economics

Once I got myself to the Atlantic coast, other centres extended invitations too. New Brunswick and Halifax centres hosted me in their cities and planned public education events to use me and the research.

At Dalhousie I was invited to address women at the university women's centre. It would be one of the last acts of a woman-only centre soon to be sacrificed to the post modern urge to "include" men in the form of the "transgendered." Vancouver Rape Relief and Women's Shelter has already won its human rights case refusing such "inclusion." On December 19th, 2003 the British Columbia Supreme Court set aside the decision of the Human Rights Tribunal.[3] The declaration of the court was that it is not discrimination for a feminist rape crisis centre to build its work and membership on the belief and practice that the shared life experience of being oppressed as women is the building block of our work.

The Avalon Centre women in Halifax were glad to tell me that they won agreement from their provincial government for a moratorium on Restorative Justice programs applied to violence against women and were working on policy to condemn all current Restorative Justice programs across Canada for their failure to uphold women's Charter rights. They hoped all of CASAC would endorse.

While on the east coast, I joined forces with the *Canadian Women's Studies Journal* and the national committee of International Women's March to construct a meeting of feminist anti-poverty thinkers including women from the National Anti-Poverty Organization, the Federation des Femmes du Quebec, Nova Scotia Fish-Net and the Antigonish Women's Centre. After a three day meeting and together with me, they wrote the Pictou Statement as another step in the dragon dance for women's sense and economic rights (in the form of a guaranteed livable income).[4] Once written we began the cross country lobbying and negotiations necessary to accumulate consensus. We knew that the Supreme Courts had recently rejected/defeated, even trounced, an economic rights perspective in the Gosselin case (Gosselin v. Attorney General of Quebec). It was time for an increased emphasis on an extra legal strategy. We planned to bring Pictou to CASAC membership as a whole. We also planned to take it to the LEAF/NAWL conference where feminist based in legal work might be glad of an alternative to lighten the despair about a neo-liberal court.

The Autonomous Women's Movement And The World March Of Women

In Quebec I was invited to a meeting on the shores of the St Lawrence of all the Calacs or anti-rape centres. Women were struggling with our need to understand, express, and reinforce ourselves as the independent/ autonomous women's movement. They brought my attention to their relationship with the work of Francine Descarries at the University of Quebec and her expression of "nous femmes." She was encouraging Diane Matte of the World March of Women to compose, in writing, the new understandings she was bringing back to Quebec from her participation in the planning and execution of the World Social Forums in Latin America and India, her meetings with the World Bank and the United Nations, her organizing with women of DAWN and other feminists in the south, and indeed, with women around the world. Diane began her activism in the eighties within Hull Rape Crisis Centre collective.

The Quebec centres are repositioning themselves. Quebec nationalist players were questioned by feminists in this time of a swing to the right but also the World March of Women allowed centres to see themselves in the world-wide francophonie and the world-wide movement. The Gomery mess, or corruption in both federalist politicians and the federal government dealings with Quebec, meshed with the uprisings of labour and the students against the Charest provincial government. Together they might have pulled women back. While the national project remains important to them, anti-rape centres seem to be very much in the struggle of redefining their work and membership in the context of new populations of immigrants of colour, the pan-Canadian autonomous women's movement and the international struggle of women.

Prostitution

The Quebecoise decided to use the LINKS report and the upcoming convention to lead the efforts to modernize our CASAC anti-prostitution policy. The report made bold statements. We had moved forward with anti-trafficking policy at our last convention in 2001. But Quebecoise were facing an upcoming Montreal sex industry trade fair which was being subsidized with federal health department money.[5] Women in Quebec centres told me that they were very frustrated with the provincial politics especially the process within the FFQ (umbrella group of women's organizations) which had facilitated under past leadership, one sex worker service group, Stella, to manoeuver the huge women's coalition of FFQ into a de-gendered neutrality, even temporary paralysis on the question of prostitution as violence against women. The anti-rape workers were preparing to call for solidarity from the rest of anti-violence workers across the country to fight the promotion of prostitution by the Canadian and Quebec government actions.[6]

Vancouver women were trying to prevent the same promotion being tolerated and instituted in the name of harm reduction. At the Raging Women conference in 2002 we exposed and challenged mayor Larry Campbell who had called for a red light district and had never retracted those statements. The pressure against protest was so fierce that hosting a forum of anti-prostitution speakers was highly controversial. We did so in conjunction with prostitutes and aboriginal leaders in October 2003 and published abolitionist opinions widely.

In November of 2004 in Ottawa, the Parliamentary Subcommittee on Solicitation Laws (the second recent attempt to decriminalize the trade) was established by the Standing Committee on Justice, Human Rights, Public Security and Emergency Preparedness. Immediately a group of Quebecers, including Diane Matte, led by Elaine Audet and Micheline Carrier, signed a letter which they published against the prostitution promotion. They also began to collect the public denunciations.[7]

The committee mandate to improve the *safety* of "sex-trade workers" and to recommend changes that would *reduce* the exploitation of and violence against "sex-trade workers" already revealed the bias of the committee assignment. According to the *Washington Post* the term "sex worker" was coined by the American pimp and pornography producer Carol Leigh. That phrasing normalizes and recasts prostitution as a choice of job and clearly serves the purposes of pimps, not us. In anti-violence centres, we know that violence is intrinsic to flesh trade and the world-wide exploitation of women and children is the very nature of this industrialization of prostitution. Daunted by the stacked-deck parliamentary process and the almost impossible time-line, we nevertheless scambled to find ways to record our positions with the parliamentary subcommittee crossing the country.[8]

There was a danger that women might have yet more roadblocks put in the way of their escape from violence by the alliance (to decriminalize and regularize) between the Liberal minority government and the N.D.P. opposition. No money is being committed to social programs supporting women and their children or to income redistribution. The federal budget approved in May 2005 did not contain the much needed 25% increase to funds for women's advocacy groups. Both parties might claim that decriminalizing the trade was an inexpensive way to be advancing "human rights" even though they would be defacto legalizing the prostitution industry. Both would likely agree to impose state "health" based regulatory powers against the women and children trapped in prostitution. While harm reduction and health projects might create numbers of jobs for middle class workers, they will not reduce prostitution or increase women's escape routes. Such outcomes are completely consistent with current neo-liberal government trends.

Hilton And The Impressarios

You will remember the Hilton case in Quebec of the boxer who tortured his wife and daughters for years with incest and beating. He remains in jail sentenced to ten years and still denying wrongdoing. The Hilton girls, Jeannie (now 21) and Anna Marie, got the Quebec court to reverse the decision to ban publication of their identities so that they could release their own book: *Le Coeur au beurre noir* or *The Heart with a Black Eye*. They report themselves damaged but moving on in their lives, although found it necessary to move to the U.S. to be sure they would not be attacked by their father's friends.

The revelation of abuse by Quebec impressarios continues. In November 2004, Guy Cloutier, TV producer, pleaded guilty to five charges for years of sexually abusing two children. In May speculation was confirmed when Nathalie Simard asked the court to release the publication ban that had been protecting her anonymity; she had been abused by Cloutier from age 11 to adulthood. She had been discovered as a talented child by Cloutier along with her brother Renee. He developed their careers to the level of household names within Quebec abusing her and at least one other child along the way. Cloutier is serving a 42-month term in prison. And, Robert Gillet, radio host, was sentenced to 30 days for "buying sex from an underaged prostitute" (we would call that child abuse, if not rape). His sentence, too, was suspended.

Sexual Harassment Leading To Death, Racial Integration And Race Relations

In Ontario the emphasis was a bit different, but the urgent solid agreement among us was not. Women in Chatham hosted the province-wide gathering of anti-rape centres and showcased their work to reveal the dangers and horrors of sexual harassment on the job. In particular, they used the coroner's inquiry into the case of a Theresa Vance, a woman worker at Sears who was harassed on the job, ignored in her plight, and murdered in the space created by state and corporate inattention to women's inequality.

Ontario women focused, too, on increasing the leadership of women of colour within their coalition and their centres. Women in the north like the women in Kenora, were hiring aboriginal women and reconstructing their relationship to aboriginal women in need and to feminists on and off reserve. Toronto had been the site of the fastest changing demographics in the country and that centre was determined to adjust their structure and practice to welcome the new groups of women resident in that city.

Together the Ontario centres were resisting the pressure to answer to the office of Victims of Crime instead of the more appropriate Ontario Women's Directorate. They worried because their funding was through the Attorney General, not the health departments, as in Quebec. As well, Ontario is the site of the greatest pressure to professionalize the work of our centres. Many shelters require degrees now. The George Brown college program had attracted many ex-collective members from the Toronto centre as instructors on the argument that the program was more feminist and progressive there than courses elsewhere. It is in fact unique in that it genders the program and keeps close ties with the community activists. Women across the country are considering again the nature of counselling, the nature of advocacy, and the relations between individual and communities of women who call us and the centres where we organize.

Jane Doe And The Toronto Police

Jane Doe's book and film have been a success. She's working in a research project regarding the usefulness of anonymity in the pursuit of justice for women raped. She was also widely circulating as a guest speaker and trainer. With her friend Bev Bains, she was still gathering up the activists in Toronto and with them pressing the Toronto police for changes using the Police Audit.[9]

Bernardo And Homalka

Paul Bernardo remains in jail and Karla Homalka was released from jail on July 4th, 2005, having served her sentence. Again people debate whether she or Paul Bernardo were the greater danger to women. Is she dangerous without him? Some recognize that the willing "Barbie Doll" version of mindless femininity she was adopting in her youth might be more dangerous than they once thought. There are always predatory men ready to use it. Rape crisis workers found themselves conflicted. We wanted to protect her from the sexism that blames her more than Bernardo by discounting the facts that he beat and raped her. We wanted to protect her from the threats of sexist violence aimed at her. But we also wanted to protect other women from the Karla who turns herself into an automaton for men, any men who will praise that femininity. Those are dangerous men.

Research On Violence Against Women And On CASAC

Enormous anti-feminist effort went into challenging the bit of government authorized research documenting the incidence of violence in Canada known as the 1993 Violence Against Women Survey. The author Holly Johnson was forced to defend her methodology. The attacks on the research and her are analysed in *Violence Against Women, New Canadian Perspectives.* In 2005 on www.Sisyphe.org *Backlash and Whiplash: A Critique of the Statistics Canada 1999 General Social Survey in Victimology* summarizes the issues as well. We are aware of a new generation of federally funded research seeking to focus Canadians on individual psychological and chemical management of women's responses to rape. But we CASAC women are building our own data bank. Some centres are digitalizing their years of crisis work for analysis. In Alberta, Lise Gotell and her team at the University of Alberta are collecting the data we as anti-rape centres had supplied from across the country about the nature and work of anti-rape centres. She was chronicling the lack of application by police and crown of the law reform work of the last decade.

"Marthas And Henrys"

Across Alberta more than 200 women have joined the listserve called *Martha's Monthly* (so named as Premier Klein refers to the "ordinary" Albertans as "the Marthas and the Henrys") and the March 2005 created quite a stir. Opposition parties read the *Martha* letters into the House and more than a few female MLAs are proud members of *Martha's Monthly.* This clever use of new technology as a resistance strategy appealed to me especially when *Martha* took on violence issues. Manitoba women still relied on the only anti-rape centre in Winnipeg. It operates as part of Klinic a long standing progressive health organization. And Saskatchewan women held one of the more important gatherings of aboriginal feminists in the last few years.

Coroner Inquiry, RCMP In Alberta

Jan Reimer, Co-ordinator of the Alberta Council of Women's Shelters was invited to the CASAC convention too but she was preoccupied in the spring of 2005 supporting battered women and shelter workers. They were preparing to intervene in the coroner inquiry into another murder of a battered woman. The femicide of Betty Fekete and her child Alex and the suicide of her husband Josif was a vivid reminder of the Heron case in

B.C. and of the repeated scenarios with the RCMP. In this case, her complaints to the RCMP, of violence against her, were imagined by the officers as just her way of communicating a version of her husband as controlling and dangerous so that she could manipulate to unfairly win custody of her son. Constable Pierre Morel of the Red Deer RCMP wrote that "complainant Blagica is using any means to get the upper hand." In many cases the RCMP seem unable to train officers to begin their response to violence by believing women are reporting incidents of violence in order to seek police help.

Workers at Alberta shelters had advocated for police protection of Blagica warning the RCMP that Josif had guns and was dangerous. He had already crashed into one shelter demanding access to his wife and forcing workers to secret her through the night to a shelter in another city. Workers told the RCMP of Blagica's emotional physical and sexual abuse by her husband. Still officer Peter Calvert testified that police had "no idea of the existence of guns before the murder suicide" and that "trying to find guns would have been time-consuming and complex noting that it would have taken four or five hours and they would have had to get a search warrant." Mounties admitted they didn't follow up with charges after being told of death threats. They had received dozens of calls in the months before the deaths but understood them only as mutually accusatory: the husband had complained that his wife didn't always use the car seat and sometimes didn't make herself available with the child, and the wife had complained of beatings, rape, danger to her child, and death threats. Blagica's 3-year-old son told a shelter worker of the Central Alberta Women's Emergency Shelter staff that he knew his father was going to kill him. The staff told the inquiry how Blagica Fekete tried to protect her son from the visit to his father. Those visits were required by the courts on the basis of his father's rights and the "best interests of the child." This mother had begged child protection authorities to recognize the safety issues for her and her son. When Josif returned the child to his mother after a visit, he came with a sawed-off shot gun and killed Blagica, Alex, and then himself. The coroner's inquiry was told that after the murders, the RCMP had conducted a rigorous review of themselves. We should all accept, they seemed to argue, their assurances that every problem was now fixed.

Heron, Mooney And Vlescick, Fekete—All RCMP Failure Cases

Another coroner inquiry had also concluded. This one examined the murders of Sherry Heron and her mothe, Anna Adams, at the Mission hospital, and the suicide of her husband. At the families request I had agreed to testify but the coroner decided, based on the arguments of the lawyer representing the federal government, that it would be distracting to have the perspective of women's groups or anti-violence activists. Every incident of violence against women had to be isolated from every other. No mention was made of any other cases except by the lawyer for the family who raised the Vernon massacre as a similar incident followed by a self-examination by the RCMP. But again as in the Mooney case, the Vlescic case, the Fekete case, this death and this RCMP behaviour were completely separated from every other femicide or attempted femicide mishandled by the RCMP. The coroner's jury did its best with a lack of evidence in front of them and made the usual recommendations for training and oversight within the RCMP. And the RCMP assured us that better detachments existed and the RCMP brass had examined the situation and was already doing those changes and as they claimed in every case above, every problem was now fixed.

Bonney Mooney was shut out of the courts. Her case and our intervention were turned down. There is no further legal way for her to hold the justice system or the RCMP accountable for the abandonment of her and her daughter and the death of her loyal friend. She is left with her government saying on the one hand that she is, in the constitution, promised the rule of law, and on the other that she, when ignored by police and attacked by a vicious man, was "the author of her own misfortune."

Tyhurst And Abusive Doctors

In the Dr. Tyhurst case of sexually enslaving his patients, an aging Tyhurst was, in January, refused an opportunity to stall payment again. He was refused leave to appeal the decision against him to the Supreme Court. Still the woman is awaiting disbursement of the funds he owes her or the cost awarded by the courts.

Marilou McPhedron continues to defend herself in the Ontario case brought by doctors against her and we continue to defend the work she did, and does, to hold the medical establishment to account for abuses of women.

Pickton, Bakker, The Fujian Traffic, And Prostitution

The Pickton case lumbers toward preparedness with many a battle over legal aid costs in high profile cases since there is no pre-set schedule. It may be years before we see the thousands of pieces of evidence and learn the rest of the truth of the men who slaughtered the destitute women of the downtown eastside of Vancouver. But we know there is more than one. And we know the role of poverty, colonialism, and prostitution now.

The Native Women's Association of Canada was finally awarded the government money for their campaign to record the missing women from their communities and has created a national and international campaign. They did not settle for the money or for simply recording the horror. They have declared their position that men should be criminalized, as in Sweden, for demanding prostitution and buying sex. It seemed so appropriate that they should make this stand since it is the aboriginal women who are suffering in the greatest numbers and their suffering and the suffering of their families is being cynically appropriated in the call for legalization and regularization of the prostitution industry.

We are now faced with the opportunity and horror of the precedent-setting arrest of Donald Bakker. He was originally arrested for sex crimes against prostitutes and other destitute women in the downtown eastside of Vancouver. But when police found depictions of his child abuse in 70 videotapes of children overseas he was charged with those crimes. The location of his abuses has not been revealed yet, but it will be new to charge and try men for their sex tourism and sexual abuse abroad.

Since the arrival of the Chinese boat women in Canada, many coalitions have formed to respond to the needs of those trafficked. Still many were desperately trying to disintegrate the issues of international trafficking from domestic prostitution, or racism from prostitution or class and gender from prostitution. They were building walls that created false dichotomy between forced or "voluntary" enslavement, between child and adult "choices," between violent or "non violent rape." For us the links are made by Bakker and Pickton between sex tourism in the third world, child abuse, and violence against local prostitutes, between global economics and aboriginal women. For women of the Rape Relief collective in Vancouver, the connections between racism, tourism and prostitution, and women's equality are unavoidable, transparent.

CASAC Convention 2005

In May 2005, Vancouver welcomed some 120 frontline workers from all regions of the country to update the stories of women who call, to compare our experiences of advocacy and organizing, and to decide on new shared policy arising out of the LINKS report. We all wanted to embody, renew, and apply our approaches to ending violence against women. We needed to share our understanding of the Charter of Rights and Freedoms and to decide if there was still any promise in it. Since only a very few of those who wanted to come could attend the convention, we web cast one day of the events, prepared a permanent record, and sound recorded all three days of it for future use.[10]

We endorsed an internationalist anti-capitalist perspective as relevant to the fight against violence against women. We denounced prostitution as violence against women and have taken an abolitionist stance. We endorsed the Pictou Statement on economics including women's right to a guarantee of a liveable income. We rejected the notion of guest workers in Canada and insisted on landing needed workers. We rejected mail order bride systems and insist on protection for immigrant women violated. We rejected the model of Restorative Justice offered by the Canadian government and rejected any diversion to religious or otherwise privatized courts or tribunals.

We confirmed our expectations for police services including those to criminalize sexist violence against women, including prostitution. We confirmed our wish to protect from criminalization all the women prostituted/trafficked. We confirmed that we willingly accept progressive sentencing provisions for men convicted, but will not consider conditional sentences on sexist violence. We insist on written judgements of criminal proceedings regarding male violence against women and that we do not consider court cases fair if they do not include the equality provisions necessary for women complaining and witnessing of violence against women. Several discussions were opened including a serious discussion as to whether it is ever necessary to jail women. Perhaps the most serious was the beginning of several talks about the relationship between us and the women who call us. How shall we see ourselves? How do we display that we and the callers are equals? What about her community? Are we to see ourselves as rape experts? Are they? Equality experts? Are we to practice as paraprofessional counsellors? Political players? What does activism mean in our organizations? Since we see ourselves as political people, what are the implications for action in counselling? Can women self-define? If not what political group are we?

Day Of Feminist Dialogue

We were joined by some fifty other invited feminists for our Day of Feminist Dialogue. During that day we presented our report and our policy decisions for their consideration.

For a special deliberation of how our proposed policies would address First Nations and Aboriginal women attacked, we asked for the opinion of several key women: those delegates of our centres who are of First Nations (including women from Nippissing, and Kenora) and the three past and current elected presidents of the Native Women's Association of Canada (Sharon McIvor, Terry Brown, and Bev Jacobs) plus the president of the Metis Women's Association (Sheila Genaille) and a Metis woman researching prostitution issues (Jackie Lynn), a representative of the Experiential Women's coalition (Cherry Kingsley), ex-volunteers at Vancouver Rape Relief and Women's Shelter (Tina Beads, Mabel Nipshank), past vice-president of NAC (Fay Blaney), and, we were joined by others over the day. We received a resounding endorsement for our equality approach, and our particular policies against Restorative Justice programs, prostitution, and diversion. We were clearly instructed on our political right and obligation as more privileged women to speak up in support of aboriginal women and when necessary to speak for aboriginal women. It was a challenging radical call for feminist support and solidarity which will be difficult and which I hope we will continue to meet.

In the hour or so we devoted to examining our plan against racism, we were challenged to continue to insist on the criminalization of violence particularly by the women of colour from the Black community, from the Muslim communities, and from the South Asian community. We were urged to stick by our position to refuse the diversion to religious or otherwise privatized courts by several members, particularly by the Ottawa center delegate and the representatives from the coalition against Shari'a law in Canada. They were joined by the guest from the African Canadian legal clinic in pushing us not to give up on the fight to make fair law apply to violence against women. We must not be dissuaded from our task by the current race and class biases of the overall justice system.

Asian and South Asian women led the caucus in calling on all of us to see our anti-prosti-tution policy and our call for feminist economic justice as an anti-racist stance that could achieve strides for women both within Canada and in our international work.

We were cautioned again to watch for and resist the increased criminalization of women that is occurring worldwide. We were told horror stories of what workers used to call double charging of both the husband and wife once she calls for police assistance, now being experienced as charging only the women and dropping the charges against him. We reminded ourselves that we wanted youth treated as youth and not charged or apprehended or jailed as adults. On the other hand we wanted them to have the advan-tages of legal representation and not be jailed or criminalized "for their own good."

Women activists, including founding members of national groups, told of fathers and husbands abusing them in the most privileged families and of the failure of the sys-tem to hold those men accountable. Mary Eberts among them denounced the silence maintained by women of privilege and called on powerful women to speak up for their own sake and for the sake of the less privileged.

As the day ended we renewed our appreciation and membership in both FAFIA and the World March of Women. But we also increased our expectation that as we moved into the next meetings with those umbrella groups like LEAF and NAWL, they would better re-flect our expertise in Violence Against Women and the struggles of working class activists.

May Day Vancouver 2005

You just can't keep the women down. Especially the young ones.

Ask those tattooed and winged ones on stilts leading the Vancouver May Day parade. They came to greet the world's womanly aspirations and visions as they have been scrolled into the Women's Global Charter for Humanity. CASAC women were the organisers of the reception of the Charter to Canada. A motorcade of young women in a decorated van re-layed the Charter from the American women greeting them at the border under Interna-tional Peace Arch. These two gangs joined with other cheeky young women whose breezy skepticism by-passed the election campaigns underway in B.C. Their feminist women el-ders may be depressed at the state of equality mechanisms, but the young thumb their noses and flash their crinolins and their piercings and go directly to the street.

In their mother's electoral and judicial politics, public childcare, pay equity, an end to women's impoverishment and violence against women, are once again demanded and at best cynically promised. Listening to Canadian politicians and judges you could be led to think of these as lavish social gifts asked by special interest women's groups. Never mind they are the basics of women's economic, and social, civil, and political human rights. Even the United Nations has criticized Canada for unequal treatment of women.

The rowdy young including Erin Sandberg from North Delta and Paula Broeder of Kenora are not apolitical. Every week they answer the calls from women needing advocates. In Vancouver they gathered with 150 other anti-rape activists to challenge the grim reality of individual men's power in the disappearances of aboriginal women and the daily assaults of men on women. Then they took on the institutional attacks on women's equality-seeking services both in Victoria and in Ottawa. They crashed the meeting of equality-seeking feminist legal scholars to put in their two cents worth. They make common cause with the blue hairs and the stilt walkers, hitting the streets in celebration of the consensus of visionary messages of their peers: women writing in Spanish, French, and English, as the Women's Charter for Humanity accumulates consensus circling the globe.

They were joined by Tonika Morgan entrusted among the young to carry the Charter scroll from Vancouver to Yellowknife, Winnipeg, Ottawa, Moncton, and Quebec. She carried it in solidarity with the 30,000 women who dispatched it from Sao Paolo, Brazil on International Women's Day 2005, and with the women of Latin American and Central America as it passed. From Vancouver's joyful rowdies, she would carry it on to 15,000 women waiting to greet her, and it, in Quebec City. One of them, Barbara Legeault, will be among the young who pass the Charter hand-over-hand through old Quebec City to the parliament.

All these young women refuse to suffer any party's cynical recycling of promises of women's rights as election rhetoric. They expect to achieve. They know that parties and politicians can ill afford to ignore them. Young women take to the streets to build and claim a future in which poverty among women, and violence against women, no longer constitute the social/political norm. Dancing, they gather their babies, their lovers, their sisters, and their mothers, with them.

Notes

1. See: http://www.nape.nf.ca/media/news_news_release_223.htm.
2. See: http://www.cbc.ca/stories/2003/12/02/nippard_031202.
3. Vancouver Rape Relief Society vs Kimberly Nixon and British Columbia Human Rights Tribunal, www.rapereliefshelter.bc.ca.
4. See: www.casac.ca/text/CASAC.convention.2005.htm.
5. 2005 Carrier, Micheline. "$270,00 granted Stella for a four day event on sex work." www.Sisphe.org.
6. In Gatineau for instance a federal grant of $43,000 was awarded to help the city develop a plan for a downtown red light district.
7. See: www.Sisyphe.ca.
8. Many can be found at www.rapereliefshelter.bc.ca and at www.casac.ca.
9. See: http://owjn.org/issues/assault/audit.htm.
10. The materials we used to prepare, the policies we debated, and the outcomes are being made available at www.casac.ca.

References

Abused Women's Advocacy Project. (2000, February). *The Voices of Victims: Victim Accounts of Law Enforcement Response to Domestic Violence Data Report September 1998-1999*. Lewiston, Main: Author.

Addario, L. (1998). *Getting a Foot in the Door: Women, Civil Legal Aid and Access to Justice*. Ottawa: Status of Women Canada.

Agar, S. (2003). *Safety Planning with Abused Partners: A Review and Annotated Bibliography*. Vancouver: B.C. Ministry of Public Safety and Solicitor General and B.C. Institute on Family Violence.

Amsterdam's Street Prostitution Zone to Close. (2003, October 21). *Expatica News*.

Annan, K. (2001). Annan Calls For Global Trust Fund to Fight HIV/Aids. Speech at OAU Aids Summit, April 26, 2001. Retrieved online January 15, 2002, from United States Information Service Web Site: <www.Aegis. com/news/usis/2001/us010408.html>

Avalon Sexual Assault Centre. (1999, September 30). Position Paper. *Formal Response of the Avalon Sexual Assault Centre to Department of Justice: The Restorative Justice Program*. Halifax: Author.

B.C. CEDAW Group. (2003). *British Columbia Moves Backwards on Women's Equality*. Submission to the United Nations Committee on the Elimination of Discrimination Against Women on the Occasion of the Committee's Review of Canada's Fifth Report.

B.C. Ministry of Attorney General. (1996). *B.C. Attorney General Violence Against Women in Relationships Policy*. Victoria: Author.

B.C. Ministry of Attorney General. (1999). *Crown Counsel Policy Manual-Core Policy*. Victoria: Author.

B.C. Ministry of Attorney General. (1999). *Crown Counsel Policy Manual-Core Policy, Charge Approval Guidelines*. Victoria: Author.

B.C. Ministry of Attorney General. (2000). *Policy on the Criminal Justice System Response to Violence Against Women and Children: Violence Against Women in Relationships Policy*. Victoria: Author.

B.C. Ministry of Attorney General. (2003). *Policy on the Criminal Justice System Response to Violence Against Women and Children: Violence Against Women in Relationships Policy*. Victoria: Author.

Bailey, I. (2003, May 22). RCMP launch manhunt for B.C. Prison guard. *National Post*, p. A5.

Bailey, I. (2002, February 16). Killer Stalked Prostitutes, Police Told. *National Post*, p. A8.

Bailey, I. (2002, April 12). I Tipped Police to Pickton in 1998: Former Employee. *National Post*, p. A10.

Bohn, G. (2003, September 24). Municipalities urge Martin to Give Cities a Fair Share of Funds. *The Vancouver Sun*, p. B5.

Boland, B. and Wychreschuk, E. (1999). *Keeping an Open Mind: A Look at Gender Inclusive Analysis, Restorative Justice and Alternate Dispute Resolution*. Newfoundland: Provincial Association of Against Family Violence.

Bonnie Mooney, Michelle Mooney and an infant in her Guardian ad litem Bonnie Mooney v The Attorney General of Canada, The Attorney General of the Province of British Columbia, The Solicitor General of Canada, Corporal K.W. Curle, Constable E.W. Roberge, and Constable Andrichuk. T.V. 1-3. Provincial Court of B.C.

Boomer, R. (2002, April 18). Nova Scotia prosecutors give up on Regan case. *Vancouver Sun*, p. A6.

Boyle, C., Lakeman, L., McIntyre, S. and Sheehy, E. (1999, November). Tracking and Resisting Backlash Against Equality Gains in Sexual Offence Law. Paper presented at the WestCoast LEAF Transforming Women's Future Conference. Vancouver. B. C.

Brickman, J., Briere, J., Lungen, A., Shepard, M., and Lofchick, M. (1980, May). Winnipeg Rape Incidence Project: Final Results. Paper presented at the Canadian Association of Sexual Assault Centres, Manitoba, Canada.

Brodsky, G., and Day, S. (1998). *Women and the Equality Deficit: The Impact of Restructuring Canada's Social Programs*. Ottawa: Status of Women Canada.

Came, B., Burke, D., Ferzoco, G., O'Farreli, B., and Wallace, B. (1989, December 18). Montreal Massacre: Railing Against Feminists. *Macleans Magazine*.

Cameron, B. (1997, December). *Rethinking the Social Union: National Identities and Social Citizenship*. Ottawa: Canadian Centre for Policy Alternatives.

Cameron, D. (1999, September 02). The Social Union Pact is Not a Backward Step for Quebec. *The Globe and Mail*.

Campbell, K. (1996). *Time and Chance: The Political Memoirs of Canada's First Woman Prime Minister*. Toronto: Doubleday Canada.

Canadian Association of Elizabeth Fry Societies and Canadian Association of Sexual Assault Centres. Conference proceedings, Ottawa, October 1-3, 2001. CD. Victoria: Time and Again Productions, 2001. Available online CASAC Web Site: <www.casac.ca/conference01/cd_order02.htm>.

Canadian Association of Sexual Assault Centres (2003). Canadian Association of Sexual Assault Centres Constitution. Retrieved online June 2003 from the CASAC Web Site: <www.casac.ca/about/constitution. htm>.

Canadian Association of Sexual Assault Centres. (2001). Renewed CASAC Constitution. In unpublished minutes.

Canadian Association of Sexual Assault Centres. (2000, June 16-17). Meeting of the Ad Hoc Planning Committee of CASAC. Ottawa.

Canadian Intelligence Service Canada Report. (1998). Canadian Intelligence Service of Canada Web Site: <www.cisc.gc.ca/AnnualReport1998/ Cisc1198en/asian98.htm>.

Canadian Women's March Committee. (2000). Its Time For A Change! The World March of Women 2000. *Canadian Women's Studies* 20 (3) 21-23.

Canadian Women's March Committee. (2000). *Lobby Guide*. Guide prepared for the World March of Women in the Year 2000. Available online from the World March of Women Website: <www.canada.marchofwomen.org/>.

Caputi, J. (1987). *The Age of Sex Crime*. Ohio: Bowling Green State University Popular Press.

CBC News-Indepth background, Martin O'Malley, CBC News Online. Retrieved online March 11, 2002 from CBC website: <www.cbc.ca/news/indepth/background/hilton_dave.html>.

CEDAW. (2003). *The Fifth Periodic Report Of Canada*. Retrieved online March 2003 from Rape Relief Web Site: <www.rapereliefshelter. bc.ca/issues/cedaw_Jan2003.pdf>.

Centre for Feminist Legal Studies Newsletter. (2003). Editor: Summer Edition, 2(3), 1-8.

Centre for Research on Violence Against Women and Children. (2003, October). Editor: 1, 1-8.

Chief Coroner, Province of Ontario. (1998). *Inquest into the Deaths of Arlene May and Randy Iles, February 16-July 2 1998: Jury Verdict and Recommendations*. Toronto: Coroners Courts.

Clark, L., and Lewis, D. (1977). *Rape: The Price of Coercive Sexuality*. Toronto: The Women's Press.

Connell, B. (2000, July 18). *Violence Against Women Sharing Our Stories: Changing the World*. Ad Hoc Committee meeting for the Canadian Association of Sexual Assault Centres at Kenora Sexual Assault Centre. Kenora, Ontario.

Crnkovich, M., Addario, L., and Archibald, L. (2000). *From Hips to Hope: Inuit Women and the Nunavut Justice System*. Research and Statistics Division, Ottawa: Department of Justice Canada, cat. 2000-8e.

Crnkovich, M. (1995, October). The Role of the Victim in the Criminal Justice System Circle Sentencing in Inuit Communities. Paper Presented at the Canadian Institute for the Administration of Justice Conference, Banff, Alberta.

Cross-Sectoral Violence Against Women Strategy Group. (2000, September). *Media Release: Women Seek Emergency Measures on Violence Against Women.* Toronto: Author.

Culbert, L., Skeleton, C., and Ramsey, M. (2003, May 22). Shooting Suspect Depressed; Mother: Police Seek Estranged Husband of Dead Woman. Electronic version, *The Vancouver Sun.*

Culbert, L. (2003, Nov. 13). RCMP's Learned gets new posting: The force's top spokesman was accused of an off colour remark, *The Vancouver Sun*, p. A15.

Culbert, L. (2003, September 24). Families Say They're Left Out After Talking to Media. *The Vancouver Sun*, p. B3.

Daley, S. (2001, August 12). New Rights for Dutch Prostitutes, but No Gain. *New York Times*, pp. A1, 4.

Daniels, C., and Brooks, R., Eds. (2001). *Feminists Negotiate the State: The Politics of Domestic Violence.* Lanham, Maryland: University Press of America.

David, F. Speech delivered at General Assembly. Retrieved online June 9, 2002, from World March of Women Web Site: <www.ffq.qc.ca/ marche2000/en/ commun-2000-06-09.html>.

Dawson, M. (2001, December). *Examination of Declining Intimate Partner Homicide Rates: A Literature Review.* Ottawa: Department of Justice Canada, cat. 2001-10e.

Day, S. (2000). The Indivisibility of Women's Human Rights. *Canadian Woman Studies, 20* (3), 11-16.

Declaration on the Elimination of Violence Against Women General Assembly Resolution. (1993). United Nations Web Site: <www. Genderandpeacekeeping.org/resources/5_ DEVAW.pdf>.

Department for Women. (1996). *Heroines of Fortitude: The Experiences of Women in Court as Victims of Sexual Assault.* New South Wales, Australia: Author, ISBN 073105204.

Department of Health and Welfare. (1991). *The War Against Women*: First Report of the Standing Committee on Health and Welfare, Social Affairs, Seniors and the Status of Women to the House of Commons. Ottawa: Author.

Department of Justice. (1999, April). News Release: Minister of Justice Tables Legislation Strengthening the Voice of Victims of Crime and Backgrounder: Federal Legislation Strengthening the Voice of Victims of Crime. Ottawa: Author.

Department of Justice. (2000, May 7). *The Changing Face of Conditional Sentencing: Symposium Proceedings.* Ottawa: Author.

Department of Justice. (2000, August). News Release: Minister McLellen Announces New Funds to Help Victims of Crime and Backgrounder: Victims Fund. Ottawa: Author.

Department of Justice. (2003, November 3-5). Moving Forward: Lessons Learned from Victims of Crime: Conference. Ottawa.

Department of Justice. (1999). *Handbook for Police and Crown Prosecutors: Criminal Harassment.* Ottawa: Author.

Direct Action Against Refugee Exploitation (DAARE). (2001). *Movements Across Borders: Chinese Women Migrants in Canada.* Vancouver: Author.

DisAbled Women's Network Ontario. *Kimberly Rogers Alert: Judicial Review Decision In CAEFS v Dr David Eden, Coroner.* DAWN Web Site: <http://dawn.thot. net/ KimberlyRogers/ judicial_review.html>.

Dobash, E., and Dobash, R. (Eds). (1998). *Rethinking Violence Against Women.* Sage: Thousand Oaks.

Dobash, E., and Dobash, R. (1990). How Theoretical Definitions and Perspective Affect Research and Policy. In D.J. Besharov (Ed). *Family Violence: Research and Policy Issues.* Washington: AEI Press, pp. 108-129.

Dobash, E., and Dobash, R. (1992). *Women, Violence and Social Change.* London and New York: Routledge.

Doe, J. (2003). *The Story of Jane Doe: A Book About Rape.* Toronto: Random House Canada.

du Bois, B. (1983). Passionate Scholarship: Notes on Values, Knowing and Method in Feminist Social Science. In Bowles, G., and Klein, R. (Eds). *Theories of Women's Studies.* London and Boston: Routledge and Kegan Paul, pp. 105-115.

Duncan, C. (2003, October). Raging Women: Fighting the Cutbacks in B.C. Paper presented at the Raging Women's Conference by Vancouver Women's Health Collective. Vancouver.

Dworkin, A. (2003). Landscapes of the Ordinary: Violence Against Women. Morgan, R. (Ed). *Sisterhood is Forever.* New York: Washington Square Press, pp. 58-69.

Eckerg, G. (2002). *Campaign Against Trafficking Women.* From the Regeringskansliet Web Site: <www.naring.regeringen.se/fragor/jamstalldhet/aktuellt/ trafficking.htm>.

Edleson, J. (2003). Should Childhood Exposure to Adult Domestic Violence be Defined as Child Maltreatment Under the Law. In Jaffe, P.G., Baker, L., and Cunningham, A. (Eds). *Ending Domestic Violence in the lives of Children and Parents: Promising Practices for Safety, healing and Prevention.* New York: Guilford Press, (In Press).

Eyherabide, E., and Shess, P. (2000, July 2). Spousal Abuse: How to Stop the Killers. Law-Enforcement Officers Must Treat All Acts of Domestic Violence as a Crime, Say the San Diego District Attorneys Pioneering Spouse Protection. *The Globe and Mail*, p. A11.

Family Court of Nova Scotia. (1989). *Family Court Act Section Five: Powers and duties of the Judge-Regulations of the Family Court in Nova Scotia.* St John: Author.

Federal-Provincial-Territorial Ministers Responsible for the Status of Women. (2002). *Assessing Violence Against Women: A Statistical Profile.* Ottawa: Author, cat. SW21-101 /2002E.

Feminist Alliance for International Action (FAFIA). (2003). *Canada's Failure To Act: Women's Inequality Deepens.* Submission to the United Nations Committee on the Elimination of Discrimination Against Women on the Occasion of the Committee's Review of Canada's Fifth Report.

Fine, M., Weis, L., Weseen, S., and Wong, L. (2000). For Whom? Qualitative Research, Representations, and Social Responsibilities. In Denzin, N. and Lincoln, Y. (Eds). *Handbook of Qualitative Research.* Thousand Oaks: Sage Publications, pp. 107-131.

Flaskas, C., and Hounslow, B. (1980). Government Intervention and Right-Wing Attacks on Feminist Services. *Scarlet Woman Magazine.*

Fraser, N. (2001). Recognition Without Ethics? *Theory, Culture and Society*, 18 (2-3), 21-42.

Freeze, C. (2003, November 18). Report on RCMP Backs Decriminalizing Sex Trade in Canada. *The Globe and Mail*, p. A10.

Fry, Hedy. (1998, March 3). Statement by The Honourable Hedy Fry Secretary of State, Multiculturalism, Status of Women, to the 42nd Session of the Commission on the Status of Women. New York: Permanent Mission of Canada to the United Nations.

Gadd, J. (1995, December 2). More Women, Children Using Shelters. *The Globe and Mail*, p. A9.

Gouvernement du Québec. (1996). Agression a Caractere sexuel. Directive. Enquete criminelle. Surete du Québec. Author.

Gouvernement du Québec. (1995). Guide des practiques policieres. Agression Sexuelle. Author.

Gulyas, M. (2002, December 31). Proposed Abuse Policy Worry Chiefs: Amendment Would No Longer Make Charge Automatic. *Delta Optimist*, p. 11.

Hadley Inquest Jury Recommendations. (2002, February 20). Retrieved online July 24, 2003, from the Ontario Women's Justice Network Web Site: <www.owjn.org/isses/w-abuse/ hadley2.htm>.

Hamilton, G. (2001, February 8). Hilton's mother "heartbroken" by sex charges, *National Post*, p. A9. Montreal Watches as Fighting Hiltons dealt latest blows (2001, March 18), *The Province*, p. A36.

Harnett, C. (1999, August 15). Go Home: We Asked You to Have Your Say About the Latest Wave of Migrants to Reach our Shores. Your Response was Huge, the Message was Clear: Send them back immediately. *Times Colonist*, p. A.1.

Huang, R., Appelby, T. (2000, June 21). Baby Saved as Husband Shoots Wife. *The Globe and Mail*, p. A3.

Hughs, D. (1999). The Internet and the Global Prostitution Industry. *Women's Space*, 4(2), 28-31.

Hume, M. (2002, May 7). 54 lives and 54 mysteries in B.C.: 'the Mind Works Overtime' as Police Search Pig Farm. *National Post*, p. A1.

Hunt For Killer Goes Province Wide. (2003, May 22). *Penticton Herald*, p. A2.

James, A., and Price, J. (1999, November). *No Safe Harbour: Confronting the Backlash Against Fujian Migrant*. Working papers series #1 and #2. Vancouver, Asia Pacific Research Networks.

Jay, S. (2003, March 3). Reject Red Light Districts as a Solution to Violence Against Women. Presentation Raging Women's Conference. Vancouver: Canada.

Jayaratne, T. (1983). The Value of Quantitative Methodology for Feminist Research. In Bowles, G., and Klein, R. (Eds). *Theories of Women's Studies*. Boston: Routledge and Kegan Paul, pp. 140-161.

Jenish, D. (1996, July 22). Bernardo: How Police Bungled the Murder Case. *MacLeans Magazine*, p. 40-41.

Jiwani, Y. (2000). The 1999 General Social Survey on Spousal Violence: An Analysis. *Canadian Woman Studies*, 20 (3), 34-40.

Johnson, H. (1993). *Violence Against Women Survey*. Ottawa: Statistics Canada.

Justice with Dignity Campaign Committee. Justice With Dignity: Remembering Kimberly Rogers. Elizabeth Frye Website: <www.elizabethfry.ca/rogers/ 2.htm>.

Justice For Girls. (2001). Statement of Opposition to the Secure Care Act. Justice for Girls Web Site: <www.justiceforgirls.org/publications/pos_ securecareact.html>.

Kostash, M. (1980). Long Way From Home: The Stories of the Sixties Generation in Canada. Toronto: J. Lorimer and Co.

Kwan, K. (2001, February 20). Abused Wife Wants Cops to Pay. Vancouver: *The Province*, p. A3.

Lakeman, L. (1993). *99 Federal Steps Toward an End to Violence Against Women*. Toronto: National Action Committee on the Status of Women.

Lakeman, L. (1999, June 22). Celebrating 25 years of Transition House Work at Women's Emergency Shelter. Address celebrating 25 years, Ontario, Canada.

Lakeman, L. (1989). Mass Murder: The Sexual Politics of Killing Women. Online: <www. rapereliefshelter.bc.ca/dec6/leearticle.html>.

Lakeman, L. (1985, February 27). Who killed Linda Tatrai? A speech delivered in Vancouver. Online: <www.rapereliefshelter. bc.ca/herstory/rr_files85_linda.html#02>.

Lakeman, L. (2000). Why Law and Order Cannot End Violence Against Women and Why the Development of Women's (Social, Economic, Political, and Civil) Rights Might. *Canadian Woman Studies*, 20 (3), 24-33.

Lakeman, L. (2002). Farewell address to Madame Justice L'Heureux-Dubé. CASAC Web Site: <www.casac.ca/issues/farewell_heureux-dube.htm>.

Lakeman, L. (1999). A Consideration of Feminist Process. In Meister, J., and Masuda, S. (Eds). *DAWNing: How to Start and Maintain a Group*. Vancouver: Dawn Canada, pp. 85-98.

Landsberg, M. (2003, September 28). Tories Waging a Sinister War on Women. *Toronto Star*.

Lee, A. (2000). Working with Refugee Women. *Canadian Woman Studies*, 20 (3), 105-107.

Levan, A. (1996). *Violence Against Women*. In Brodie, J. (Ed). Women and Canadian Public Policy. Toronto and Fort Worth: Harcourt Brace and CO., pp. 320-355.

Lowman, J. (Ed). (1998). Prostitution Law Reform in Canada. In *Toward Comparative Law in the 21st Century*. Institute of Comparative Law in Japan, Tokyo: Chuo University Press, pp. 919-946.

Luciw, R. (2000, June 23). Risk Assessment Could have Saved Slain woman: Advocacy groups. *The Globe and Mail.*

Lunney, D. (2001, May 3). 911 Tapes Released (sisters died) Tapes Release Lauded. 911 Tragedy Broadcast Publicly. *Winnipeg Sun.*

MacLeod, L. (1987). *Battered But Not Beaten...: Preventing Wife Battering in Canada.* Ottawa: Canadian Advisory Council on the Status of Women.

MacPherson, D. (2000). A Framework for Action: A Four Pillar Approach to Drug. Vancouver: City of Vancouver.

Makin, K. (2002, February 15). Top Court Revives Charges Against Regan: Ruling Exposes Sharp Division Among Justices as Majority Decides Ex-premier Should Face Sexual-Assault Allegations. *The Globe and Mail*, p. A3.

Malenfant, L. (2001). Hilton's Grounds for Appeal: The Report Newsmagazine. Newsmagazine Web Site: <www.fathersforlife.org/php/ hilton1.htm>.

Mardorossian, C. (2002). Toward a New Feminist Theory of Rape. *Signs: Journal of Women in Culture and Society*, 27 (3), 743-776.

Martin, J. (1989). Martin's Annual Criminal Code: Incorporating R.S.C. 1985. Aurora: Canada Law Book, INC.

McIntyre, S. (1996). Feminist Movement in Law: Beyond Privileged and Privileging Theory. In Jhappan, R. (Ed) *Women's Legal Strategies in Canada.* Toronto: University of Toronto Press, pp. 42-98.

McIntyre, S. (1994). Redefining Reformism: The Consultations that Shaped Bill C-49. In Roberts, J., and Mohr, R. (Eds). *Confronting Sexual Assault. A Decade of Legal and Social Change*, Toronto: University of Toronto Press, pp. 293-327.

Middleton, G., and Berry, S. (2002, June 25). Police First Suspected Pickton Early as 1997. Vancouver: *The Province*, p. A4.

Middleton, G. (2000, February 10). I played "Piggy's Palace." Vancouver: *The Province*, p.A6.

Ministry of Industry. (2002). *Strengthening Voluntary Sector Capacity Through Technology*: Report of the Joint Table on Information Management/Information Technology of the Voluntary Sector Initiative. Ottawa: Author, cat. Iu4-10/2002.

Ministry of Supply and Services. (1991). *Family Violence in Canada: A Call to Action.* Ottawa: Author, cat. H72-21/66-1991.

Ministry of Supply and Services. (1993). *Changing the Landscape: Ending Violence-Achieving Equality.* Final Report of the Canadian Panel on Violence Against Women. Ottawa: Author, cat. sw451/1993E.

Morgan, R. (1990, c1989). *The Demon Lover: On the Sexuality of Terrorism.* New York: Norton.

Morris, M. (1999). *The Other Side of the Story: A Feminist Critique of Canada's National Response to the UN Questionnaire on the Implementation of the Beijing Platform for Action.* Paper prepared for the Canadian Feminist Alliance for International Action.

Morton, B. (2000). The Reality of the Past, Present, and Future Human Rights and Poverty in Canada. *Canadian Woman Studies*, 20 (3), 60-63.

Municipalities Urge Martin to Give Cities a Fair Share of Funds: Heads of Municipal Organization Tours Downtown Eastside and Calls its Problems a Canadian Issue, not a Vancouver Issue. (2003, September 24). *The Vancouver Sun*, p. B5.

National Association of Women and the Law. (2002, March 7-10). Women, The Family and The State. Conference. Ottawa: NAWL.

National Council of Welfare. (1995). Legal Aid and the Poor. Online: <www.ncwcnbes.net/ htmdocument/reportlegalaid/reportlegalaid. htm>.

911 Calls unheeded; John Dunlop Murdered Two Sisters: Pleads Guilty. (2001, March 13). Winnipeg: *Canadian Newswire.*

New Brunswick Public Prosecution Manual. (1996). New Brunswick Public Prosecution Manual Chapter X- Family Violence. Fredricton: Author.

New Foundland Attorney General and the Solicitor General. (1996). *Crown Policy Manual: Directive of the Attorney General and the Solicitor General Regarding Spousal/Partner Assault.* Author.

Oglov, V. (1997). *Restorative Justice Reforms to the Criminal Justice System.* Draft Discussion Paper. Prepared for the B.C./Yukon Society of Transition Houses.

Pemberton, K. (2003, May 24). Mission Murder Suspect Shoots Self. *Times Colonist*, p. A6.

Pence, E. (1989). *The Justice System Response to Domestic Assault Cases: A Guide for Policy Development.* Duluth: Domestic Violence Intervention Project.

Perreaux, L. (2001, May 3). "You are lying to me." 911 Operator. *National Post*, p. A3.

Poverty and Human Rights Project. (2002, October 31). Written Submission. A Framework to Improve the Social Union for Canadians: An Assessment of the Implementation of SUFA from a B.C. Perspective. Vancouver: Author.

Proffit, N. (2000). Women Survivors of Woman Abuse: An Exploration of Their Personal Transformation and Engagement in Collective Action for Social Change. Doctoral Dissertation. Wilfrid Laurier University, Ontario.

Prostitutes and Other Women for Equal Rights (P.O.W.E.R.). (1993, May 4). *Prostitutes and Policing.* Written Submissions by P.O.W.E.R. to the Hon. Wallace T. Oppal. Commission of Inquiry into Policing in British Columbia. Vancouver: Author.

Province of British Columbia. (2003). *Search Warrant Application.* Chilliwack R.C.M.P., Police file # 2003-8475.

R V Godoy. (1999). Supreme Court of Canada.

Ramsey, M. (2003, May 22). Guard Who Saw Killings Praised. *The Vancouver Sun*, p. A4.

Rape Relief Files-1986 Prostitution: Legal History. Retrieved online May 2003 from Rape Relief Web Site: <www.rapereliefshelter.bc.ca/ herstory/rr_files86.html>.

Razack, S. (1991). *Canadian Feminism and the Law: The Women's Legal Education and Action Fund and the Pursuit of Equality.* Toronto: Second Story Press.

Redstockings. (1975). *Feminist Revolution: An Abridged edition with Additional Writings.* New York: Random House.

Regroupment Quebecois Des Centres D'Aide Et Lutte Contre Les Agressions A Caractere Sexual. (2001, May 25). Base D'Unite. Assemblee Generale Annuelle.

Richards, G. (2003, May 28). Woman Slain in Hospital Feared Husband's Wrath. *The Globe and Mail*, pp. A1, A7.

Rigakos, G. (1994). *The Politics of Protection: Battered Women, Protective Court Orders and the Police in Delta.* Burnaby: Simon Fraser University.

Schmitz, C. (1998, May 27). Whack the Complainant at Preliminary Inquiry. *Lawyers Weekly.*

Sheehy, E.A. (1999). Legal Responses to Violence Against Women in Canada. *Canadian Woman Studies*, 19 (1-2), 62-73.

Sheehy, E. A. (1995). *What Would a Women's Law of Self-Defence Look Like.* Ottawa: Status of Women Canada.

Sidel, R. (1996). *Keeping Women and Children Last: America's War on the Poor.* New York: Penguin.

Silman, J. (1987). *Enough is Enough: Aboriginal Women Speak Out.* Toronto: Women's Press.

Skelton, C. (2002, February 9). Robert Pickton's 1997 bail-hearing transcript. *The Vancouver Sun*, p. A5.

Smith, A. (Interviewer). (2003, May 22). *CBC Morning News* [Television broadcast]. Canada: Public Broadcasting Service.

Solicitior General National Reference Group Women's Issues Conference. (1998, January 23). Consultation with Solicitor General Andy Scott. Vancouver, B.C.

Special Joint Committee on Child Custody and Access. (1998). *For the Sake of the Children*: Report of the Special Joint Committee on Child Custody and Access. Ottawa: Author.

Statistics Canada. (2001). *Family Violence in Canada: A Statistical Profile*. Ottawa: Author, cat. 85-224-XIE.

Statistics Canada. (2002). *Family Violence in Canada: A Statistical Profile*. Ottawa: Author, cat. 85-224.

Status of Women in Canada. (1995). *Setting the Stage for the Next Century: The Federal Plan for Gender Equality*. Ottawa: Author, cat. SW21-15/1995.

Statutes of Saskatchewan. (1994). Saskatchewan Victim's of Domestic Violence Act. Regina: Author.

Still, L. (1992, April 24). Drunkeness Proposed as a Defence. *The Vancouver Sun*, p.3.

Sullivan, M., and Jeffreys, S. (2001). *Legalising Prostitution is Not the Answer: The Example of Victoria, Australia*. Coalition Against Trafficking in Women, Australia and USA. Retrieved online October 2002 from CATW Web Site: <www.catwinternational. org>.

Sullivan, G. (1982). Funny Things Happen on Our Way to Revolution. *Aegis: Magazine on Ending Violence Against Women*, spring (4), 12-22.

Timeline. (2003, February 11). *Timeline 1970-1979*. Retrieved online June 8, 2003, from Women space web site: <http://herstory. womenspace. ca/timeline.html>.

Timeline. (2003, February 11). *Timeline 1990-1999*. Retrieved online June 8, 2003, from Women's Space Web Site: <http://herstroy. womenspace. ca/timeline3.html>

Trainor, C. (1999). *Canada's Shelter's for Abused Women*. Ottawa: Statistics Canada, cat. 85-002-XPE.

Update From the House from Libby Davies. (2003, October).

Vancouver Police Department. (2001, May 29). Vancouver Police Department Regulations and Procedures Manual-Relationship Violence 32.01 Violence in Relationships-General Policy. Vancouver: Author.

Vancouver Police Department. (1999, June 20). *Vancouver Police Department Regulations and Procedures Manual- Major Incidents 18, 19, Sexual Offences*. Vancouver: Author.

Vinneau, D. (1992, October 12). No Vote called a threat to Women. *Toronto Star*, p. A2.

Wife-Abuse Issues Subject of Conference. (1993, October 25). Montreal: *The Gazette*, p. A8.

Wilson, B. (1993). *Touchstones for Change: Equality Diversity and Accountability*. Ottawa: Canadian Bar Association.

Women, Law and the Administration of Justice Conference. Vancouver, June 1, 1991.

Women We Honour Action Committee. (1992). *Women Killing: Intimate Femicide in Ontario 1974-1990*. Toronto: Author.

Women's Internet Conference. (1997, October 18-21). Retrieved online June 6, 2002, from Women's Space Web Site: <http://womenspace. ca/confer/>.

Women's Legal Education and Action Fund. (1996). *Equality and the Charter: Ten Years of Feminist Advocacy before the Supreme Court of Canada*. Toronto: Emond Montgomery Publications.

Woods, J. (1998). *Recommendations for Amendments to "E" Division R.C.M.P. Operational Policies Pertaining to Relationship Violence and the Processing of Firearms Applications*. Royal Canadian Mounted Police.

World March of Women. (2002). *Women on the March: Focus on the Actions and Demands of the World March of Women*. Retrieved online June 2001 from <www.ffq.qc.ca.narche2000/ en/index.html>.

World March of Women Coordinating Committee. In World March of Women in the Year 2000 (1999). *The Advocacy Guide to Women's World Demands*. Montreal: Author.

Yllö, K., and Bograd, M. (Eds). (1990). *Feminist Perspectives on Wife Abuse*. Newbury Park, California: Sage Publications.

Index

GIRLHOOD: Redefining the Limits
Yasmin Jiwani, Claudia Mitchell, Candis Steenbergen, editors

Girlhood is a collection of essays on girls, girlhood and girl culture. Drawing from the works of national and international scholars, this book focuses on the multifaceted nature of girls' lived experiences. Examined is racism, sexism and classism; girlhood and girl gangs; the power and politics of schoolgirl style; encounters with violence; chatrooms; sexuality; and identity formation and popular culture. This groundbreaking collection offers a complicated portrait of girls in the 21st century: good girls and bad girls, girls who are creating their own girl culture and giving a whole new meaning to "girl" power.

YASMIN JIWANI is an Assistant Professor in the Department of Communication Studies at Concordia Univeristy, Montreal, and author of *Discourses of Denial: Mediations of Race, Gender, and Violence in Canadian Society*. CLAUDIA MITCHELL, Ph.D., is a James McGill Professor in the Faculty of Education, McGill University, and co-author of *Seven Going on Seventeen: Tween Studies in the Culture of Girlhood* (with J. Reid-Walsh). CANDIS STEENBERGEN is a Ph.D. candidate in Studies in Society and Culture from Concordia University, and former editor of *good girl magazine*.

224 pages ♀ paper ISBN: 1-55164-276-X $24.99 ♀ cloth ISBN: 1-55164-277-8 $53.99

RAGING GRANNIES: Wild Hats, Cheeky Songs, and Witty Actions for a Better World
Carole Roy

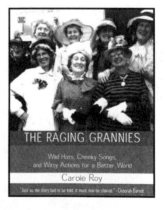

Bursting with adventures, protest songs, photographs, Granny profiles, and Granny wisdom, this is the tale of the Raging Grannies: their beginning and growth, the invention of their identity, the educational and bold potential of their activism, and their impact on issues, stereotypes, media, and people.

> Unique in form and content...[*The Raging Grannies*] fills a gap in feminist literature. Roy's examination of strategies of satire and humour, in particular, is ground-breaking.
> —Deborah Barndt, co-editor of *Just Doing It: Popular Collective Action in the Americas*

CAROLE ROY is a long-time activist. She holds an MA in Women's Studies, from York University, and a Ph.D. in Adult Education, from University of Toronto.

355 pages ♀ paper ISBN: 1-55164-240-9 $24.99 ♀ cloth ISBN: 1-55164-241-7 $53.99

WOMEN AND RELIGION
Fatmagül Berktay

While taking women's subjectivities and their reasons for their taking
to religion into account, this book focuses mainly on the *functions* of
religion, the way it relates to women; its contribution to gender differences; and the status of women within it, particularly the relationship
between gender on the one hand, and power and social control on the
other, and within this context, the meanings attributed to the female
body. The author examines why, in all three monotheisms the gender
of God is male and what the impact of this is on our thoughts *vis a vis*
gender definitions, the nature of authority and power structures.

Undertaken as well, is an exposition of contemporary Fundamental-
ism in both its Protestant and Islamic variants (in America and Iran).

FATMAGÜL BERKTAY is an associate professor with the Department of Philosophy, and
teaches feminist theory at the Women's Research Center, both of the University of Istanbul, Tur-
key. She is a contributor to *Being a Women, Living and Writing*.

240 pages ♀ paper ISBN: 1-55164-102-X $24.99 ♀ cloth ISBN: 1-55164-103-8 $53.99

See also:

ECOLOGY OF EVERYDAY LIFE: Rethinking the Desire for Nature, *Chaia Heller*
EMMA GOLDMAN: Sexuality and the Impurity of the State, *Bonnie Haaland*
FEMINISM: From Pressure to Politics, *Angela Miles, Geraldine Finn, editors*
FINDING OUR WAY: Rethinking Eco-Feminist Politics, *Janet Biehl*
WOMEN AND COUNTER-POWER, *Yolande Cohen, editor*
WOMEN AND REVOLUTION, *Lydia Sargent, editor*

send for a free catalogue of all our titles

**BLACK
ROSE
BOOKS**
C.P. 1258, Succ. Place du Parc
Montréal, Québec
H2X 4A7 Canada

or visit our website at http://www.web.net/blackrosebooks

to order books
In Canada: (phone) 1-800-565-9523 (fax) 1-800-221-9985
email: utpbooks@utpress.utoronto.ca

In United States: (phone) 1-800-283-3572 (fax) 1-651-917-6406

In UK & Europe: (phone) London 44 (0)20 8986-4854 (fax) 44 (0)20 8533-5821
email: order@centralbooks.com

Printed by the workers of
MARC VEILLEUX IMPRIMEUR INC.
Boucherville, Québec
for Black Rose Books